IMAGES
of America

BARBOURVILLE AND KNOX COUNTY

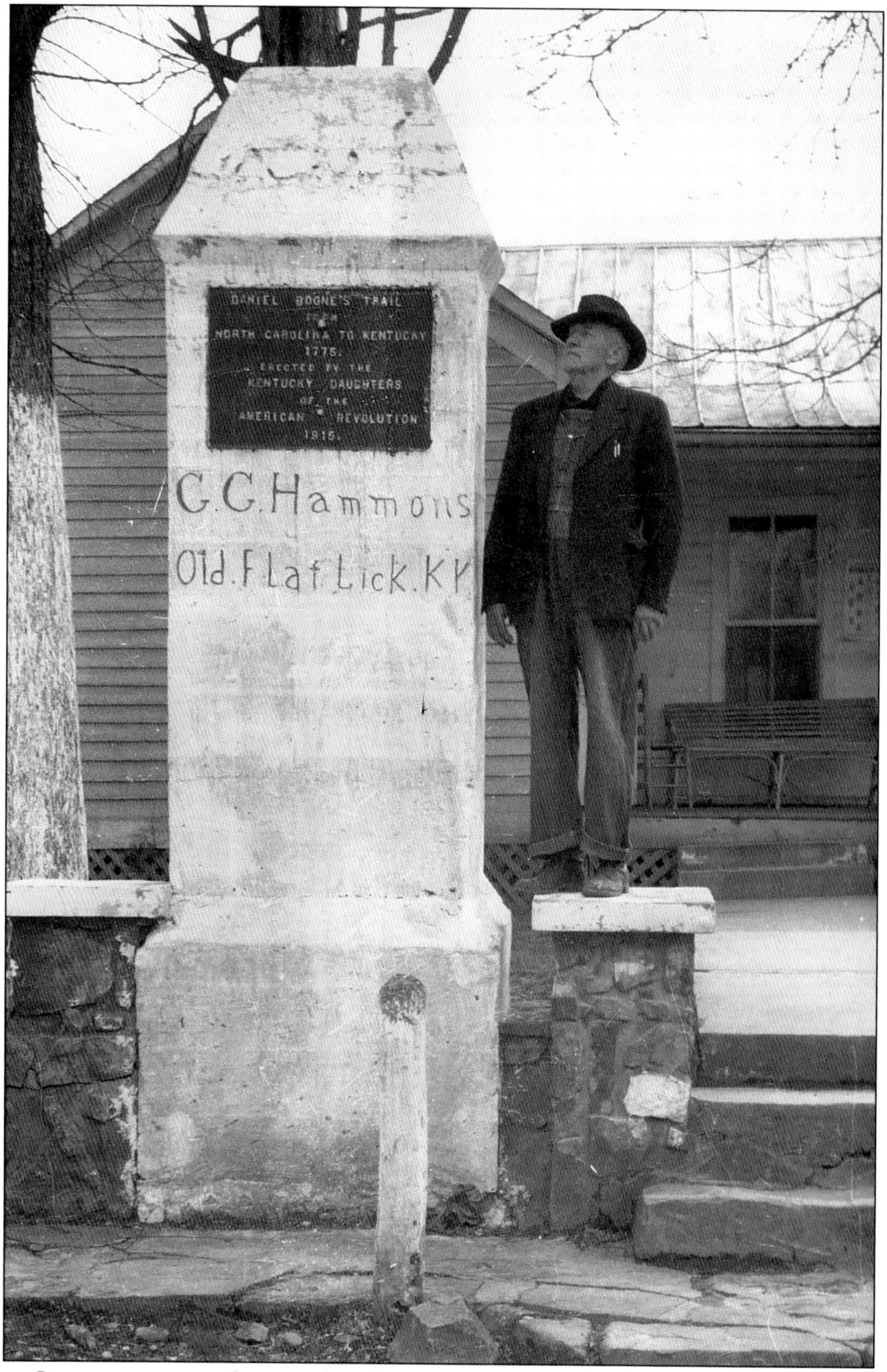

Knox Countians are proud to say that the Old Wilderness Road runs through their county. Daniel Boone blazed this trail through Knox County in 1775. Flat Lick resident G.G. Hammons proudly stands by a Daniel Boone trail marker placed here by the Daughters of the American Revolution in the year 1915.

IMAGES of America

BARBOURVILLE AND KNOX COUNTY

Michael C. Mills

ARCADIA PUBLISHING

ISBN 978-0-7385-0585-5

Published by Arcadia Publishing
Charleston, South Carolina

Printed in the United States of America

Library of Congress Catalog Card Number applied for.

For all general information contact Arcadia Publishing at:
Telephone 843-853-2070
Fax 843-853-0044
E-Mail sales@arcadiapublishing.com
For customer service and orders:
Toll-Free 1-888-313-2665

Visit us on the Internet at www.arcadiapublishing.com

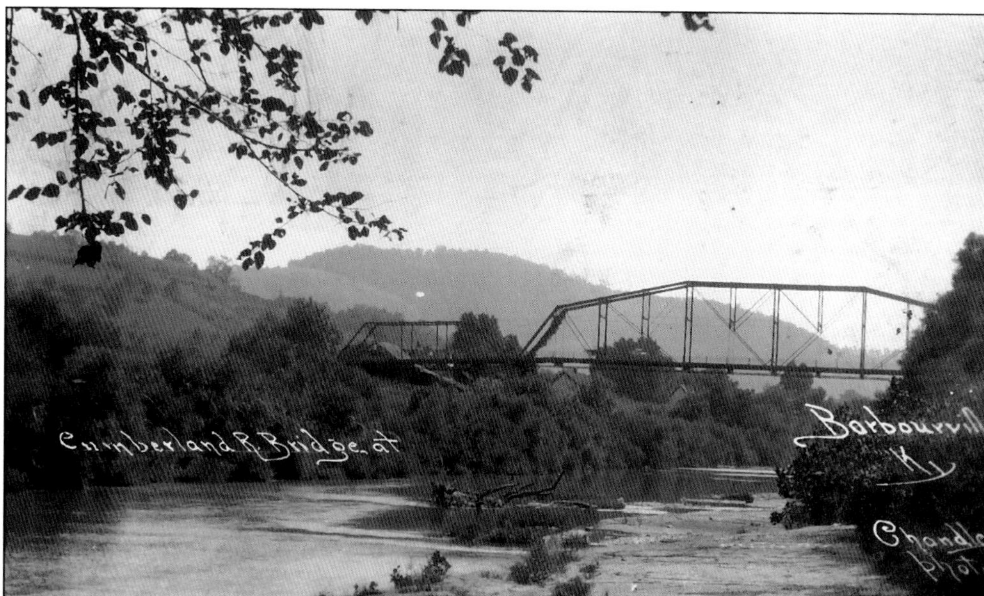

The city of Barbourville is located in the center of Knox County, KY, on the banks of the Cumberland River at the mouth of Richland Creek. The river was discovered by Dr. Thomas Walker in the year 1750. Doctor Walker followed this river through Knox County and built Kentucky's first house 5 miles south of Barbourville.

Contents

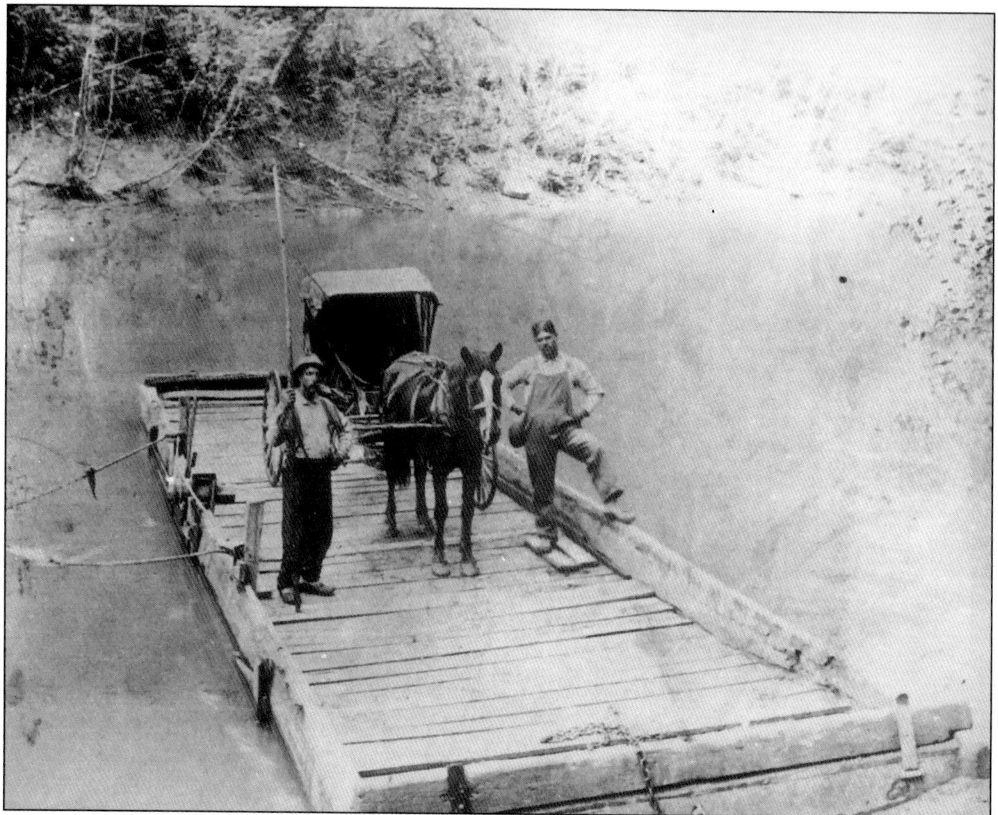
The Cumberland River ferry is pictured here.

Acknowledgments

The author would like to thank the following organizations for their preservation of historic photographs and their willingness to share their images of America with future generations to enjoy:

The Cumberland Gap Historical Park
The Knox County Historical Museum
The Filson Club
The Kentucky Historical Society
The *Louisville Courier Journal*
The Louisville and Nashville Railroad
Union College
Barbourville High School
Knox Central High School

I would also like to thank the many citizens of Barbourville and Knox County who have shared their photos with me through the years.

Introduction

Knox County, KY, was created in 1799 and included most of present-day southeast Kentucky. Its boundaries reached from Madison County to the north and to the Cumberland Gap in the south, making Knox County the gateway to the early settling of the state. Routes of travel were through the famous Cumberland Gap by way of the warrior's path to Flat Lick and Stinking Creek. Later trails were blazed by famous explorers such as Dr. Thomas Walker in 1750, as he followed the Cumberland River through Knox County and built the first log house 5 miles south of present-day Barbourville.

Daniel Boone marked out the Wilderness Road through the area in 1775, and settlements soon sprang up along the road at places such as Yellow Creek (Middlesboro), Cumberland Ford (Pineville), Flat Lick, Turkey Creek, Fighting Creek (Bimble) and at the mouth of Richland Creek, the future site of Barbourville, the county seat of Knox County. Knox County was named in honor of General Henry Knox, President George Washington's secretary of war.

The first officials of Knox County were named by the second governor of Kentucky, James Garrard, and the first court was held June 23, 1800. Magistrates voted on a motion to choose a county seat as near to the center of the county as possible; the vote resulted in a tie, with Flat Lick being considered along with the mouth of Richland Creek on the banks of the Cumberland River. To help with the decision, a landowner by the name of James Barbour offered to give the county 2 acres of land for use as a public square, and to sell 36 acres to create a town. The court accepted Barbour's offer and appointed a committee to lay out the town, which initially consisted of 78 lots, beginning on the north bank of the Cumberland River and extending six blocks from south to north and four blocks from west to east. The court then voted to name the new town Barbourville in honor of its benefactor. By the year 1802, lots were advertised for sale, and potential merchants began buying lots and building businesses. A courthouse was built in the center of the town square, which soon became the center of all town activity.

The majority of Barbourville and Knox County citizens came from North Carolina and Virginia. Many were of English decent and very independent minded. They were opposed to slavery and believed in hard work.

Economic growth was slow, as roads were very bad, and a typical farmer made only necessary trips into town. Barbourville became a trading post for travelers along the Wilderness Road during the early 1840s. During the 1840s and 1850s, the tiny town produced several men of distinction, including many congressmen and legislators who represented southeast Kentucky. Citizens were for the most part self educated, as schools would not be made available until the last half of the 19th century. The area grew slowly, as its only link to the outside world was through Cumberland Gap to the east, and Barbourville had a population of only 227 just before the Civil War.

During the Civil War, Camp Andy Johnson was set up at Barbourville to recruit soldiers from Tennessee and Kentucky. In September of 1861, one of the first small battles of the Civil War was fought here, when General Felix Zollicoffer came through Cumberland Gap to break up and burn this camp.

After the Civil War, Barbourville became more isolated, as trade routes changed from the Wilderness Road to the Ohio River routes. The town and county would soon be awakened by the coming of the L&N Railroad in the late 1880s. The mining of coal, the discovery of gas, and logging gave the county new life. Union College was founded in 1879, the Barbourville Baptist Institute was started in 1899, and a city school system began in 1890. Rural one-room schoolhouses sprang up throughout the county by the year 1900. In 1923, U.S. Highway 25-E replaced the old Wilderness Trails across Knox County, and travel and trade increased. The city of Barbourville operated one of the last horse-drawn street car systems in the United States, from 1890 to 1919.

Barbourville is located on the banks of the Cumberland River and has survived many floods during its history, including a record flood in 1946. It continued to battle floods until a flood wall was completed in 1959.

The completion of Interstate 75 near the western boundary of present-day Knox County and the four-lane road U.S. 25-E, as well as the completion of tunnels through the Cumberland Gap, have now opened Knox County and Barbourville to new industry and tourism opportunities. The sleepy little town of the 1840s has awakened to a new future with better roads, more industry, a better education system, and a solid appreciation of its place in history.

One

Knox County

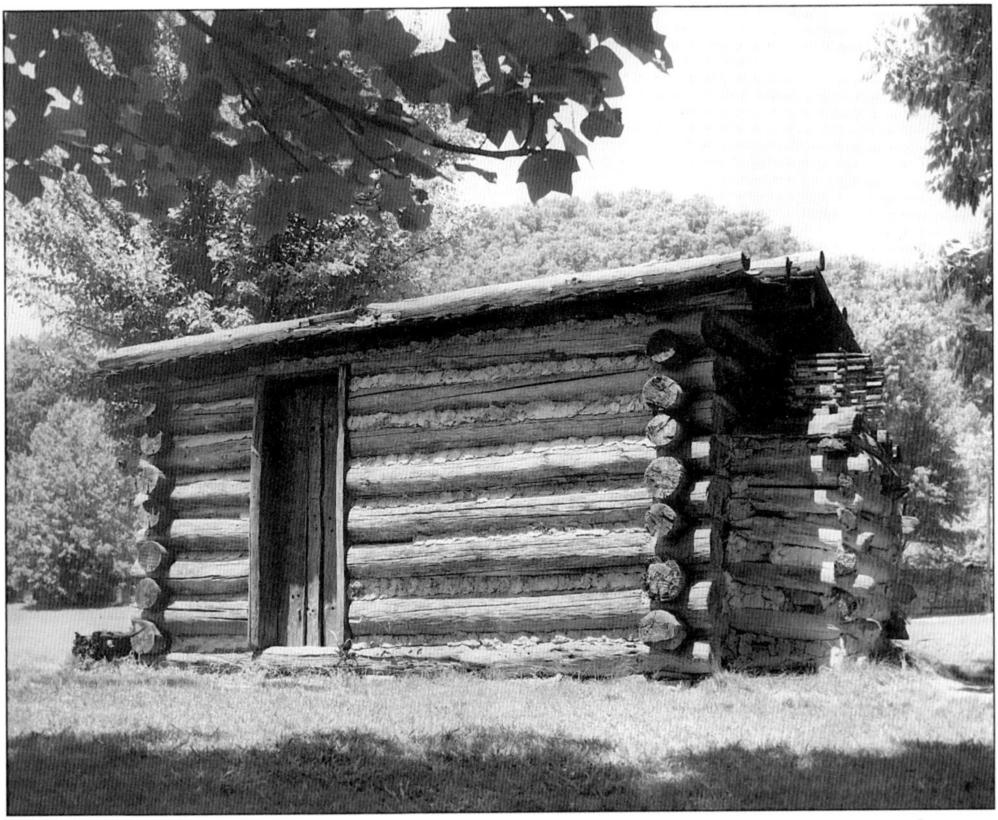

No one will ever know just who was the first explorer to visit what is now Knox County. However, we do know that Dr. Thomas Walker was the first to leave a record of his visit to this area in April of 1750. He records in his journal that he found the famous gap in the Cumberland Mountains, and that he followed it to Clover Creek (Clear Creek), where he soon discovered the Cumberland River. Dr. Walker followed the river at Cumberland Ford (Pineville) and then continued to Flat Lick, where he observed a salt lick and the approaching waters of Stinking Creek. He passed by the mouth of Richland Creek, where Barbourville would later be built. Five miles south of this site, he and his men built Kentucky's first house. In this photo we see a replica of it, which stands at the Doctor Thomas Walker State Park.

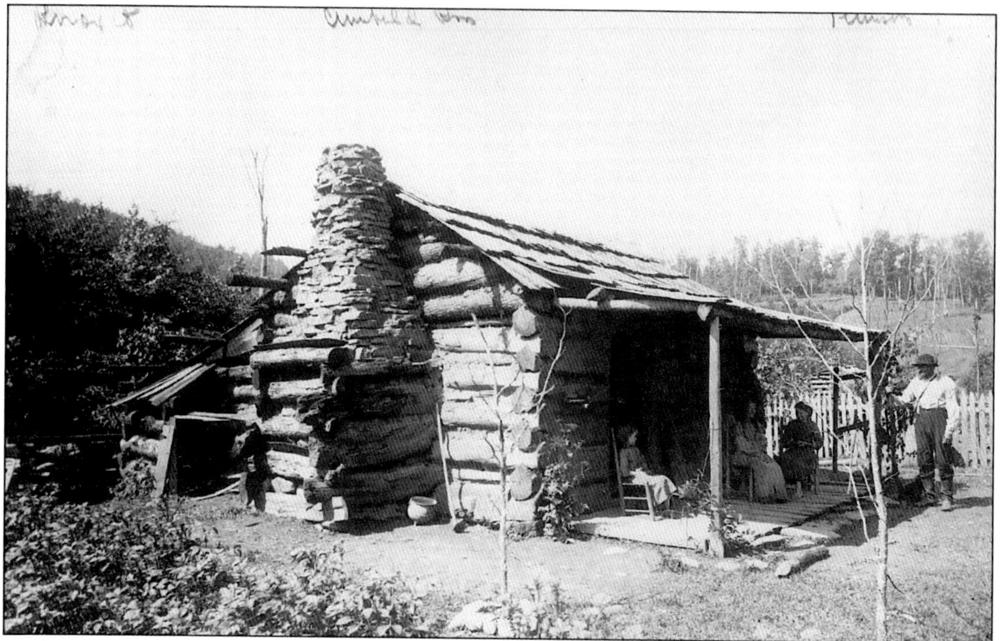

In the 1880s, Knox Countians continued to build log homes similar to the first one built by Thomas Walker. This house was built by the Moore family at Flat Lick. The cabin sat near the Wilderness Road, which was blazed through Knox County by Daniel Boone in the year 1775. (Photo courtesy of the Filson Club.)

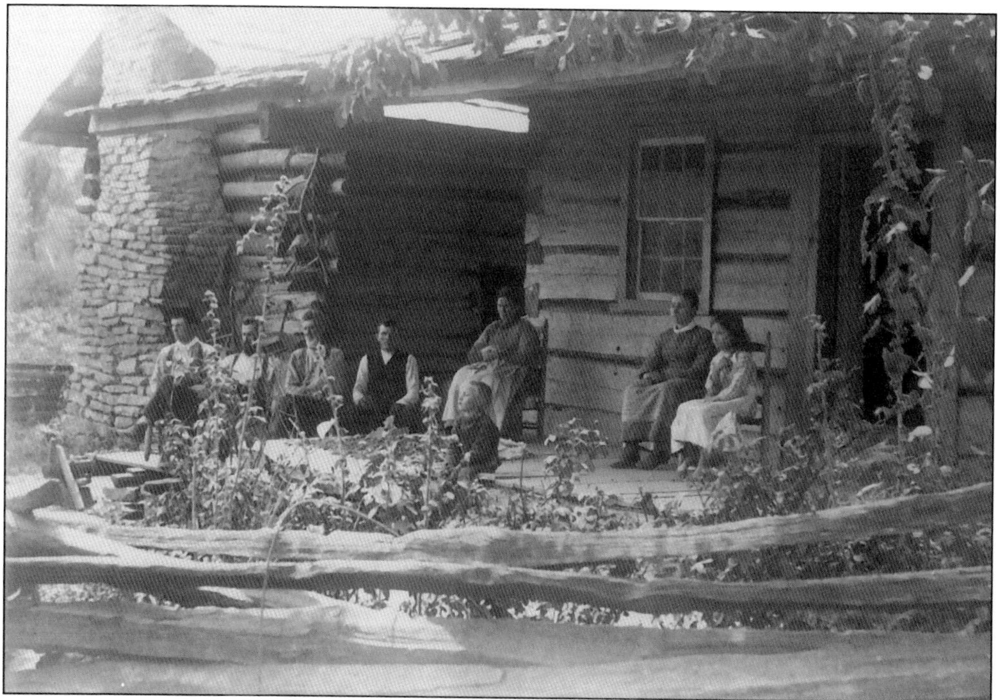

This split-log home belonged to the Fox family and was located on Goldens Creek. The front porch was important to the eight-member family, as it provided a cool resting place on hot summer afternoons. (Photo courtesy of the Filson Club.)

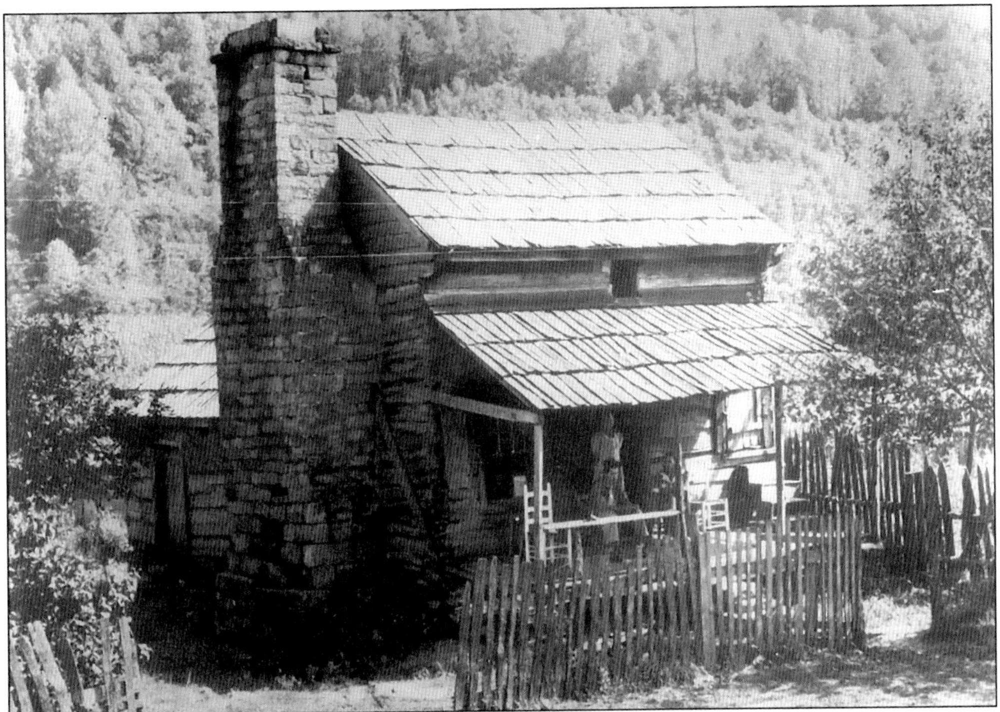

Closer to Barbourville we find the old Rasnic House. It sat on the Wilderness Road just 5 miles south of Barbourville. This house, located at Bimble, KY, was a local landmark until it burned in 1945. The cabin was also built of split logs, with a front porch and a large chimney.

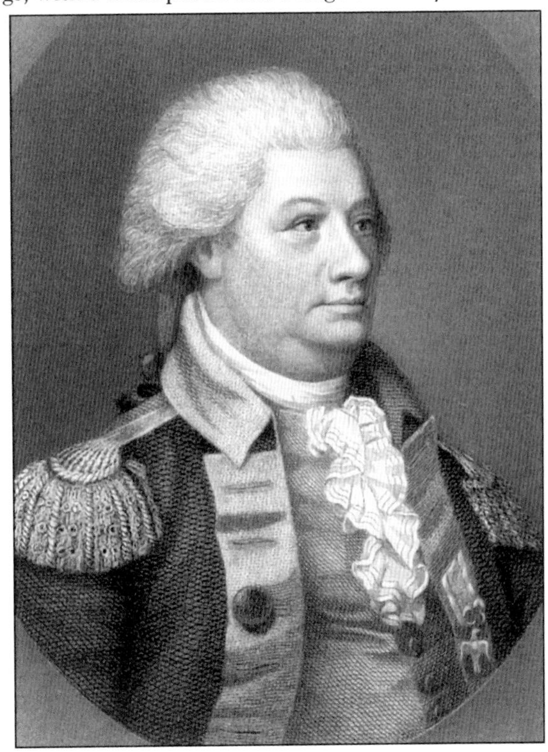

Knox County was named for General Henry Knox of Massachusetts. He was a veteran of the battle of Bunker Hill and was President George Washington's secretary of war.

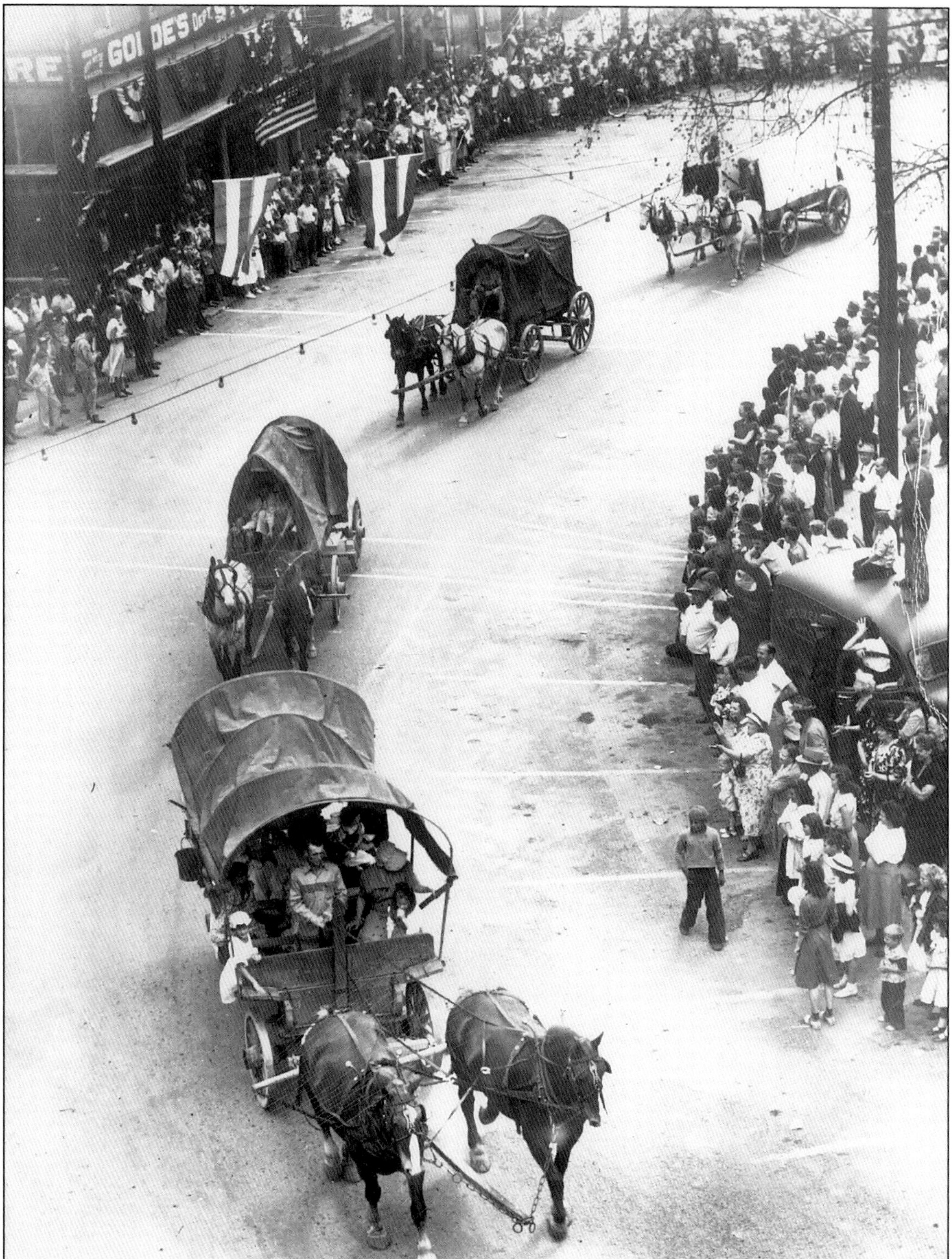

Early travel through Knox County was done on horseback and horse-drawn wagons. In 1950, Governor Flem Sampson, a resident of Barbourville, organized a celebration in honor of Dr. Thomas Walker's exploration of Knox County. The celebration featured a parade around the Courthouse Square, and citizens re-enacted the horse-and-wagon days. This pioneer parade served as a model for Knox County's most famous celebration, the Daniel Boone Festival. The Daniel Boone Festival is held each October to celebrate Daniel Boone's exploration of Knox County and southeast Kentucky.

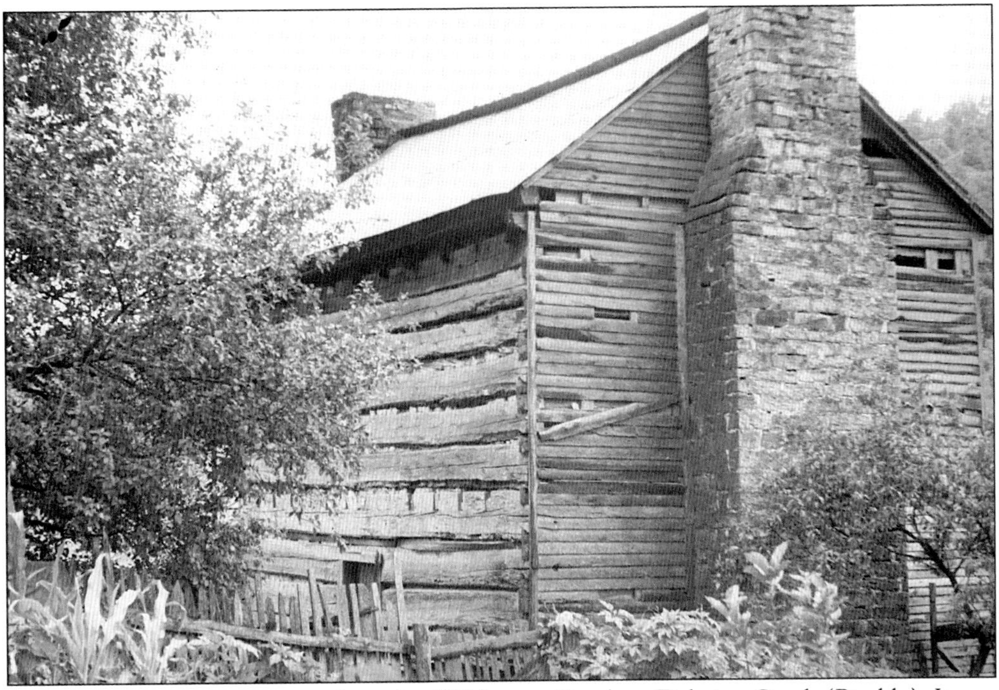

In 1807, a pioneer tavern stood on the Wilderness Road on Fighting Creek (Bimble). It was established by David Thomas. The old pioneer tavern was later used as a residence by the Ewing Callihan family. This photo reveals the split-log construction on the back wall, shortly before the old landmark was torn down.

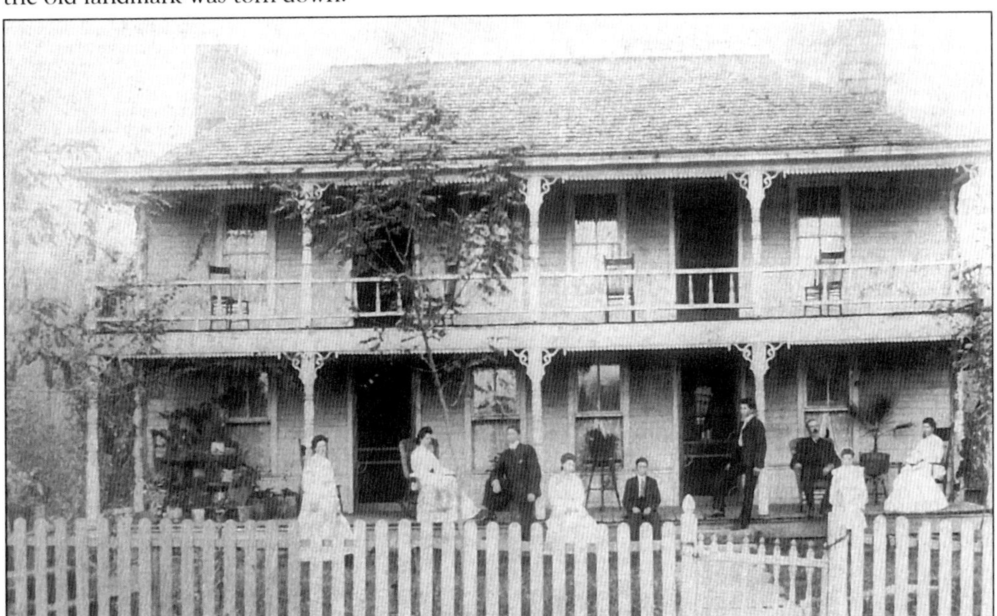

During the late 1800s and early 1900s, more elaborate houses were constructed. Here we see the Silas Woodson plantation house, which sat on the Wilderness Road near Turkey Creek. Note the siding and the two porches. Silas Woodson, seated in the rocking chair, moved to Missouri later in life and was elected governor of that state in 1872.

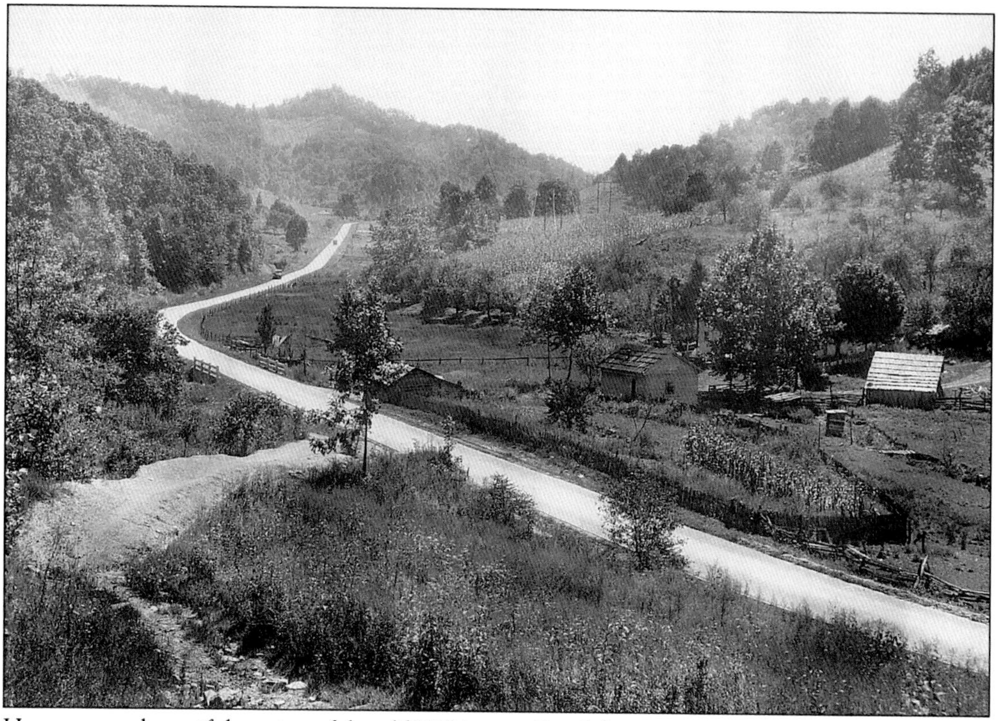

Here we see a beautiful section of the old Wilderness Road, between Four Mile and Flat Lick. This photo shows the road that became U.S. 25-E, now known as the Cumberland Gap Parkway.

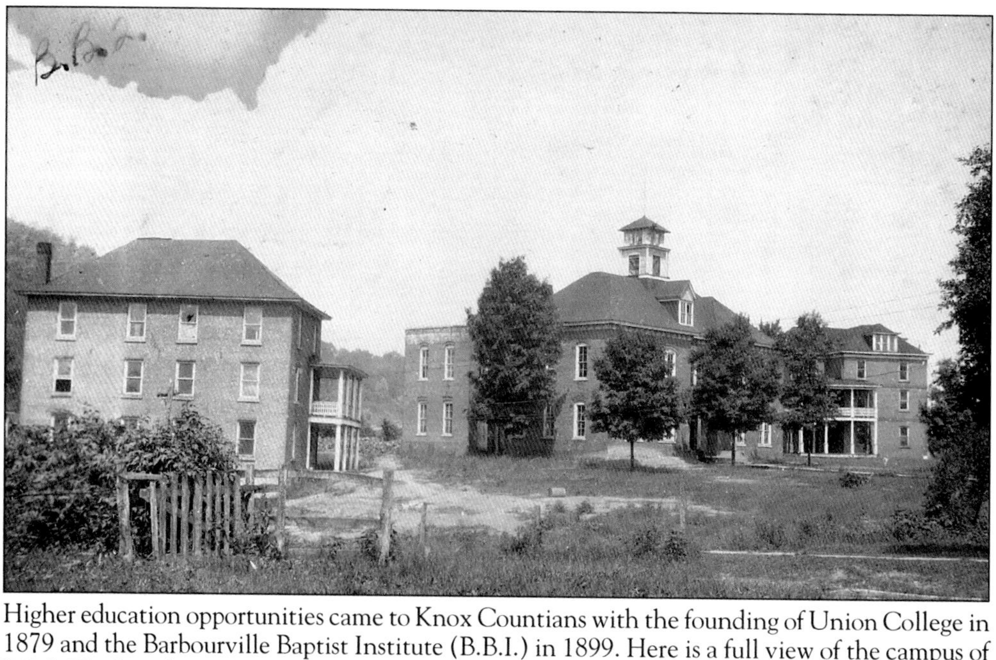

Higher education opportunities came to Knox Countians with the founding of Union College in 1879 and the Barbourville Baptist Institute (B.B.I.) in 1899. Here is a full view of the campus of B.B.I. The boarding school, located in Barbourville, featured a boy's dorm (far left), a classroom building (center), and a girl's dorm (far right). In 1935, this campus was closed, and it became the home of Knox Central High School.

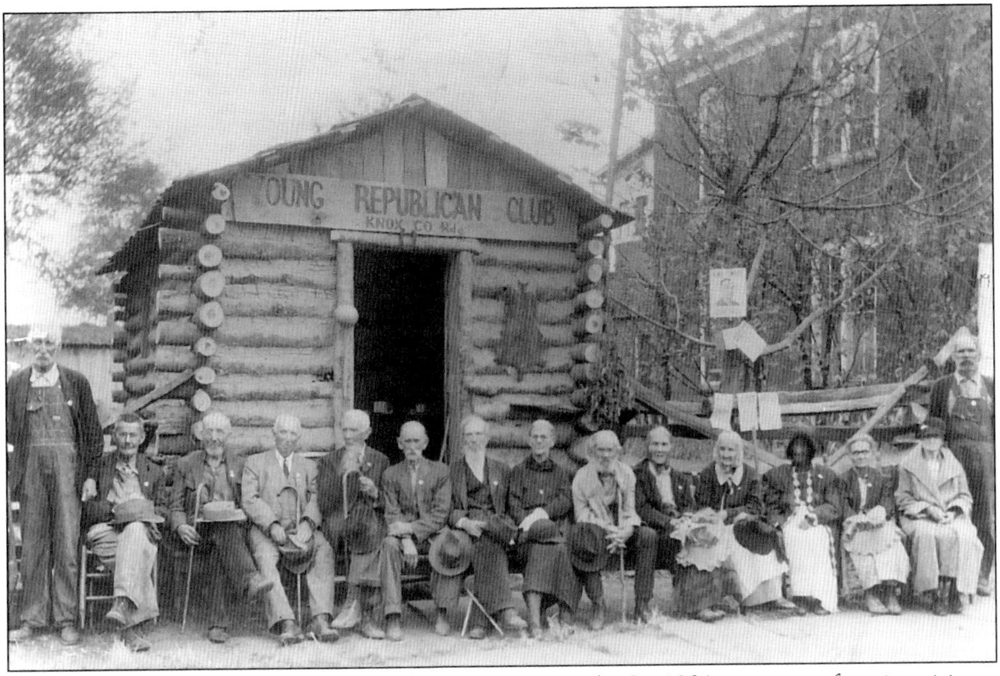

Knox County has always taken its politics very seriously. In 1931, a group of senior citizens calling themselves the Young Republicans Club built a log house on Knox Street to represent the G.O.P.

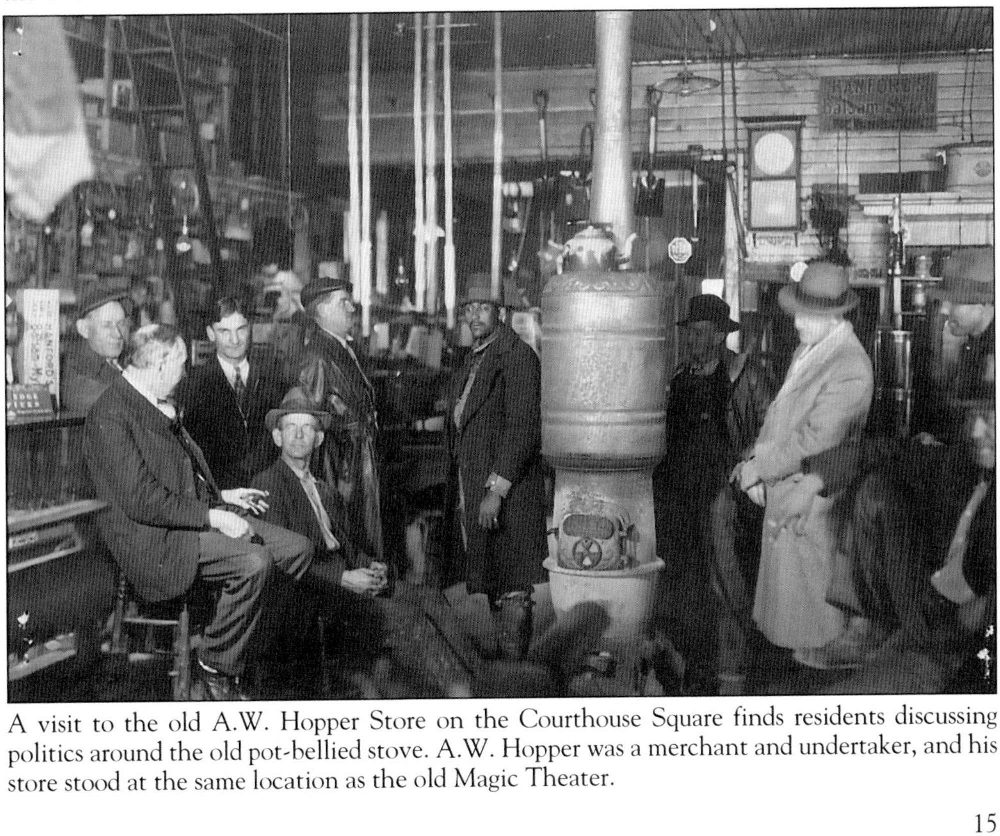

A visit to the old A.W. Hopper Store on the Courthouse Square finds residents discussing politics around the old pot-bellied stove. A.W. Hopper was a merchant and undertaker, and his store stood at the same location as the old Magic Theater.

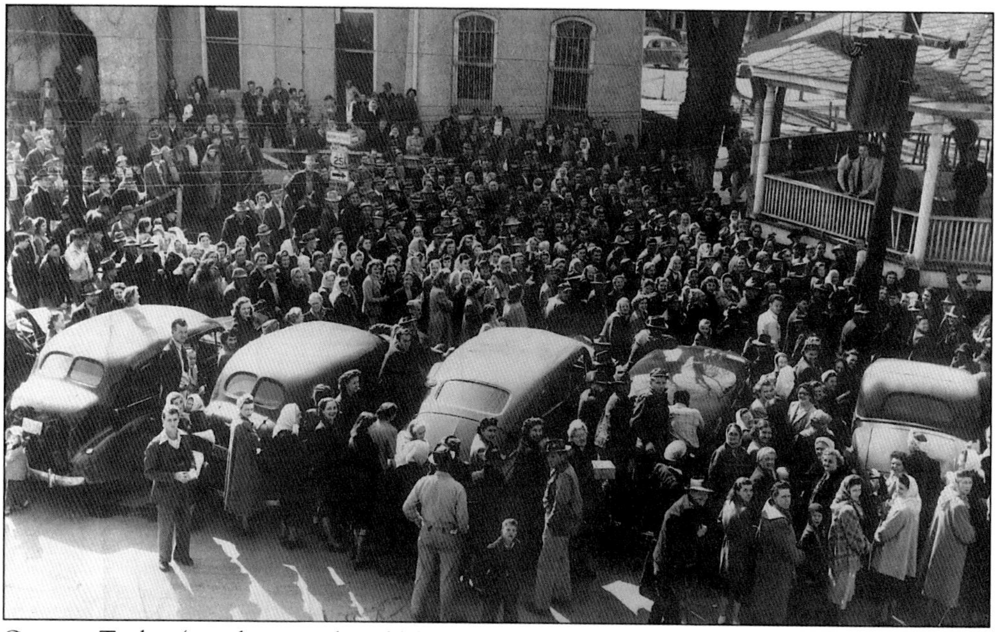

Gorman Taylor (standing on the old bandstand) reads the lucky number as a large crowd gathers for a prize drawing. Prize drawings were used to entice county residents to come to town on Saturday mornings. Most families chose to come to town only once a week to do their shopping, so during the 1940s and 1950s, it was not unusual at all to see adults and children on the Courthouse Square all day long.

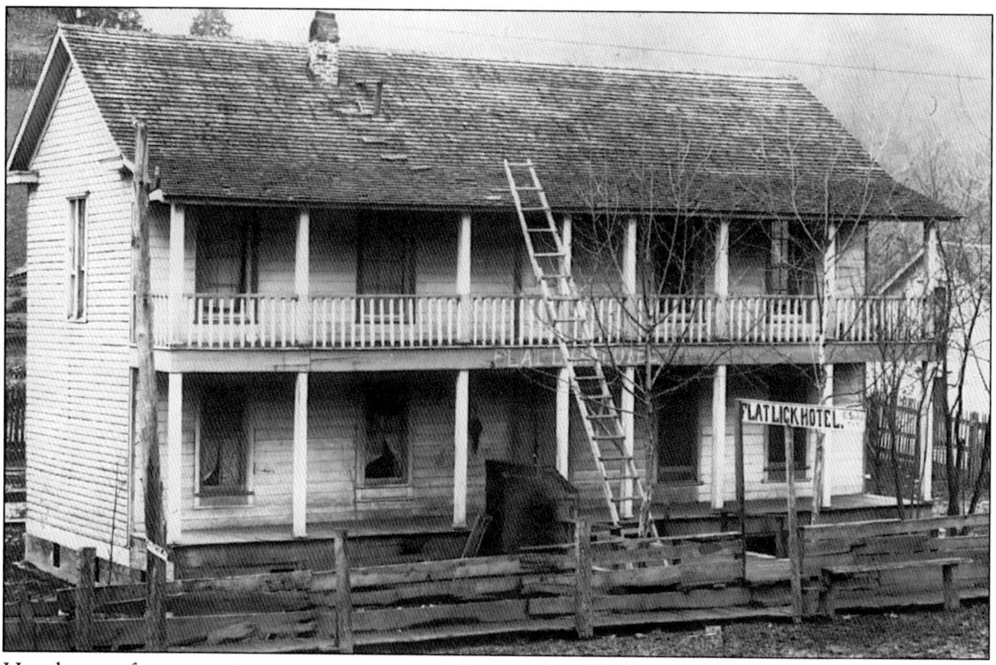

Hotels are often seen in county seat towns, but are less likely to be found in rural areas. Knox County had many taverns in its early days, and these gave way to boardinghouses in various communities around the county. Here we see the remains of the old Flat Lick Hotel in the early 1900s. (Photo courtesy of the Cumberland Gap National Park.)

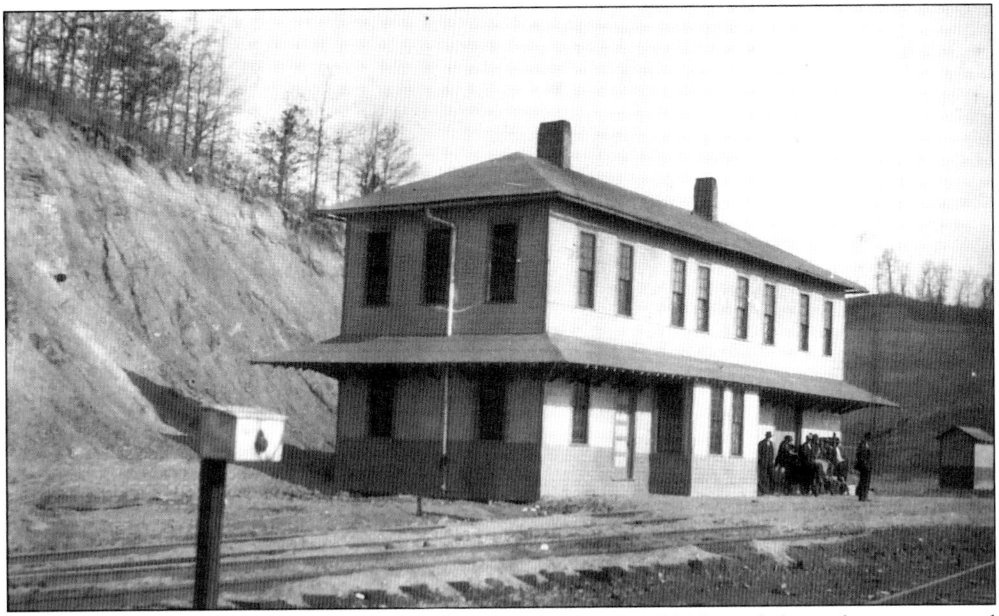

The railroad came into Barbourville and Knox County in 1888, and for a few years, coal became an important part of Knox County's economy. The L&N Railroad built a depot in Barbourville and smaller ones in the larger communities along the tracks. Here we see the old Heidrick Depot.

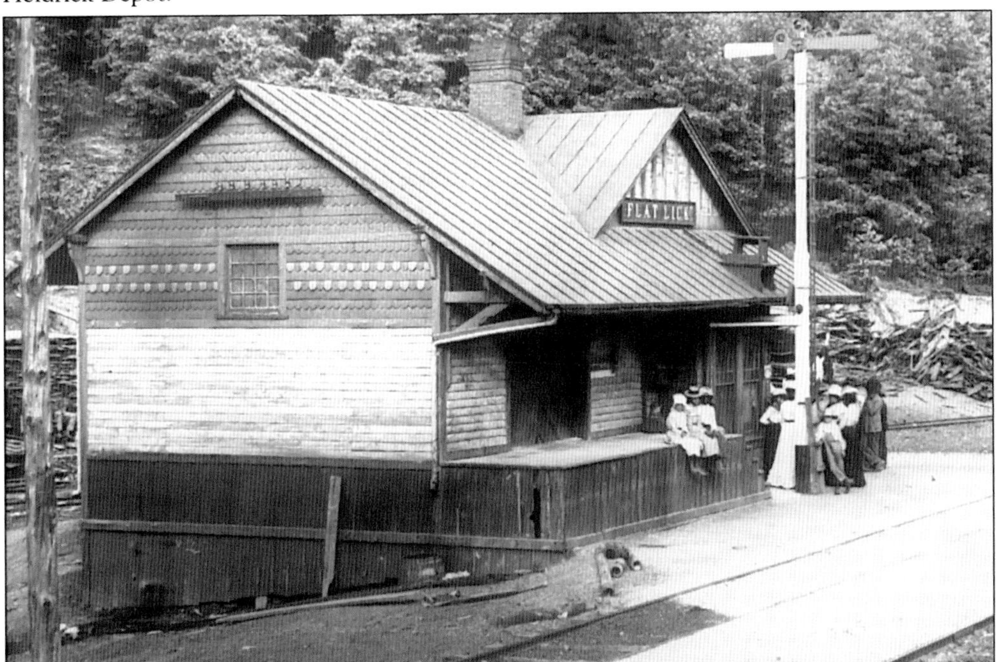

The depot at Flat Lick was a very active place. This community was one of Knox County's earliest residential areas. It was named for the salt lick there that was used by both Native-American and pioneer hunters. Flat Lick was the site of early Civil War skirmishes in 1862. Taverns were located there as early as 1803, and one of the county's earliest churches, Concord Baptist, was established there in 1815. (Photo courtesy of the Cumberland Gap National Park.)

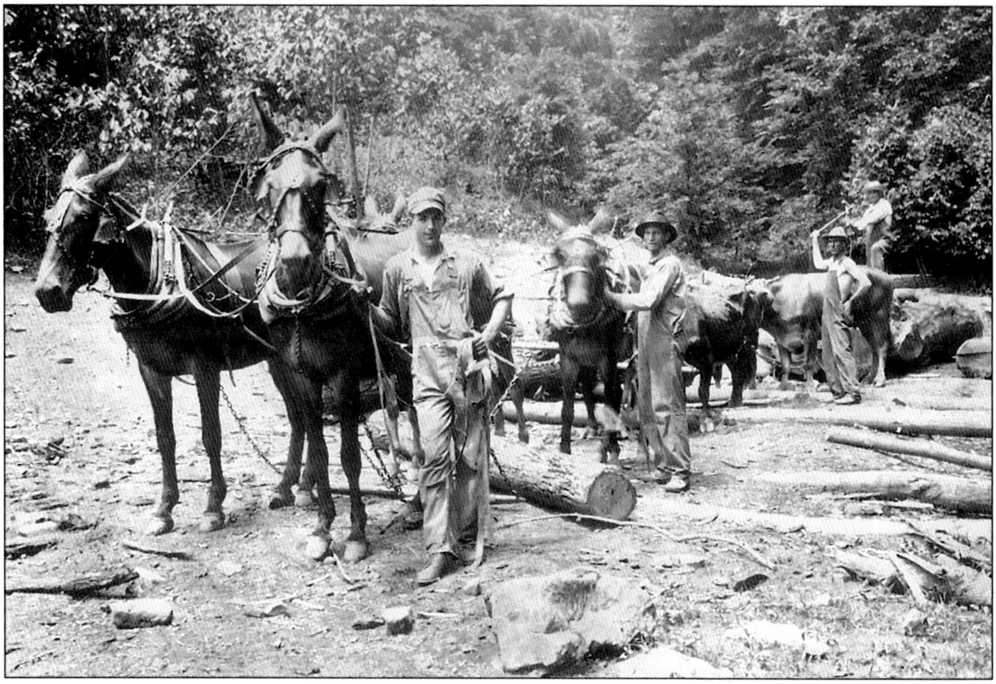

Logging was also a major part of Knox County's economy. The year is 1925, and Jay B. West, Pascal Code West, and Caleb West are shown here in the logging woods.

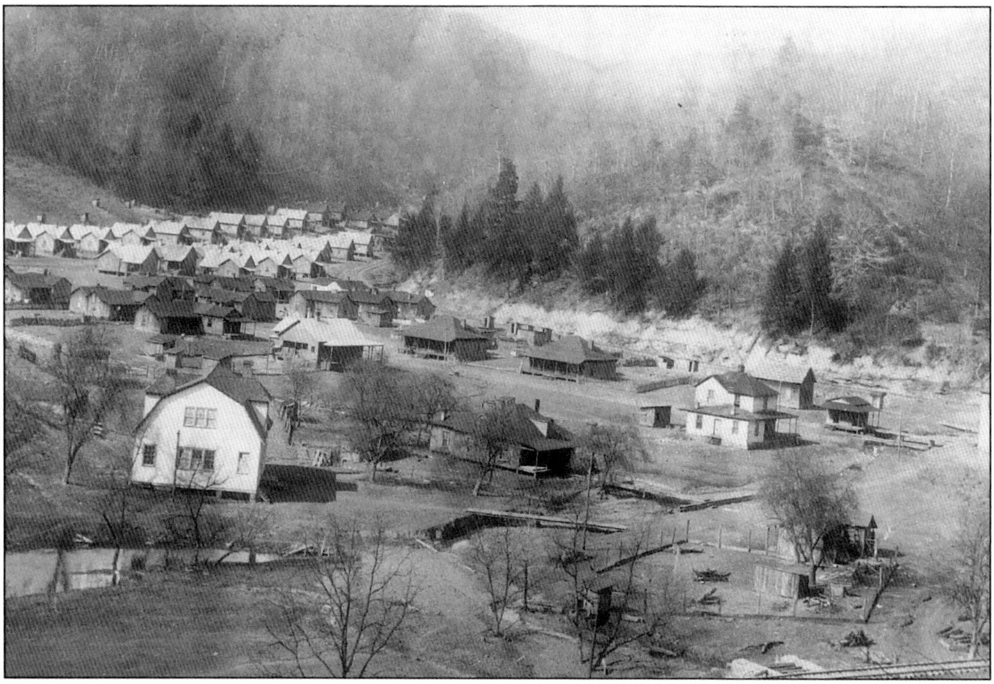

Before strip mining began in the 1960s, most Knox County coal was deep mined. The Brush Creek area was the most heavily mined area in Knox County. The Kentucky Jellico Coal Company had mines at Kay Jay, and a large coal camp was built at Warren. Here we see the Warren Coal Camp.

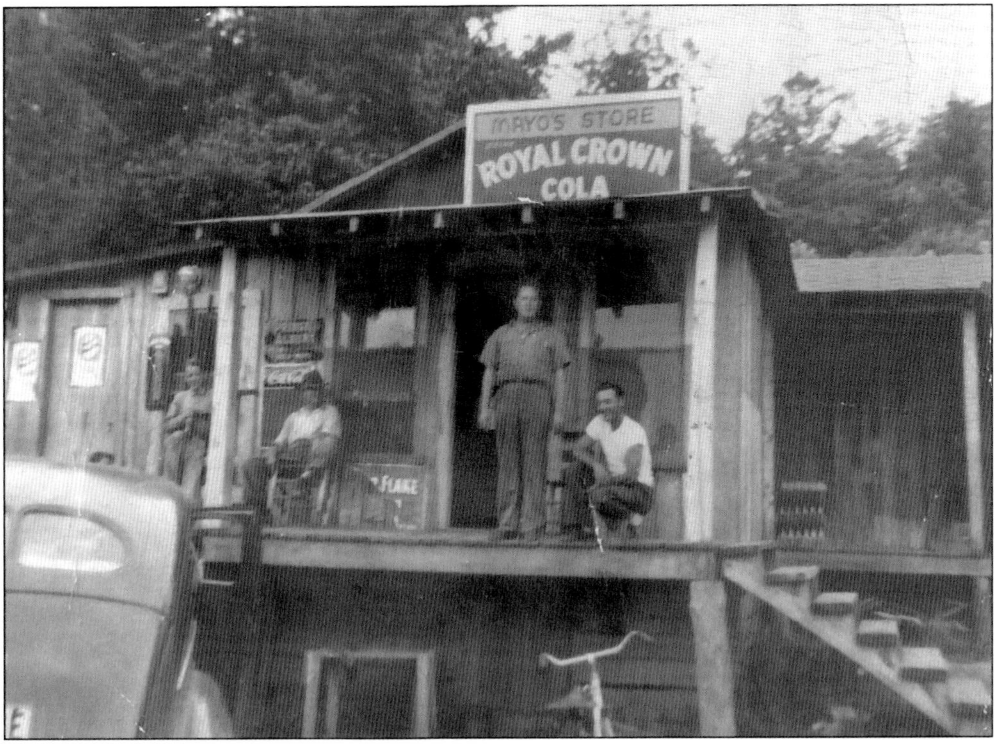

Rural family-owned grocery stores were, at one time, found in every Knox County community. Typical of these was Mayos Store at Dewitt, KY, on Stinking Creek in the 1940s. Pictured from left to right are John Walker, owner John Henry Mayo, his son, Arthur Mayo, and Rosco Baker.

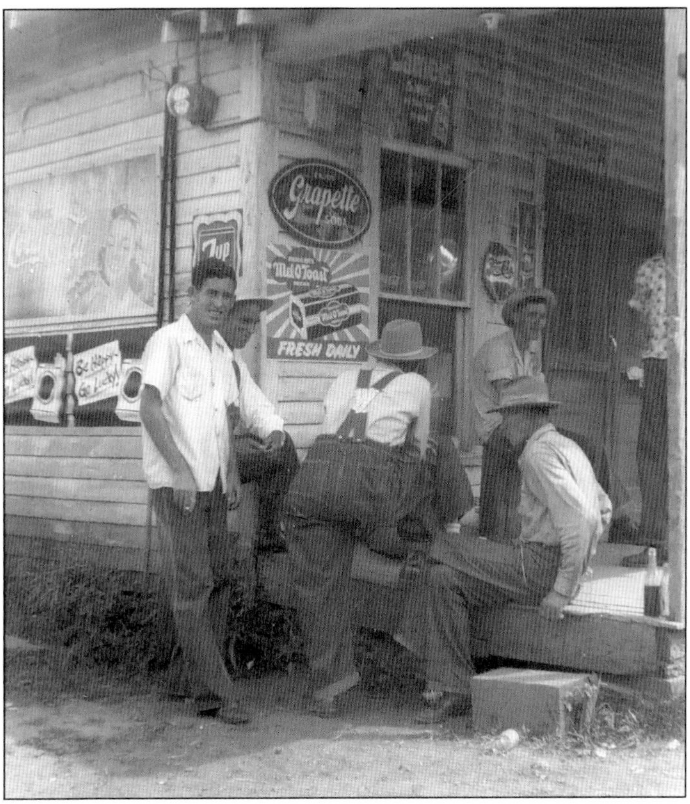

On any warm morning, throughout Knox County, one could find "loafers" congregated on storehouse porches. Talk was about everything from gardening to politics. Here William Mills gathers with a group of men at the Boyd Davis Grocery Store in Bimble, KY.

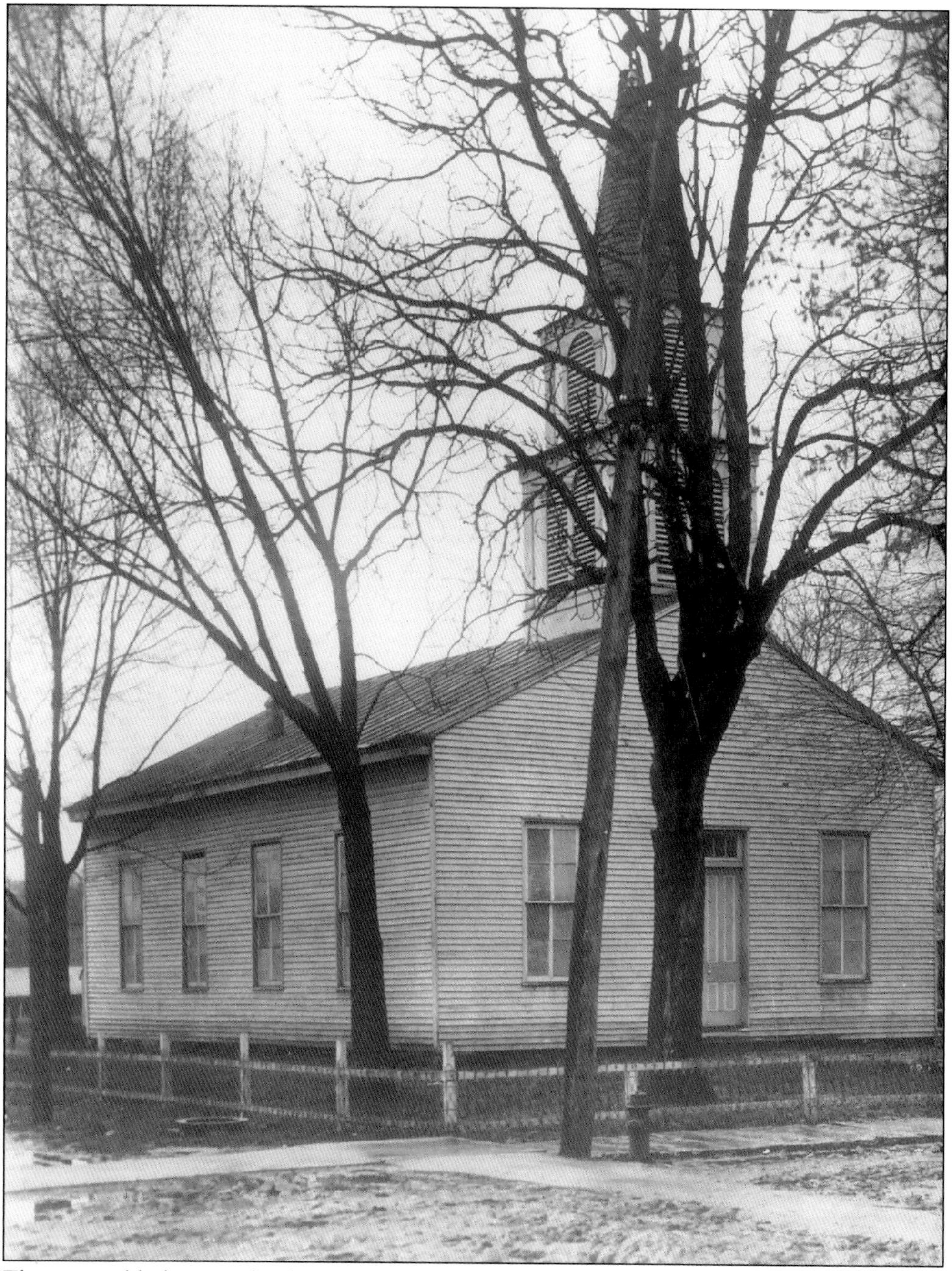

This is an old photograph of Barbourville's Christian Church. It is typical of the many rural churches in the valleys of Knox County during the 1940s and 1950s. Most Knox Countians are religious people and make Christianity an important part of their lives.

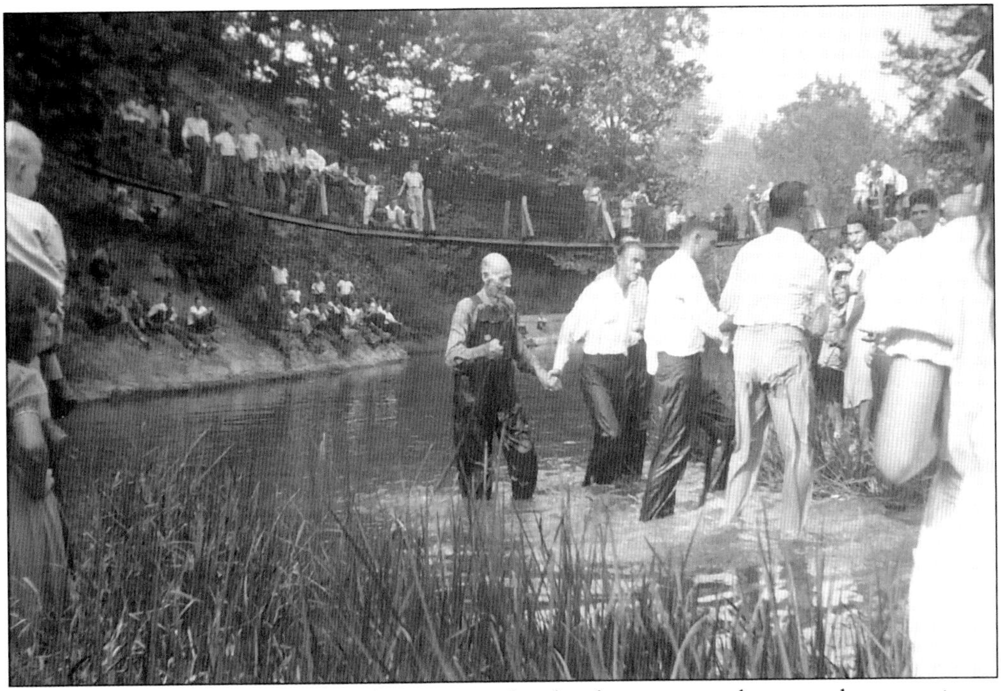

This country baptizing in the creek is a scene that has been repeated over and over again on many Sunday afternoons throughout Knox County.

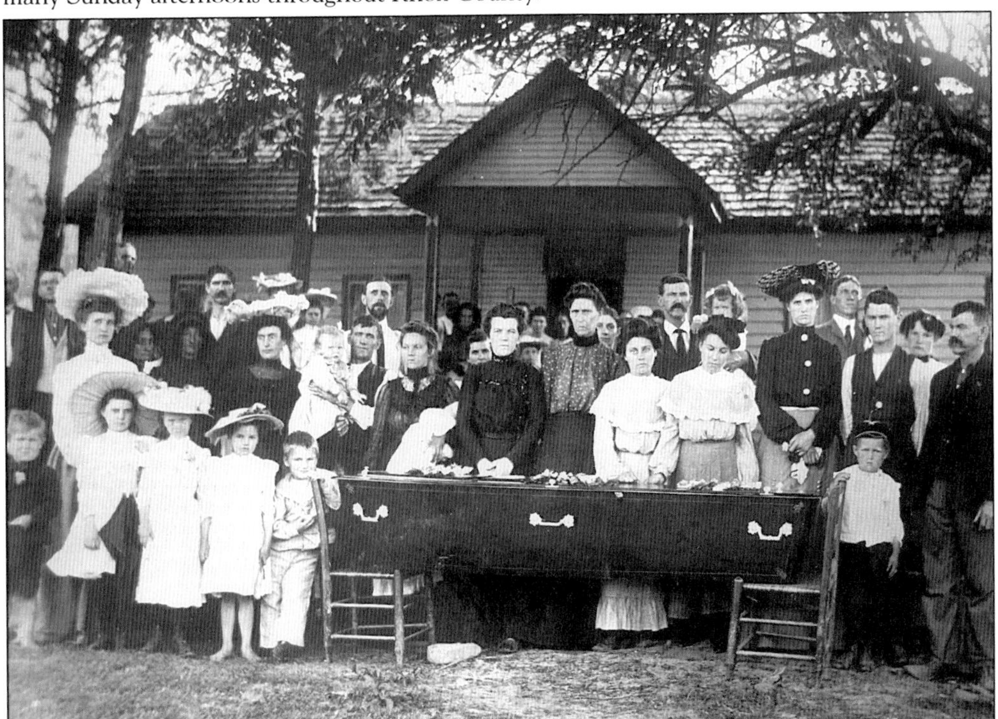

This is an interesting scene in 1904, as family and friends gather for the funeral of Thomas B. Disney at Gray, KY. Knox Countians saw death as only a passing to a better life.

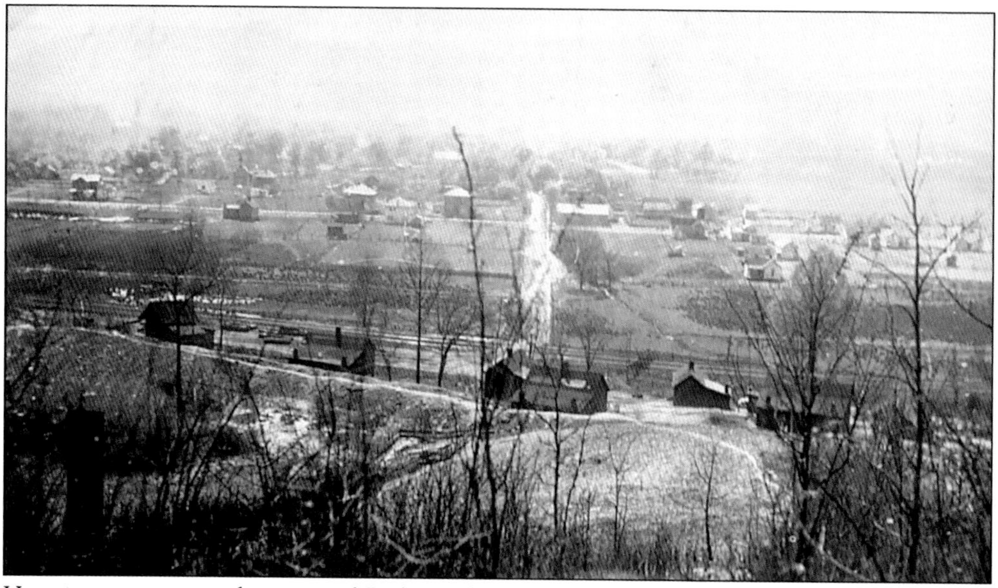

Here is a rare postcard picture of Barbourville in the early 1900s. This view was taken from Sampson Hill looking up Knox Street. The old Brick Store can be seen at the far end of the street, to the right.

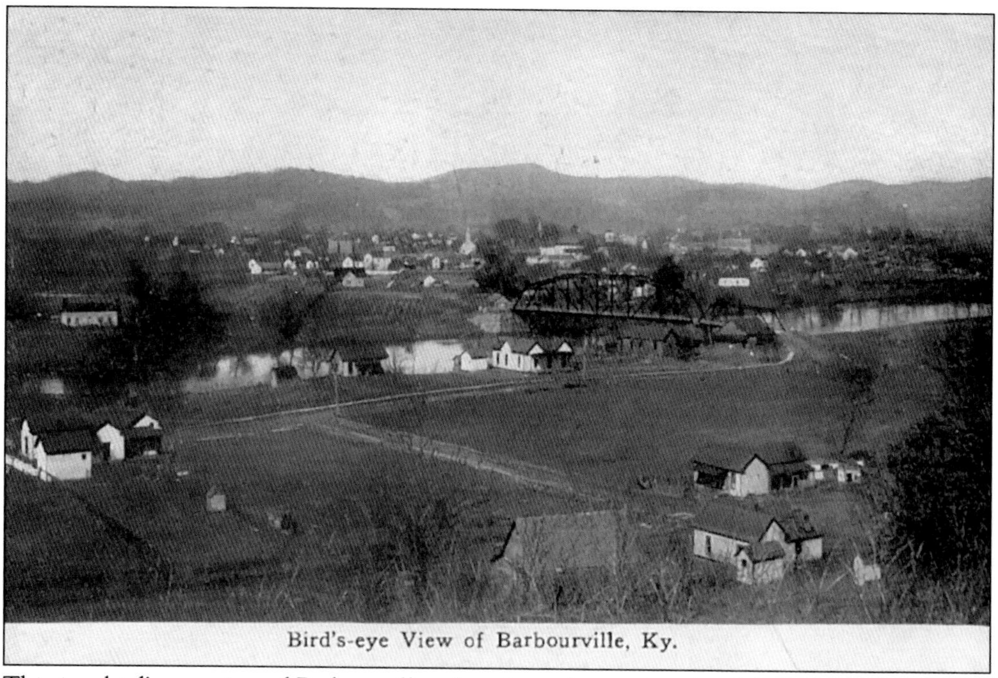

This is a bird's-eye view of Barbourville taken from the south side of the Cumberland River Bridge. Homes and farms can be seen here, during the days of annual flooding. A flood wall was built in 1959 to protect the north bank of the river. However, this caused the relocation of many families on the south side of the wall.

Two

BARBOURVILLE

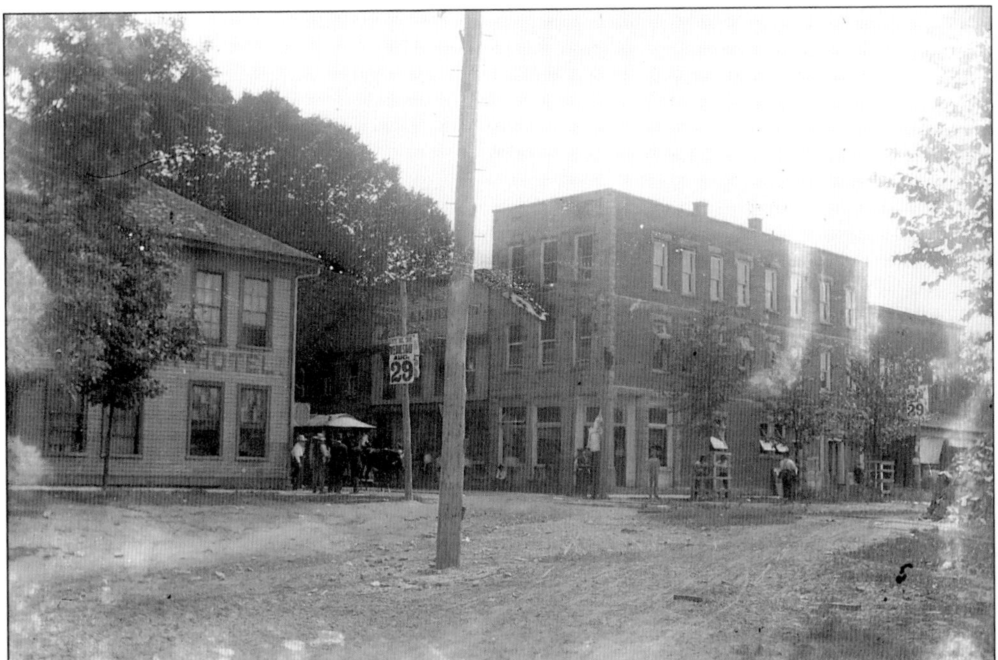

Barbourville, the county seat of Knox County, was situated along the north bank of the Cumberland River in 1800. It was originally off the main route of the Wilderness Road until 1810, when a new road was built to intersect the town. Barbourville is the only town in Knox County and is the oldest in southeast Kentucky. Early travelers to Barbourville found excellent hotels and places of business. The town was incorporated in 1890. Like most rural towns, streets were unpaved and walkways were but boardwalks. This 1906 photo shows the city before paved streets.

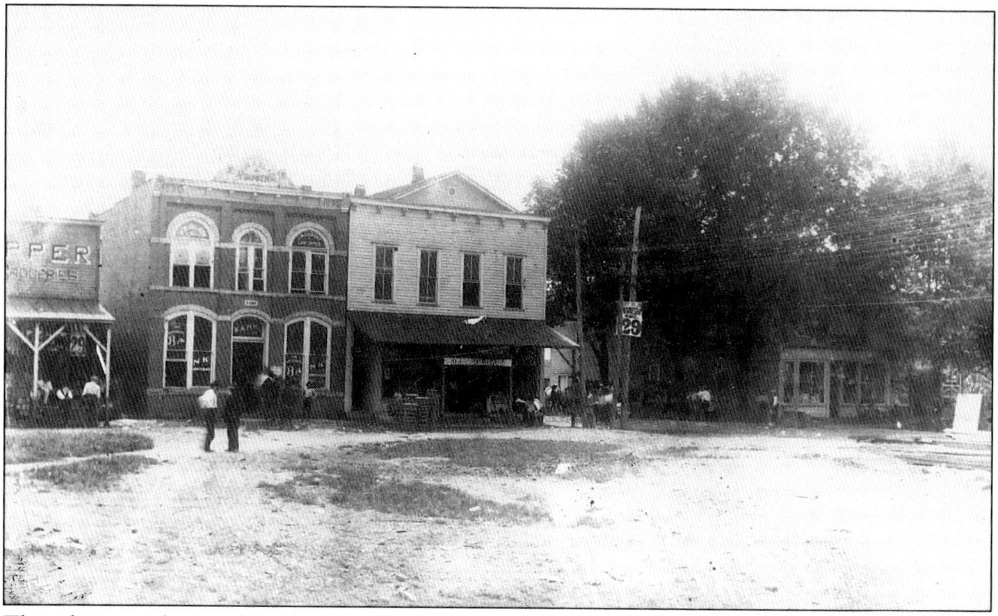

This photograph was also taken in 1906 and shows the old A.W. Hopper Building (at the left) and the John A. Black Bank, which was built in 1895. The Croley Hardware Store is pictured to the right center, and to the far right is the T.J. Pitzer Store, which later was operated as the L.C. Miller Store.

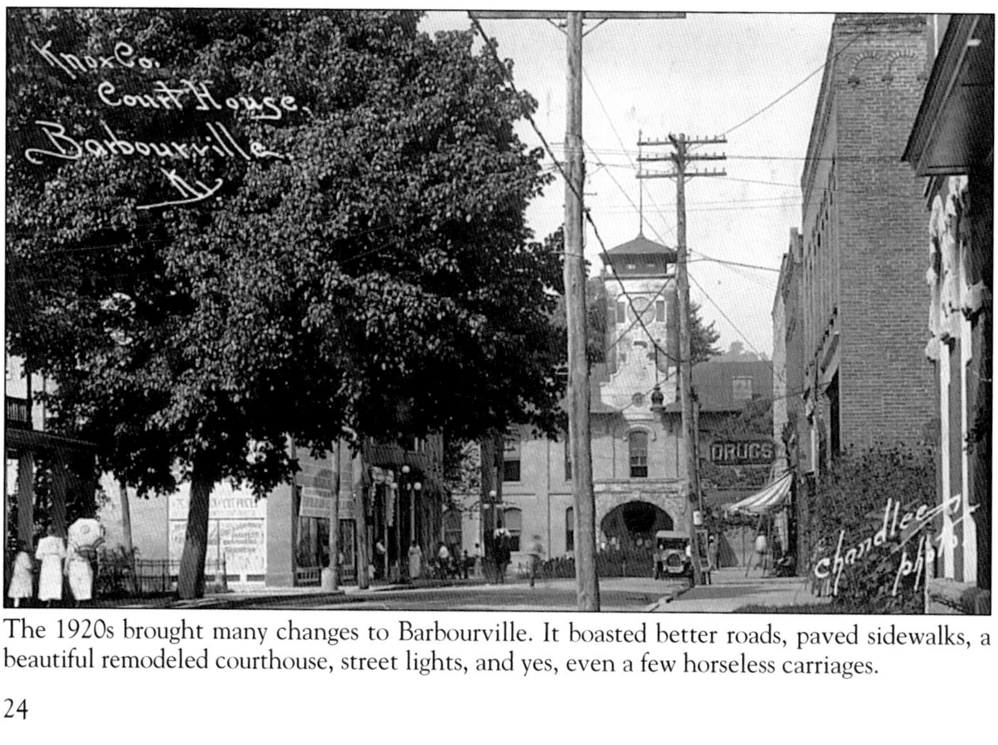

The 1920s brought many changes to Barbourville. It boasted better roads, paved sidewalks, a beautiful remodeled courthouse, street lights, and yes, even a few horseless carriages.

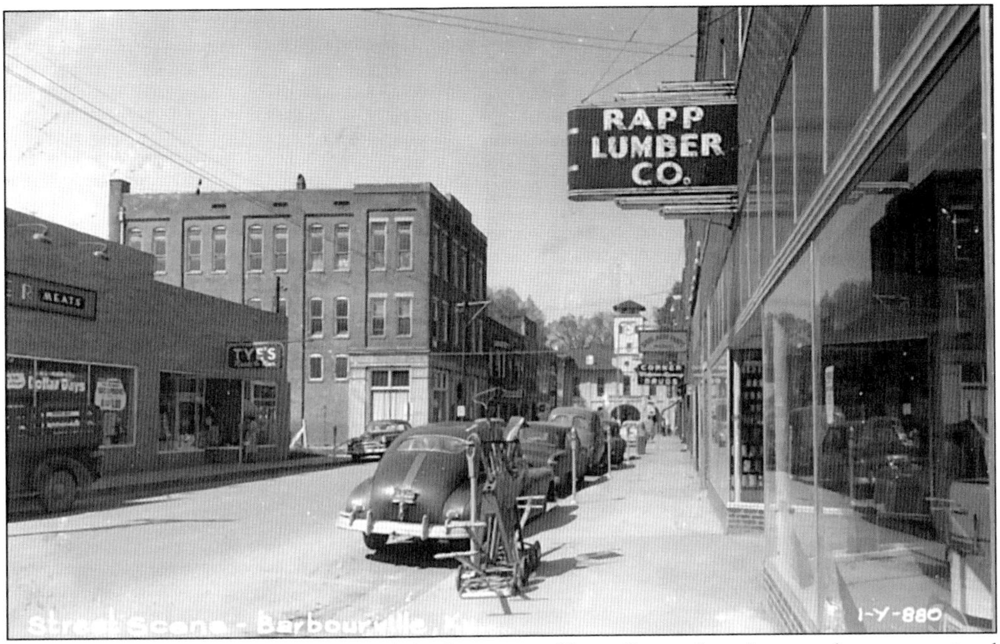

By 1950, parking meters had replaced shade trees on Knox Street, but the courthouse remained and had been joined by new businesses. On the left are the Kroger Store, Tyes Clothing Store, and Union National Bank; on the right side of the street are the Rapp Lumber Company, Knox Auto Parts, and the old Corner Drug Store.

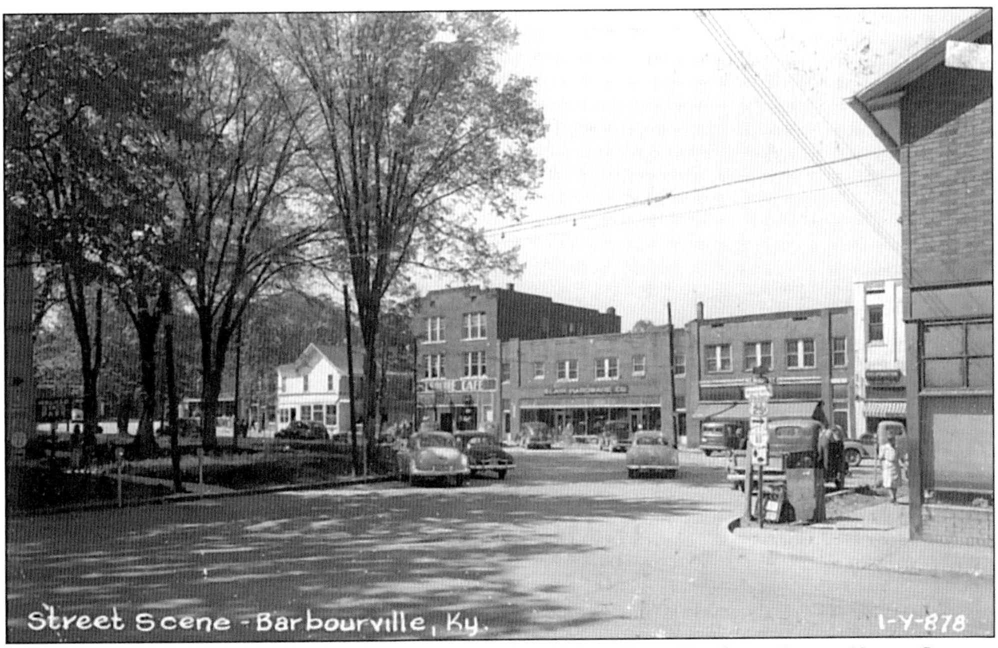

Circling Courthouse Square in 1950, we see the old Wilson Brothers Store, Knox County Supply, Blair Hardware Company, the Esquire Café, and the old Bee Hive Restaurant and Boarding House.

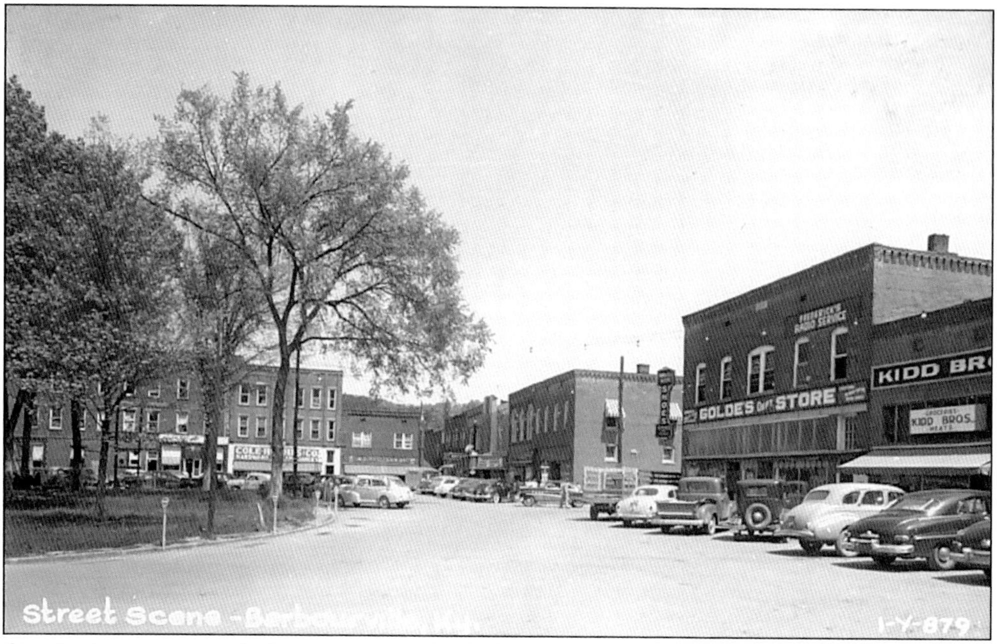

Continuing on around the square, we find the Kidd Brothers Grocery Store and Goldies Department Store in 1950. In the distance are the old Magic Movie Theatre, R.H. Williams 5 & 10 Cent Store, and Cole and Hughes Hardware Store.

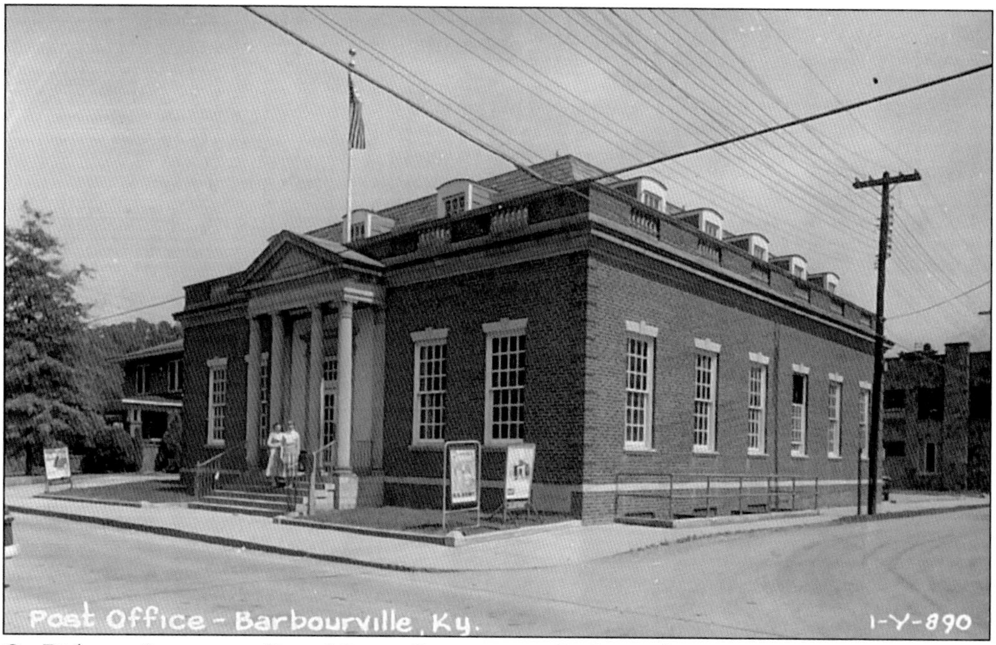

On Dishman Street, now Daniel Boone Drive, we see Barbourville's old post office building as it looked in 1950. Today, this building is home to the Knox County Board of Education.

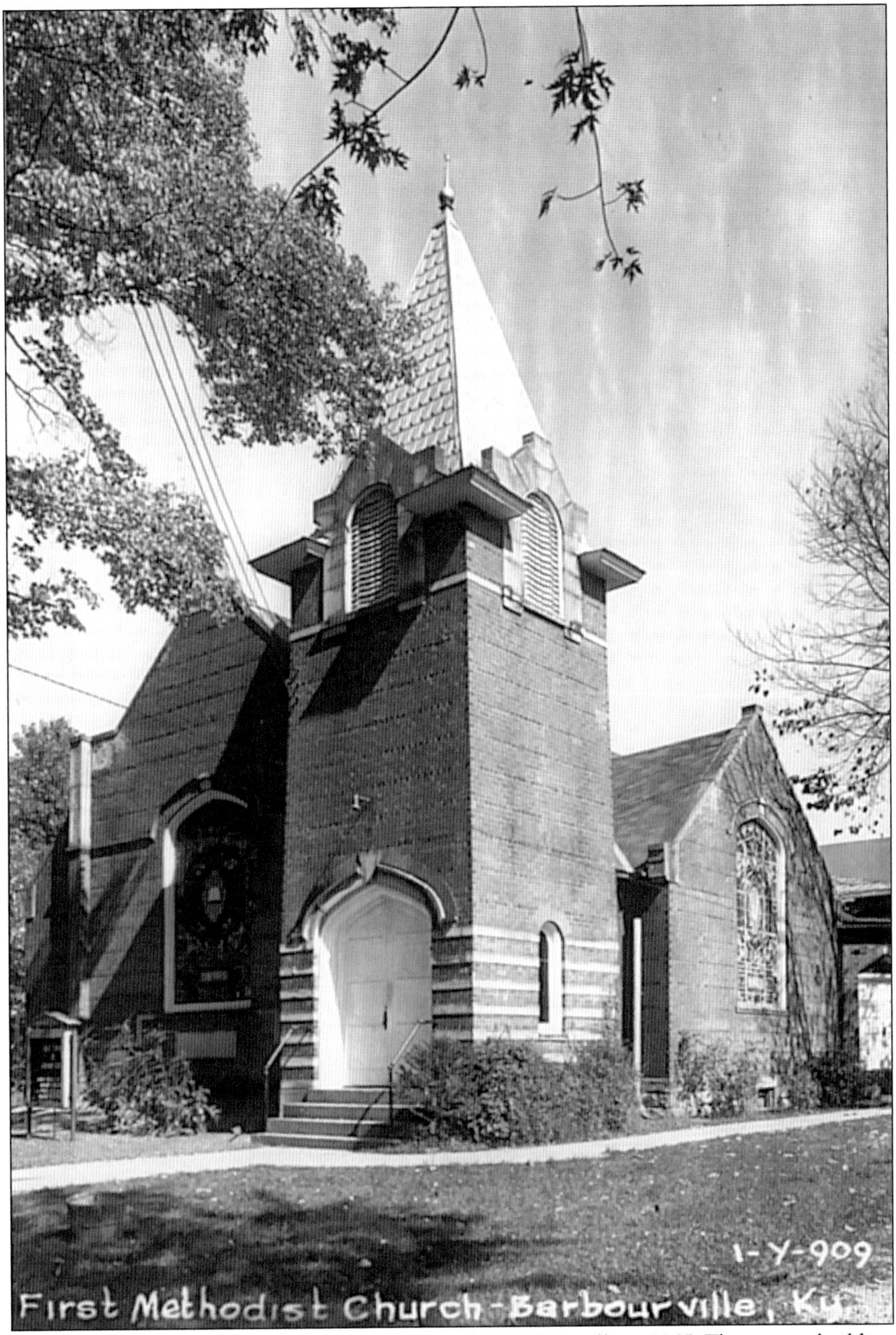

The First United Methodist Church was organized in Barbourville in 1865. The present building was built in 1907. This beautiful structure stands today on North Main Street.

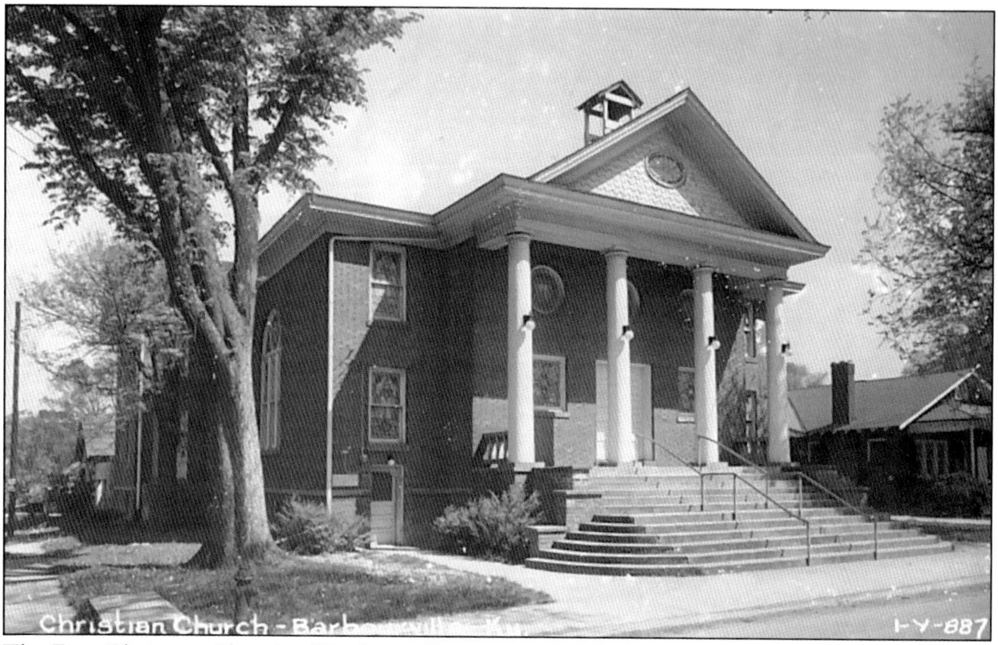

The First Christian Church of Barbourville constructed this fine building in 1915. It is located on High Street.

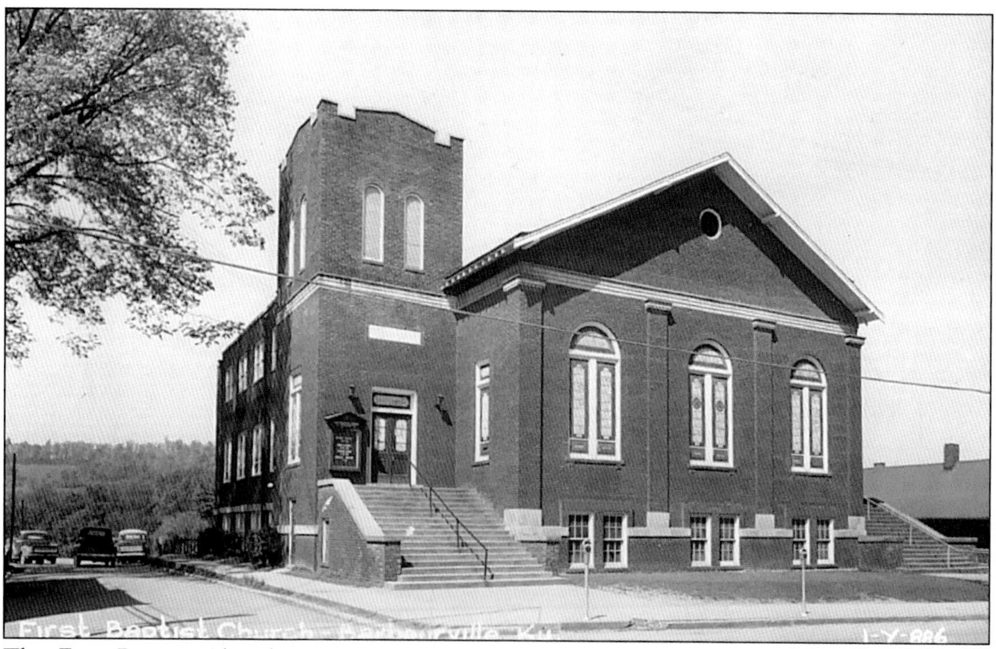

The First Baptist Church is located on North Main Street. It was originally called the Cumberland River Baptist Church and was organized on May 12, 1804. In 1974, the church built a new sanctuary on this same site.

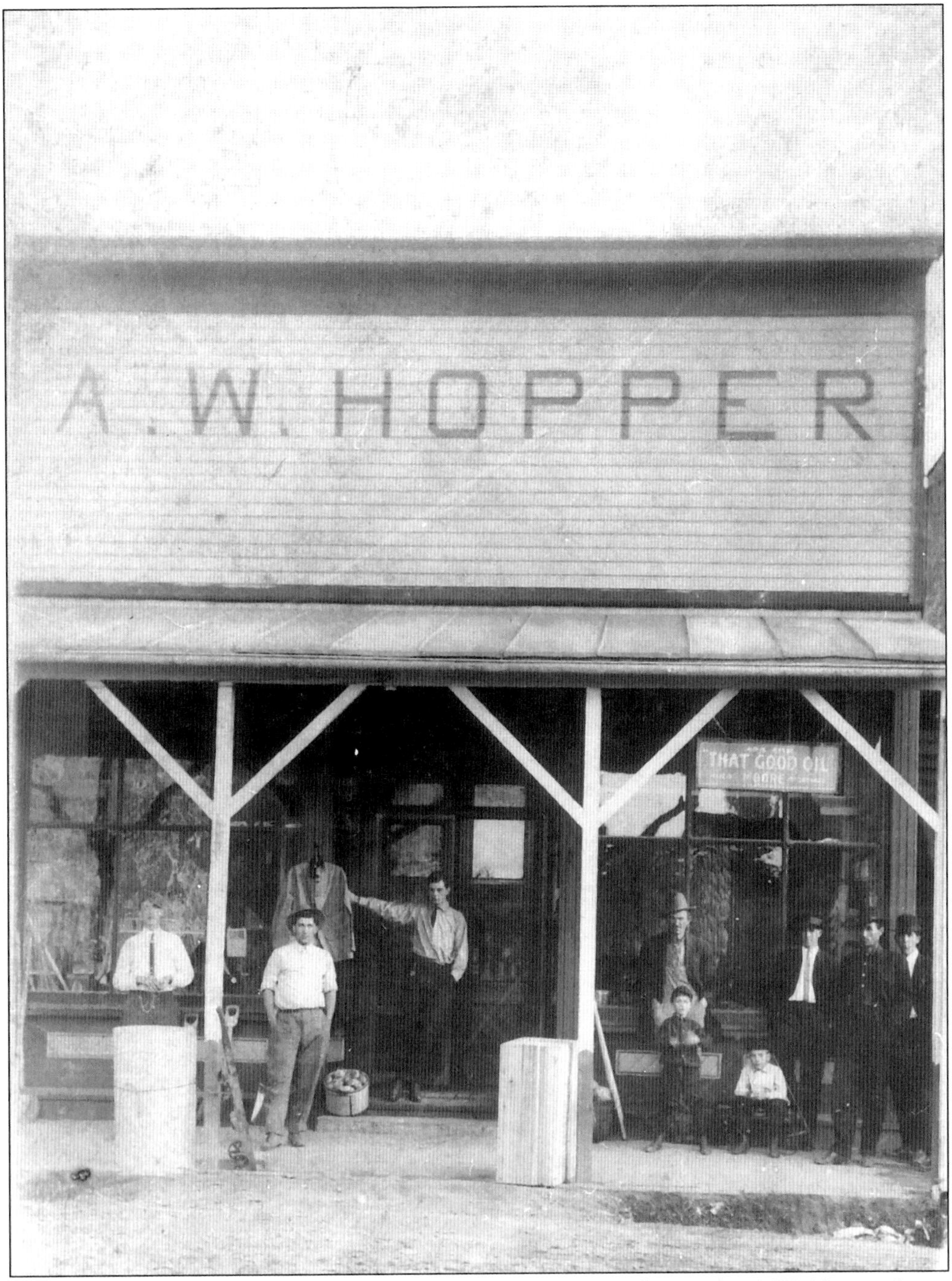

In the early 1900s, perhaps the most popular store in Barbourville was the A.W. Hopper Store. In the back, Mr. Hopper also ran a funeral parlor. This old hardware store was the site of many "get-togethers" around the old coal stove.

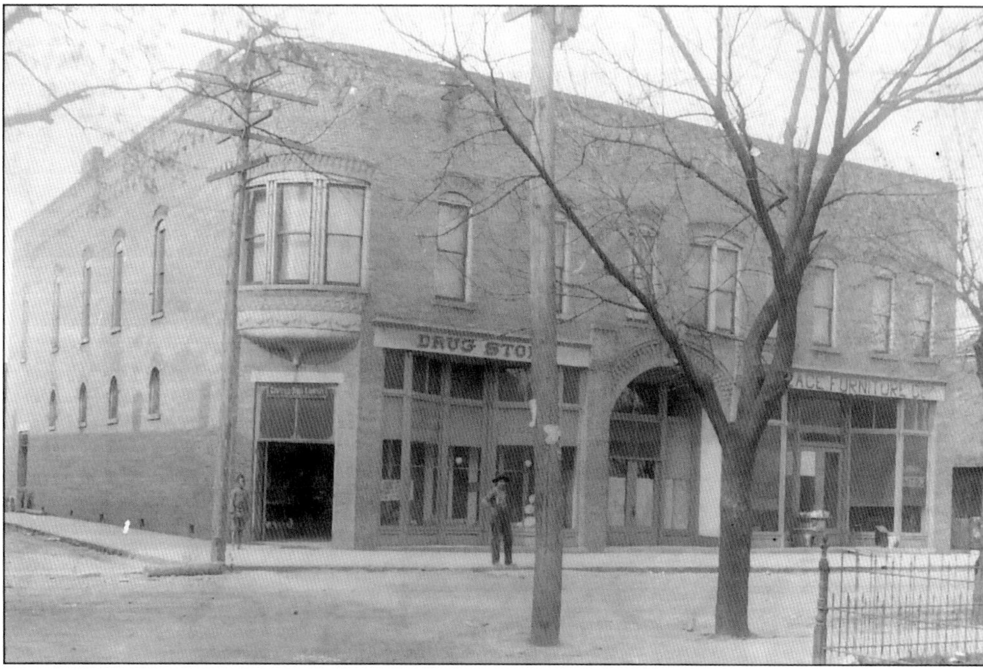

The old Corner Drug Store, once known as the Costello Drug Store, was located at the intersection of Knox Street and Liberty Street. This building was a Barbourville landmark since 1904. Many citizens remember visiting the old soda fountain there. The drug store was destroyed by fire in 1990.

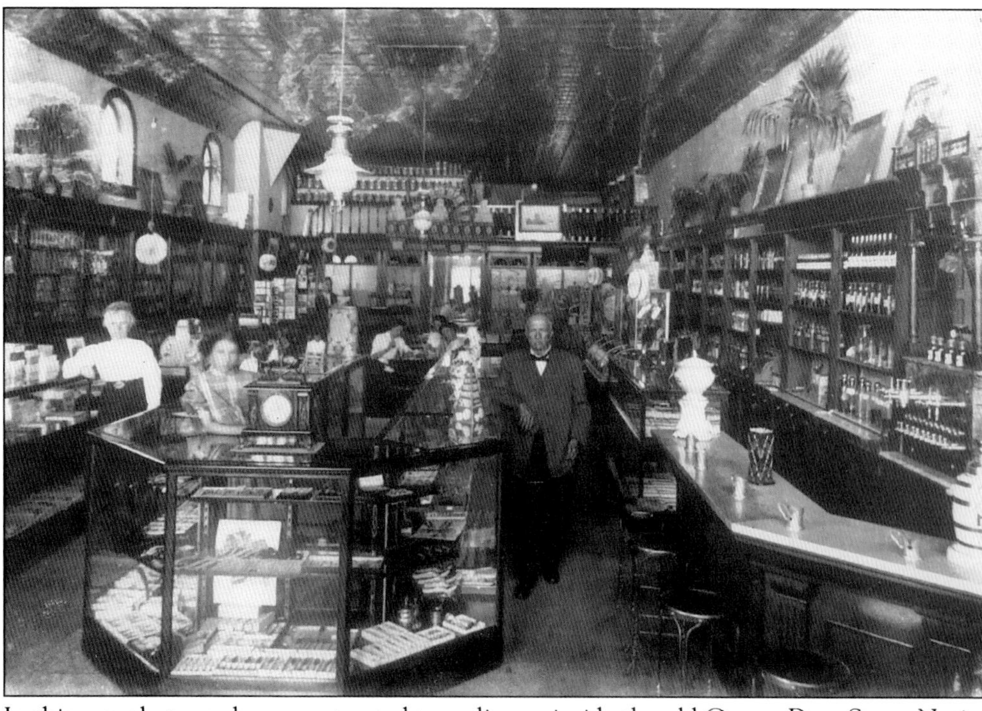

In this rare photograph, we are treated to a glimpse inside the old Corner Drug Store. Notice the tin roof tiles, its glass display cases, and everyone's favorite, the old-time soda fountain.

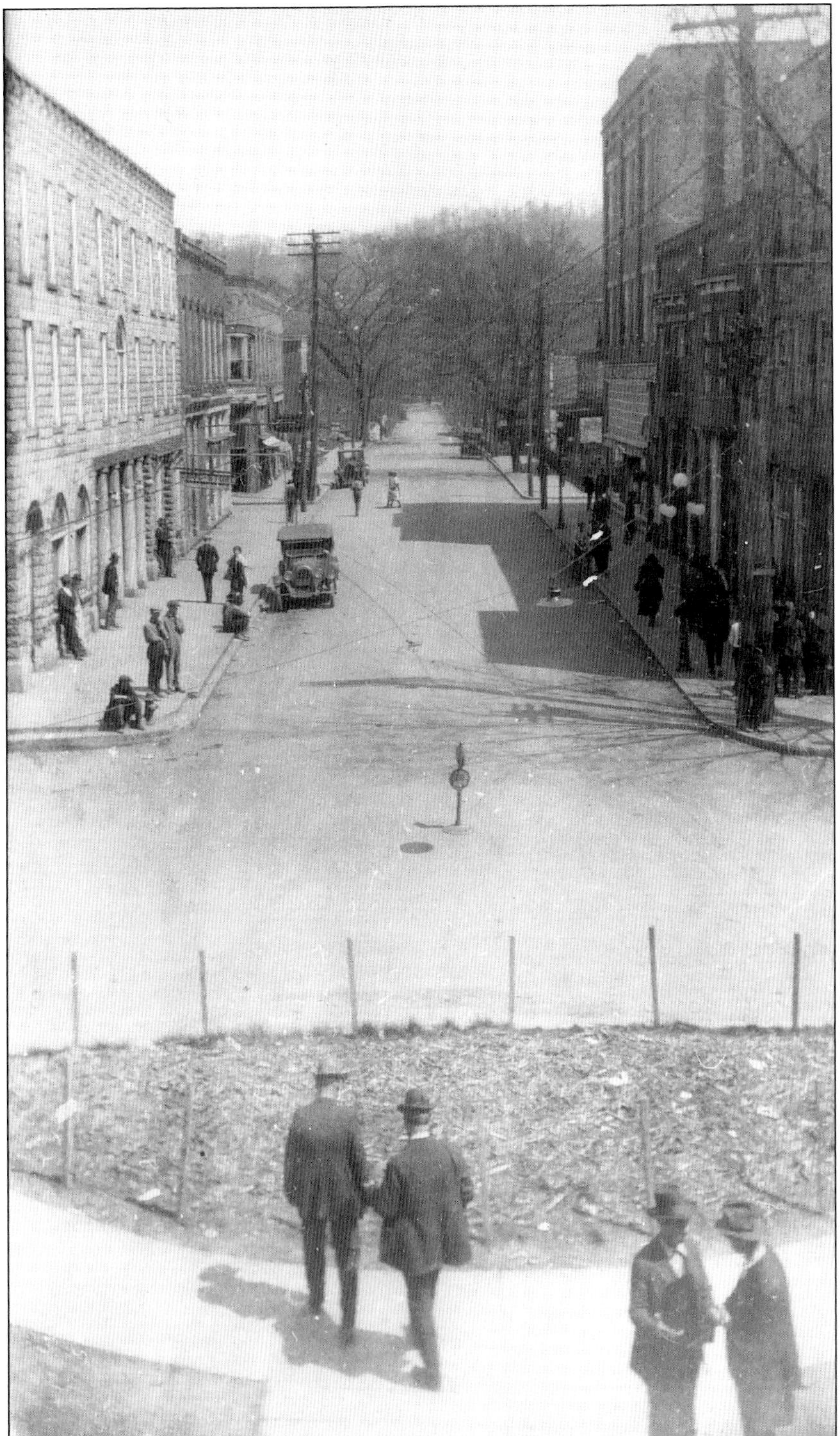

Looking down Knox Street in the 1920s, on the left are the Jones Hotel and, further down, the old Corner Drug Store; on the right are First National Bank and the New York Store. Early cars are visible. This photo was taken from atop the courthouse porch.

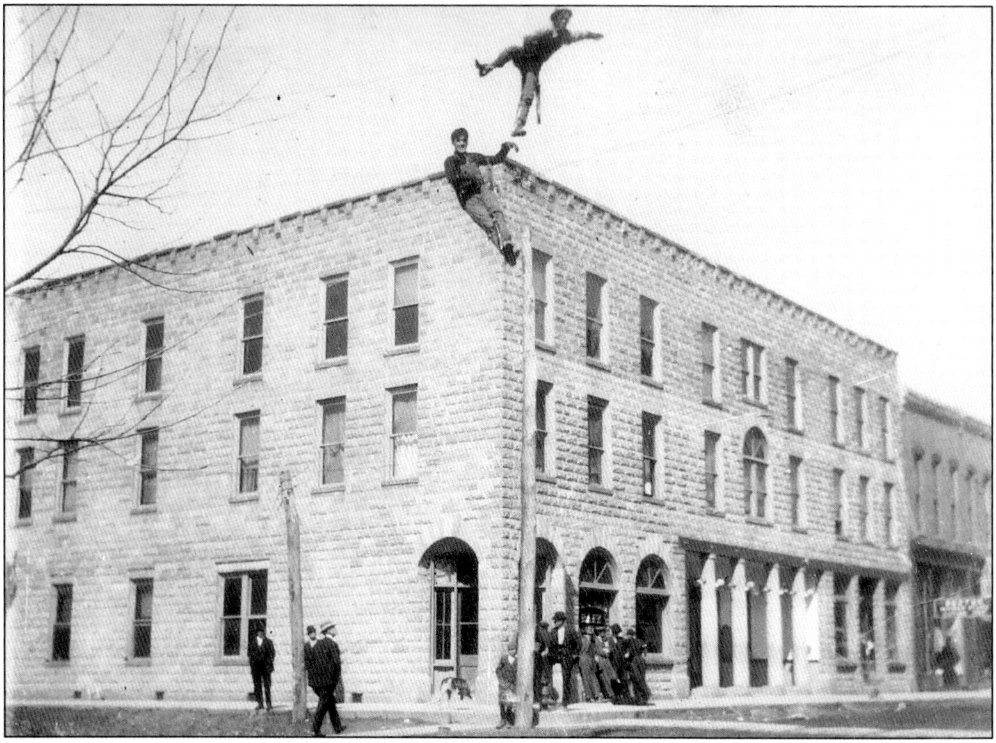

Sometime after 1880, a wood-frame hotel known as the Pitzer Hotel was built on the corner of Knox Street and Courthouse Square. Around 1910, the Pitzer Hotel was replaced by a concrete block building remembered as the Jones Hotel.

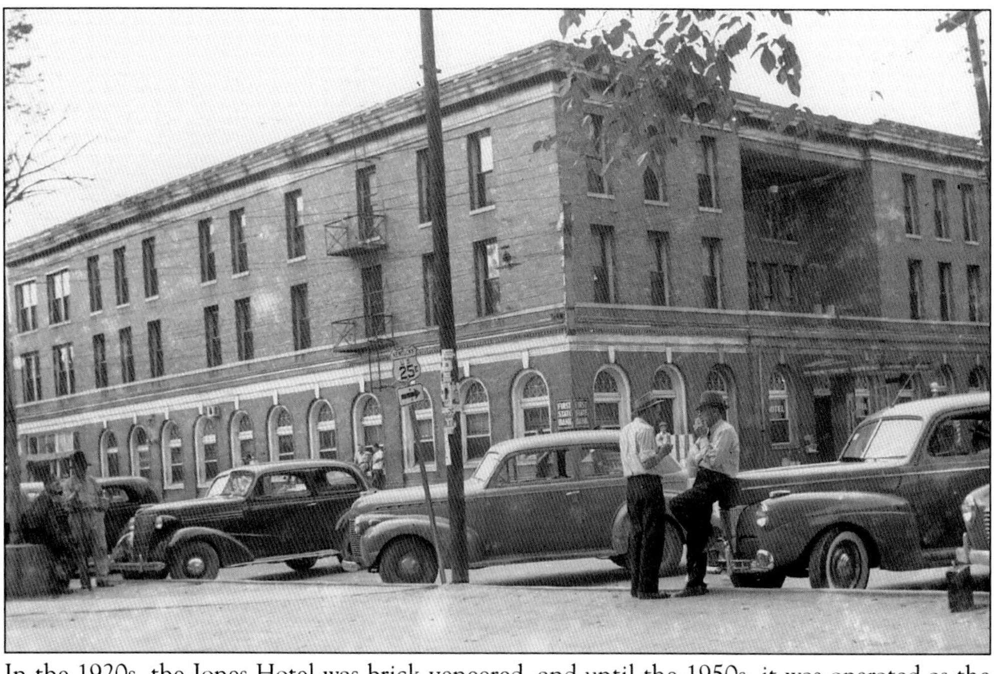

In the 1920s, the Jones Hotel was brick veneered, and until the 1950s, it was operated as the Blackstone Hotel.

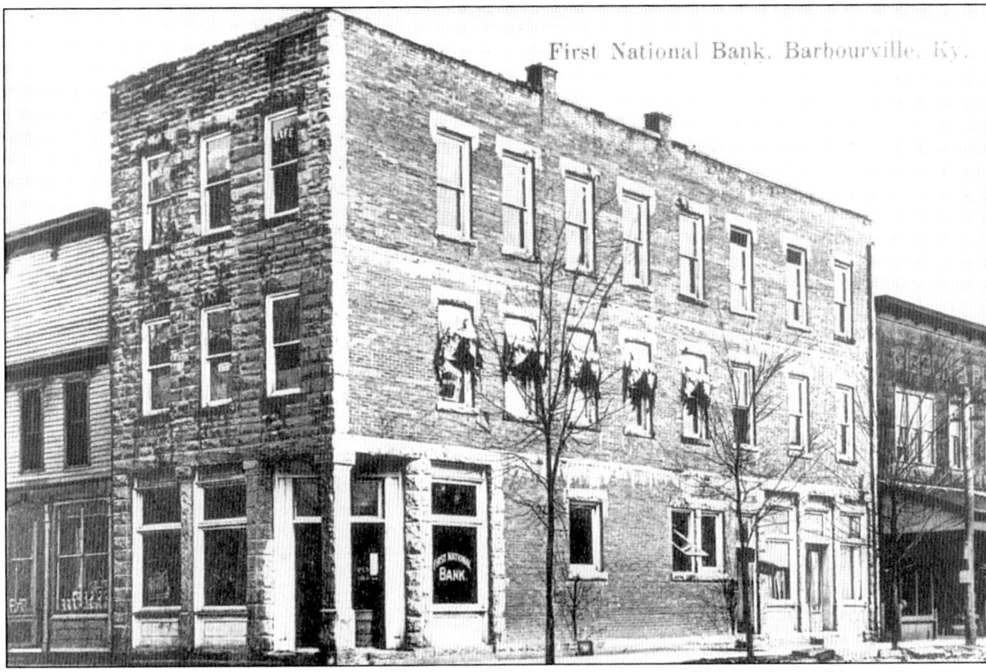

This building was the site of the First National Bank in Barbourville. In the 1950s and 1960s, it was home to the Floyd Sowders College Corner Restaurant.

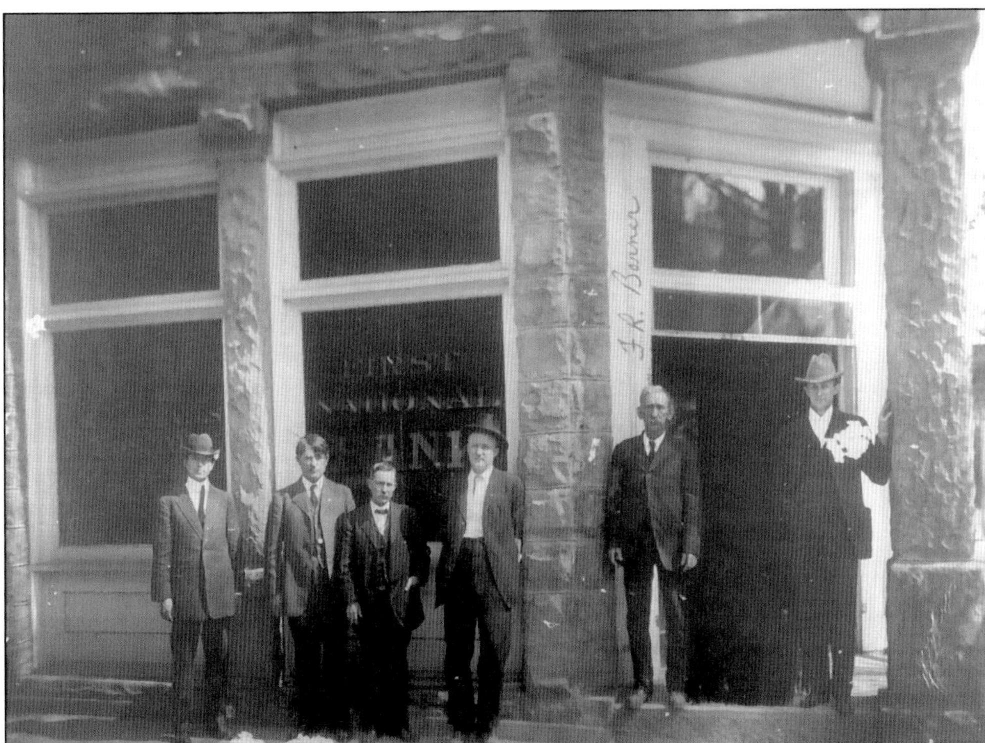

The officers of the First National Bank pose for a group photograph.

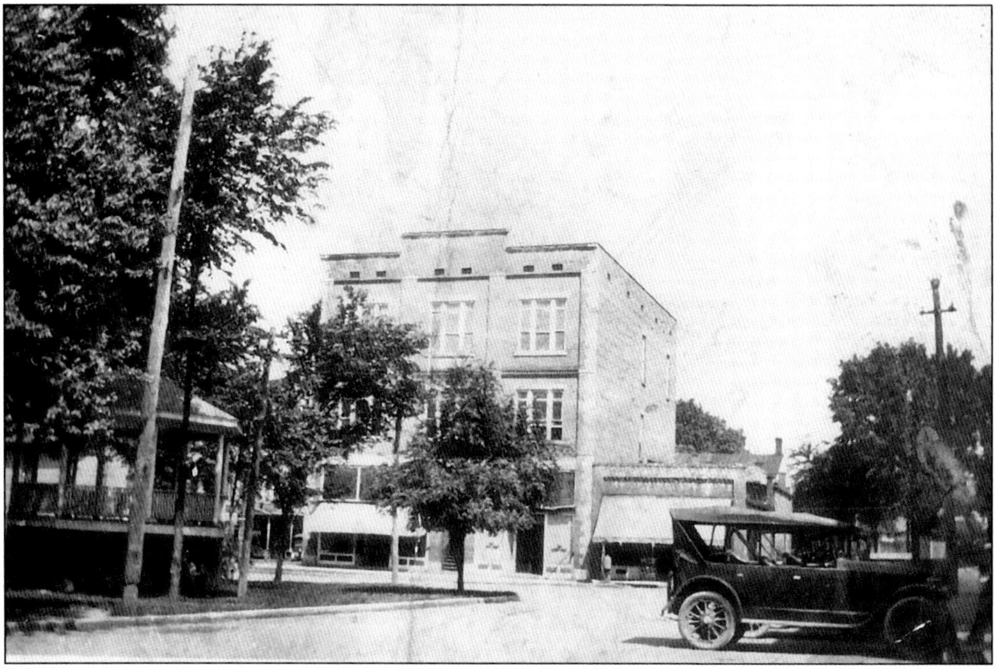

In the distance the Lawson Building, one of the city's largest buildings, is visible. The top floor is occupied by the Masonic Lodge. To the right of the Lawson Building is the Hawn Drug Store. To the left in this photo is the old courthouse bandstand, which was built in 1922.

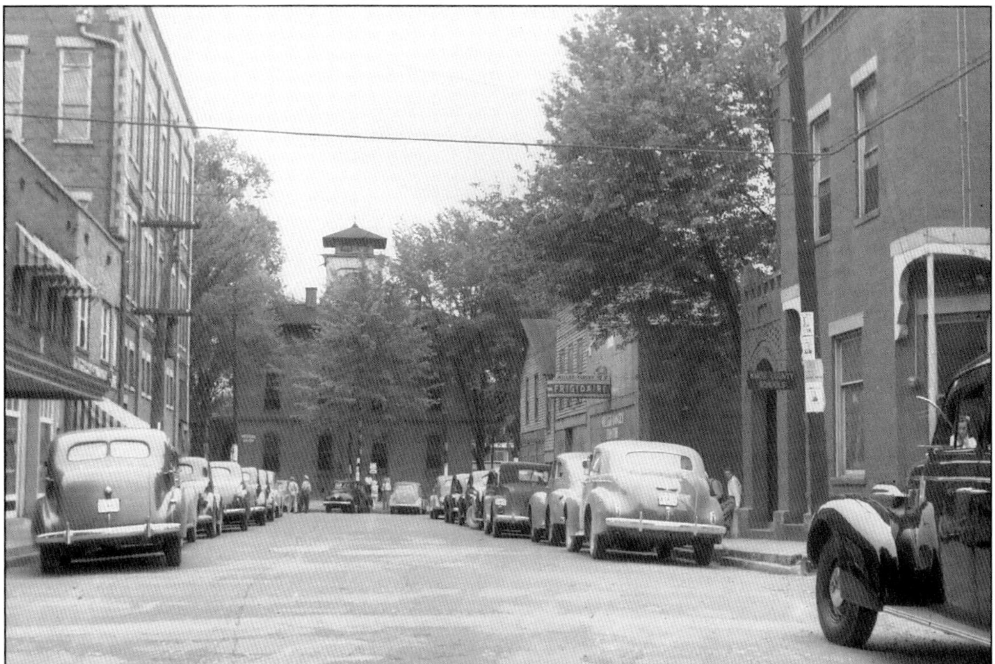

To the right in this early 1950s street scene, the office of the Knox County schools and the Miller Yancy Furniture Company are visible. To the left are the Lawson Building and, in the background, the north end of the old courthouse.

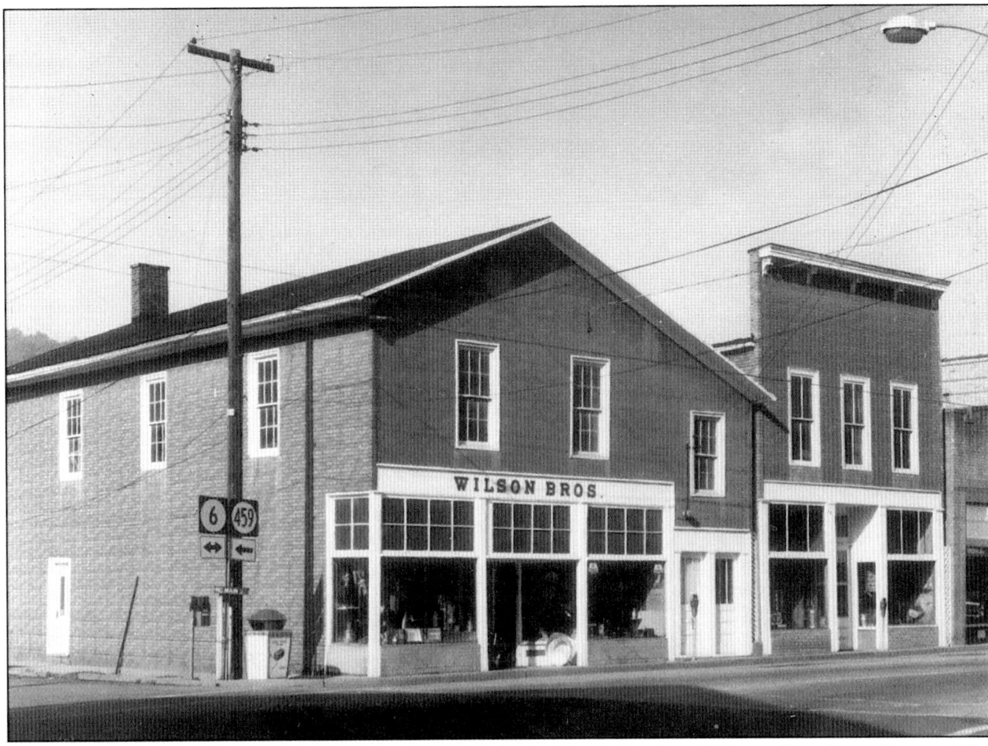

This edifice, the oldest building in Barbourville, was once the Wilson Brothers Store. The business was in operation at the end of the Civil War, and the building remains busy today as the Vintage House Restaurant. The interior has been kept as it looked in the past.

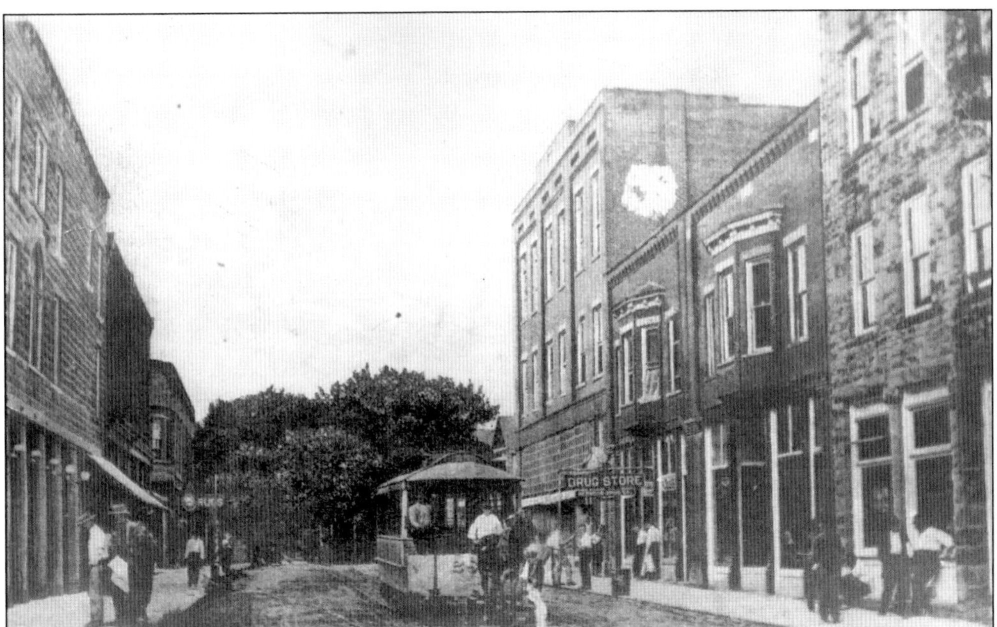

This is a 1919 view down Knox Street. Notice the old street car as it makes its way towards the Courthouse Square.

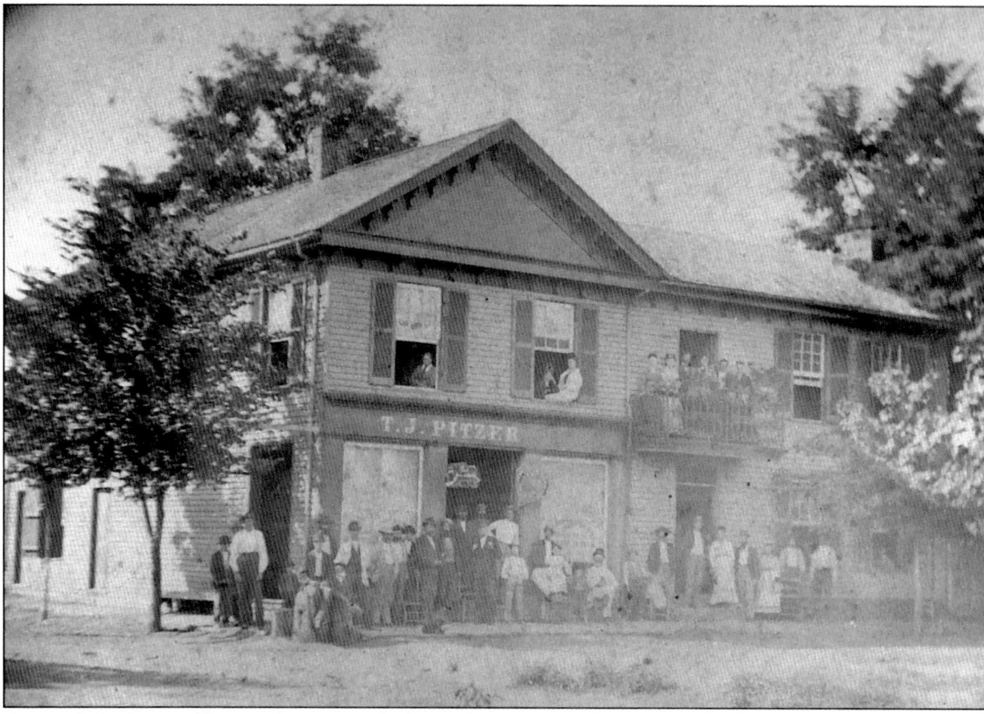

One of Barbourville's early stores belonged to T.J. Pitzer. It was located at the corner of Courthouse Square and South Main Street.

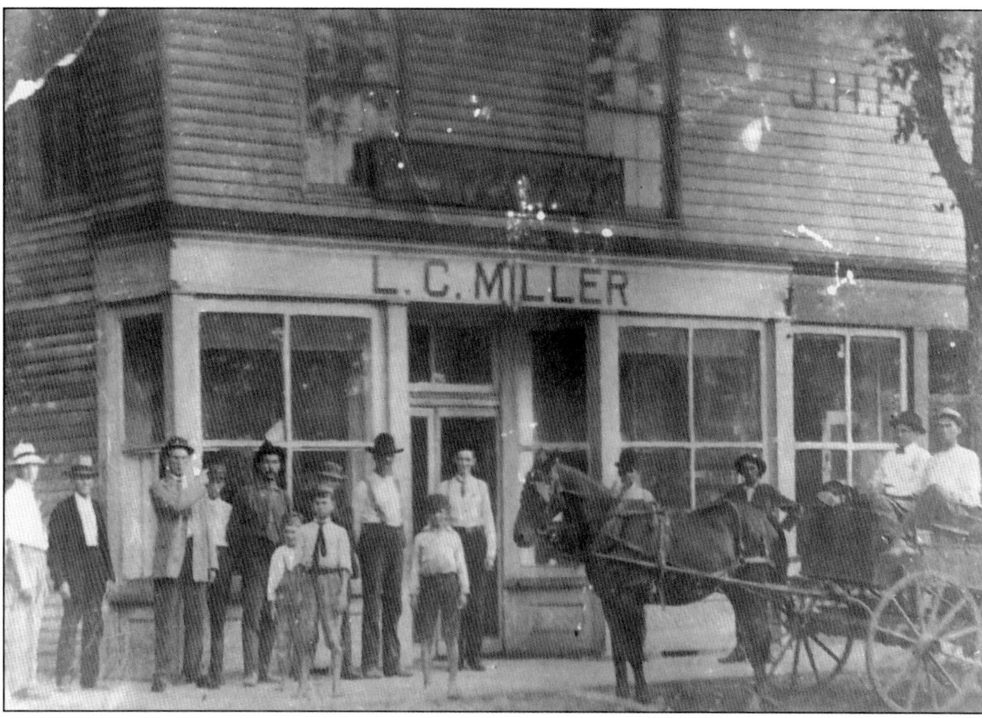

In 1906, the T.J. Pitzer Store was replaced by the L.C. Miller Store. This site would later become Goldies Department Store.

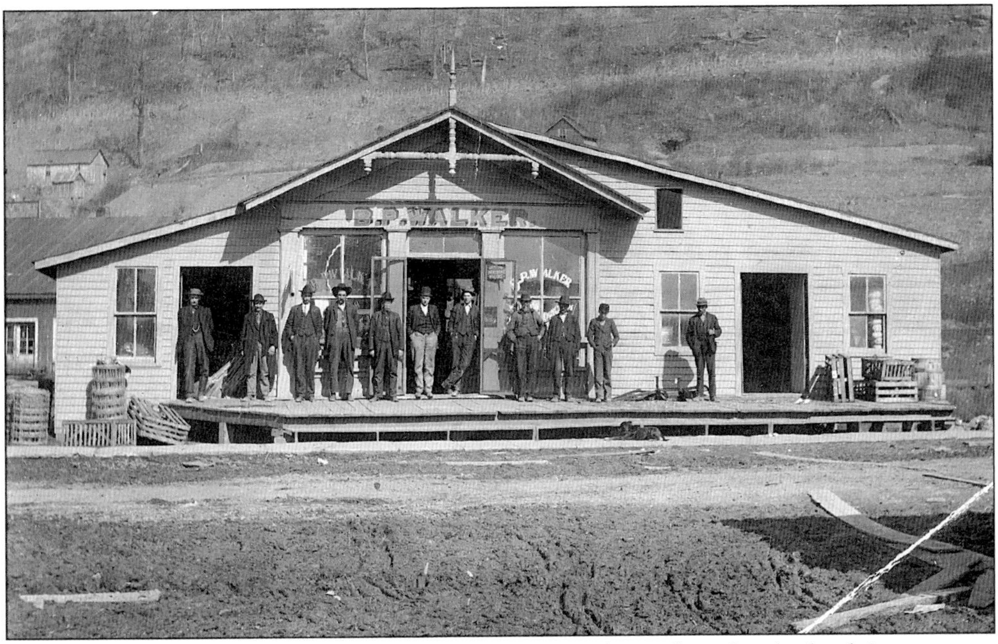

Not much is known about the B.P. Walker Store. It was located on Cumberland Avenue near the railroad depot. Mr. Walker was sheriff of Knox County in 1921.

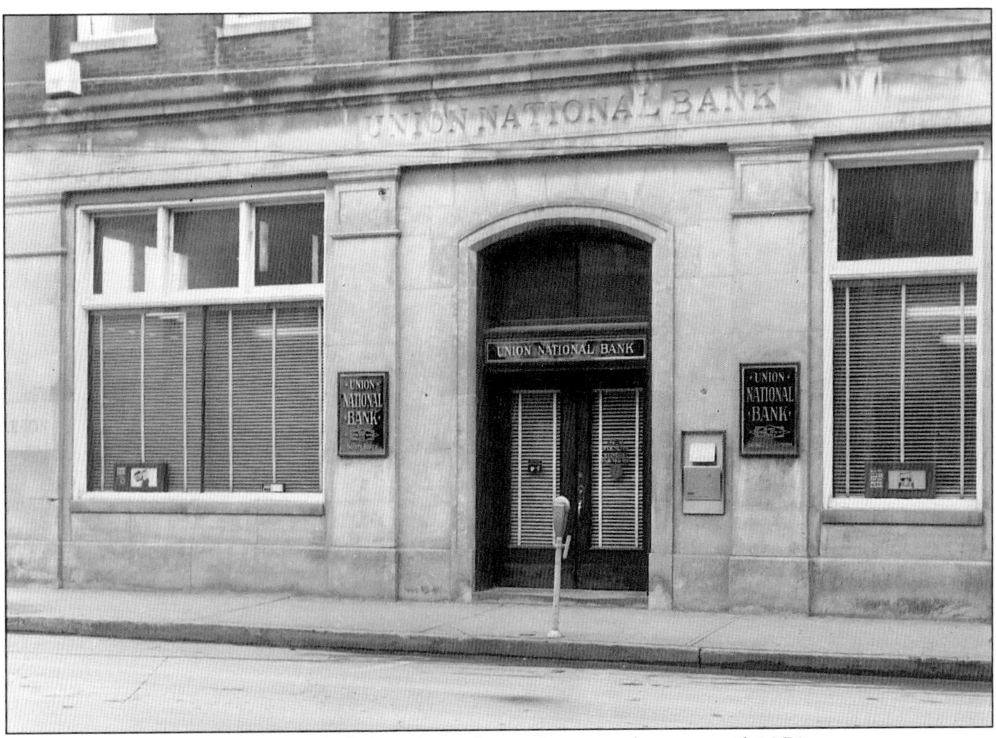

The Union National Bank called this Knox Street location home until 1971.

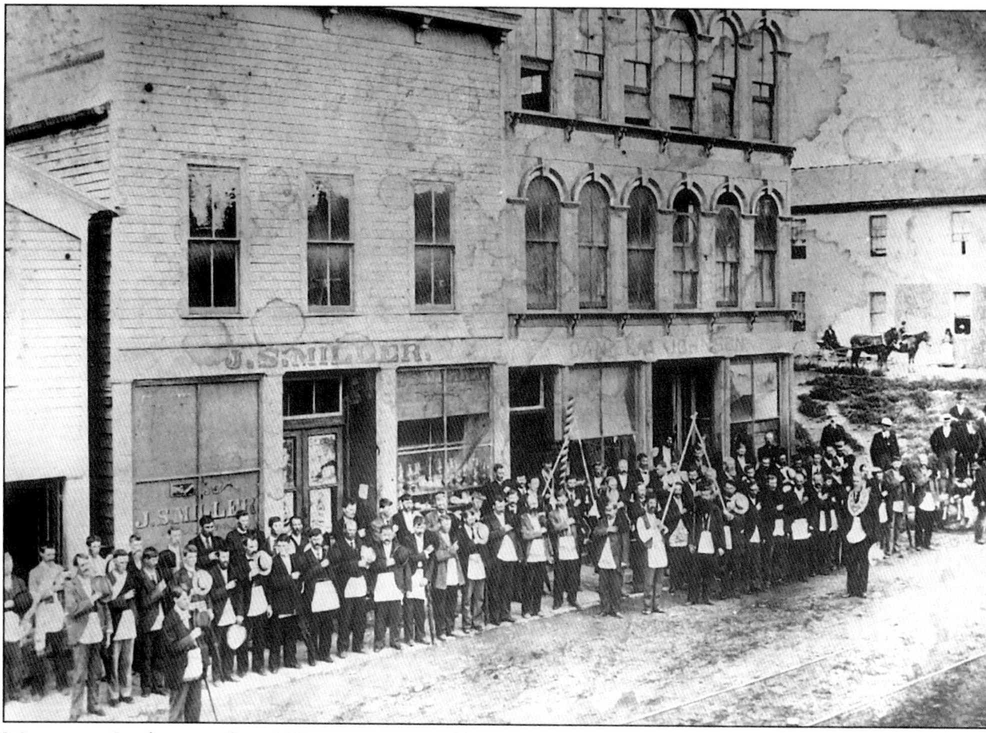

Mountain Lodge number 187 was organized here in 1848. This photo was taken in 1889 at the corner of Courthouse Square and North Main Street. The buildings from left to right are the old Wilson Brothers Store, the J.S. Miller Store, and the Daniel A. Johnson Store. The lodge held its meetings on the third floor of the Johnson Building. At the far right, the old Ben Eve Hotel is visible, which is on the present site of the First Baptist Church.

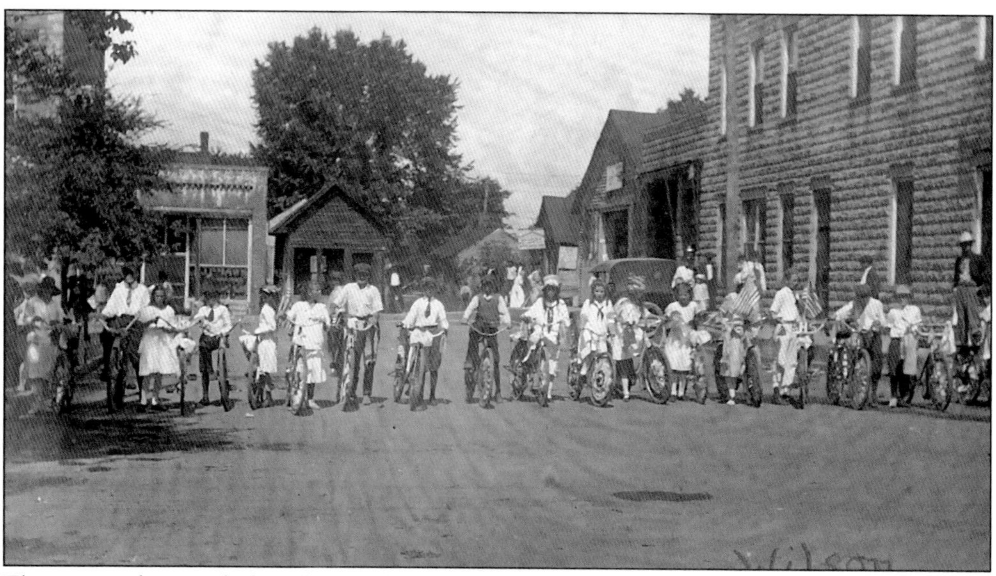

This postcard view of a bicycle parade in the 1920s gives us a rare look at the northeast corner of Courthouse Square. From left to right is the Hawn Drug Store, the old Miller Woodson Law Building (in the background), the Tye Livery Stable, and the Jones Hotel.

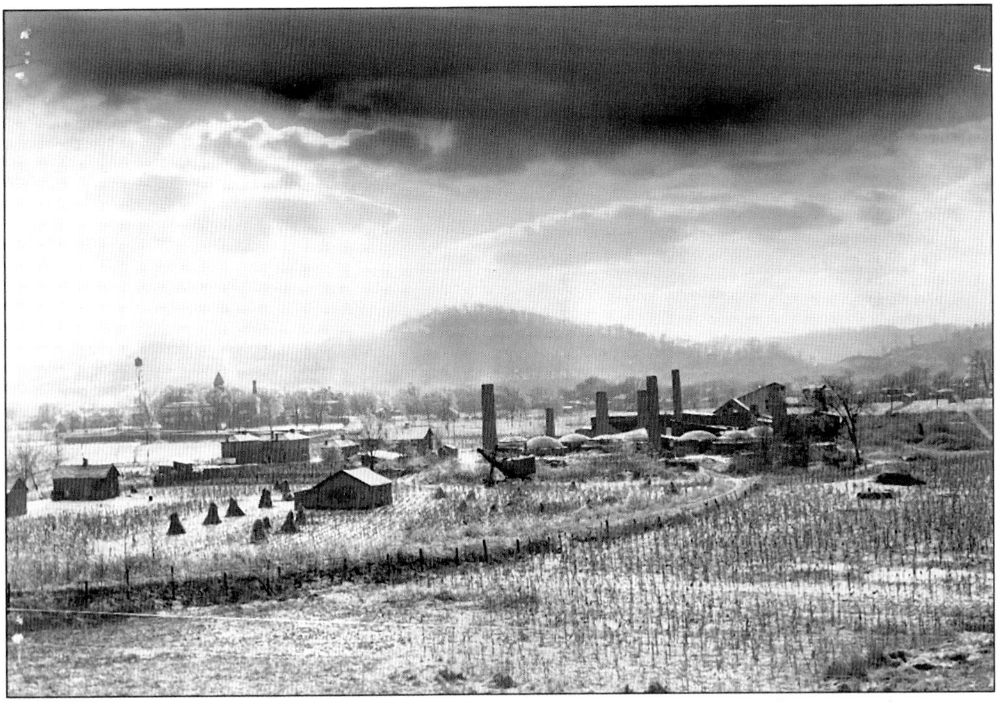

The Barbourville Brick and Tile Company began making bricks in 1900 and continued operating until the 1950s. Today, this site is home to Barbourville's beautiful city park.

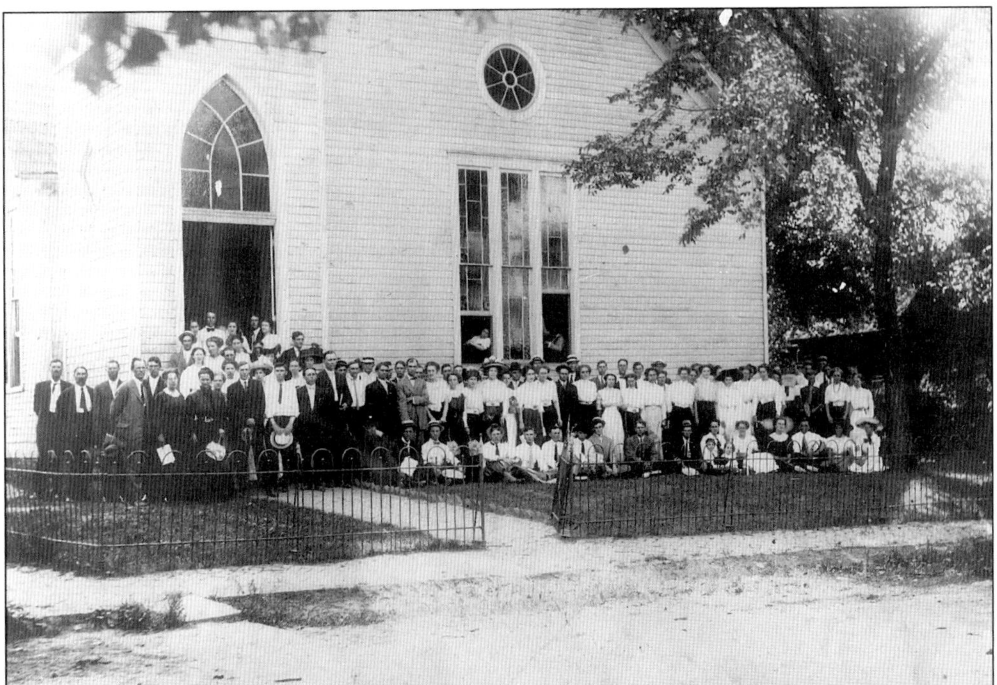

The First Baptist Church of Barbourville was once located on Pine Street. Here the congregation poses for a picture.

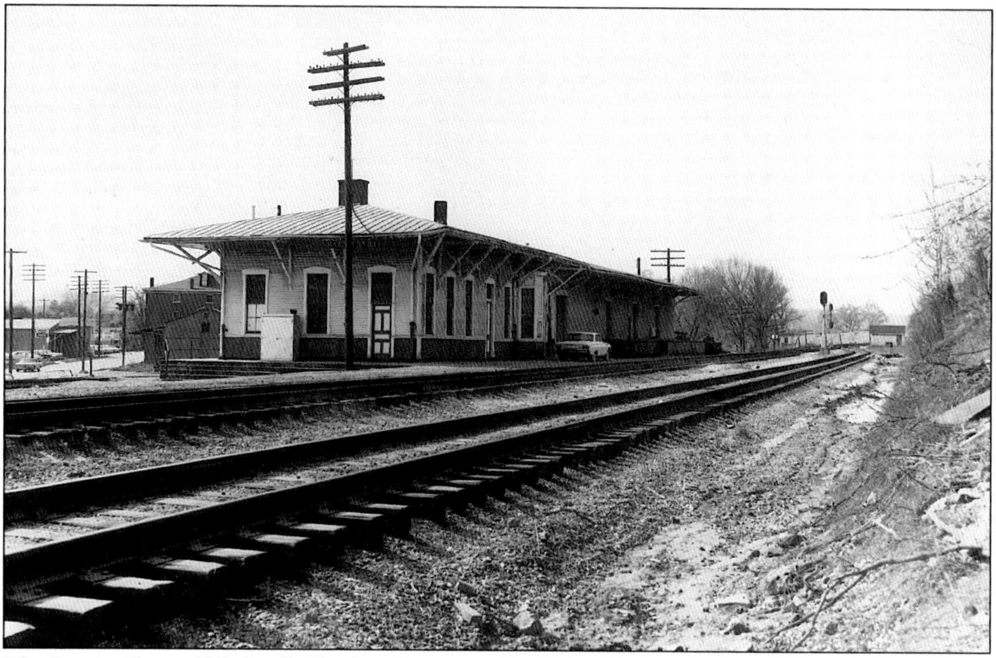

The Louisville and Nashville Railroad came to Barbourville in 1888, and soon after, a double track was laid. A box car served as the first depot until a permanent building was constructed. The depot looked like this in the 1950s and 1960s, but has since been torn down.

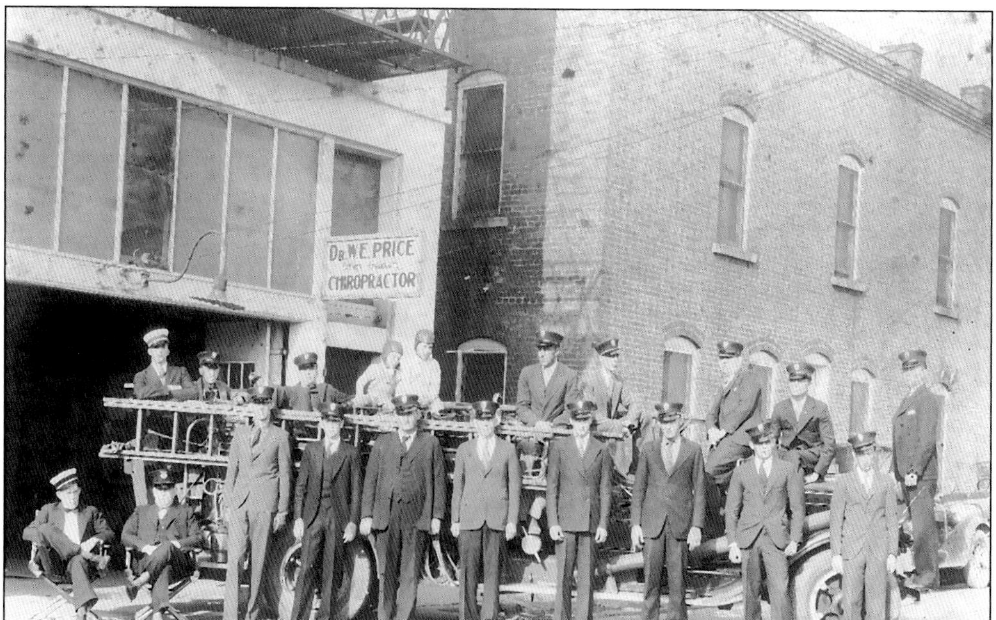

The Barbourville Fire Department was organized from an original fire brigade. Bert Churchill was the fire chief. The fire station here was located in the National Theater Building on Liberty Street. This picture was taken in 1932.

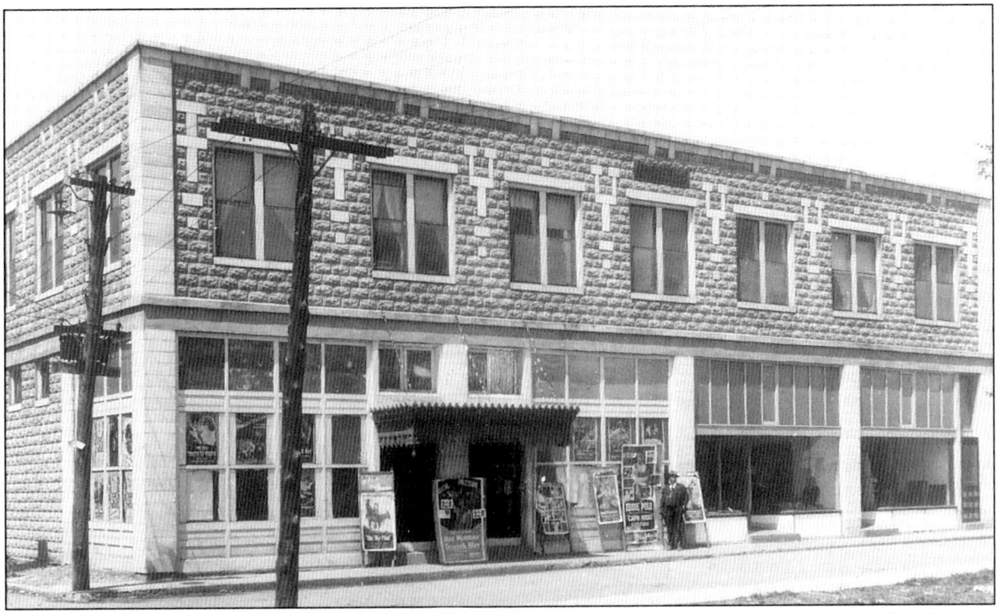

The National Theater opened on March 8, 1923. This theater was destroyed by fire in January 1938.

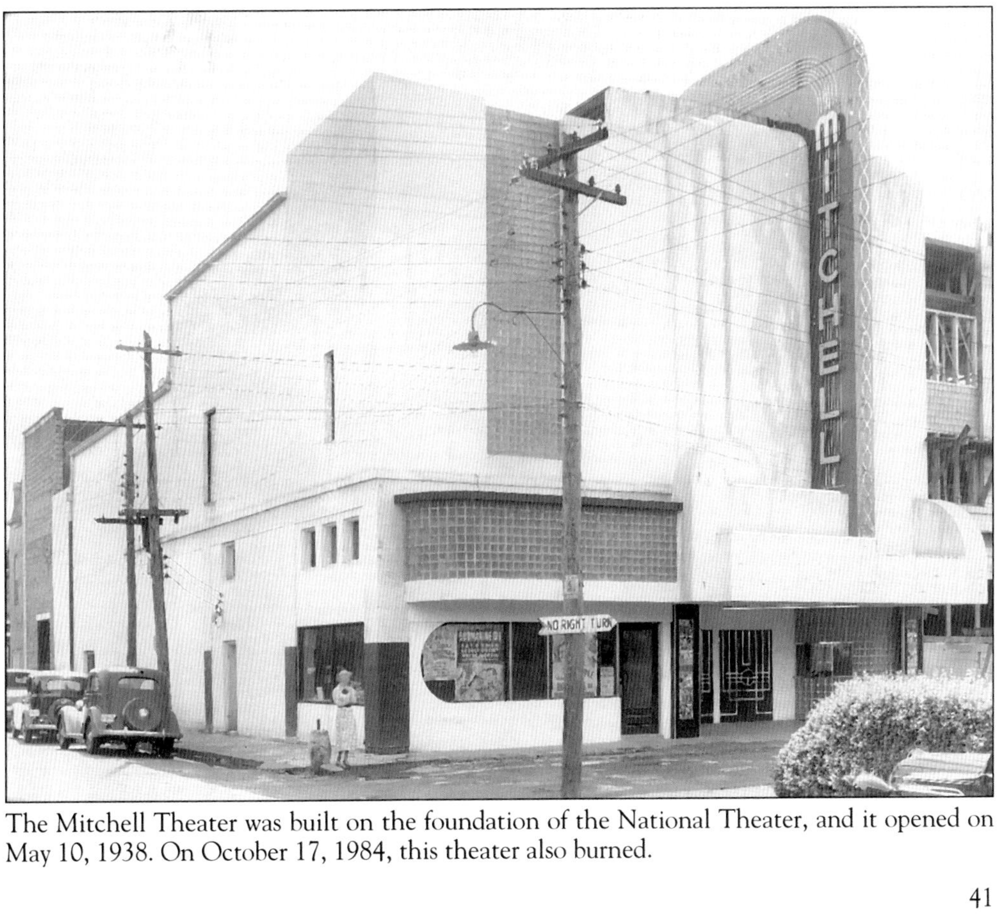

The Mitchell Theater was built on the foundation of the National Theater, and it opened on May 10, 1938. On October 17, 1984, this theater also burned.

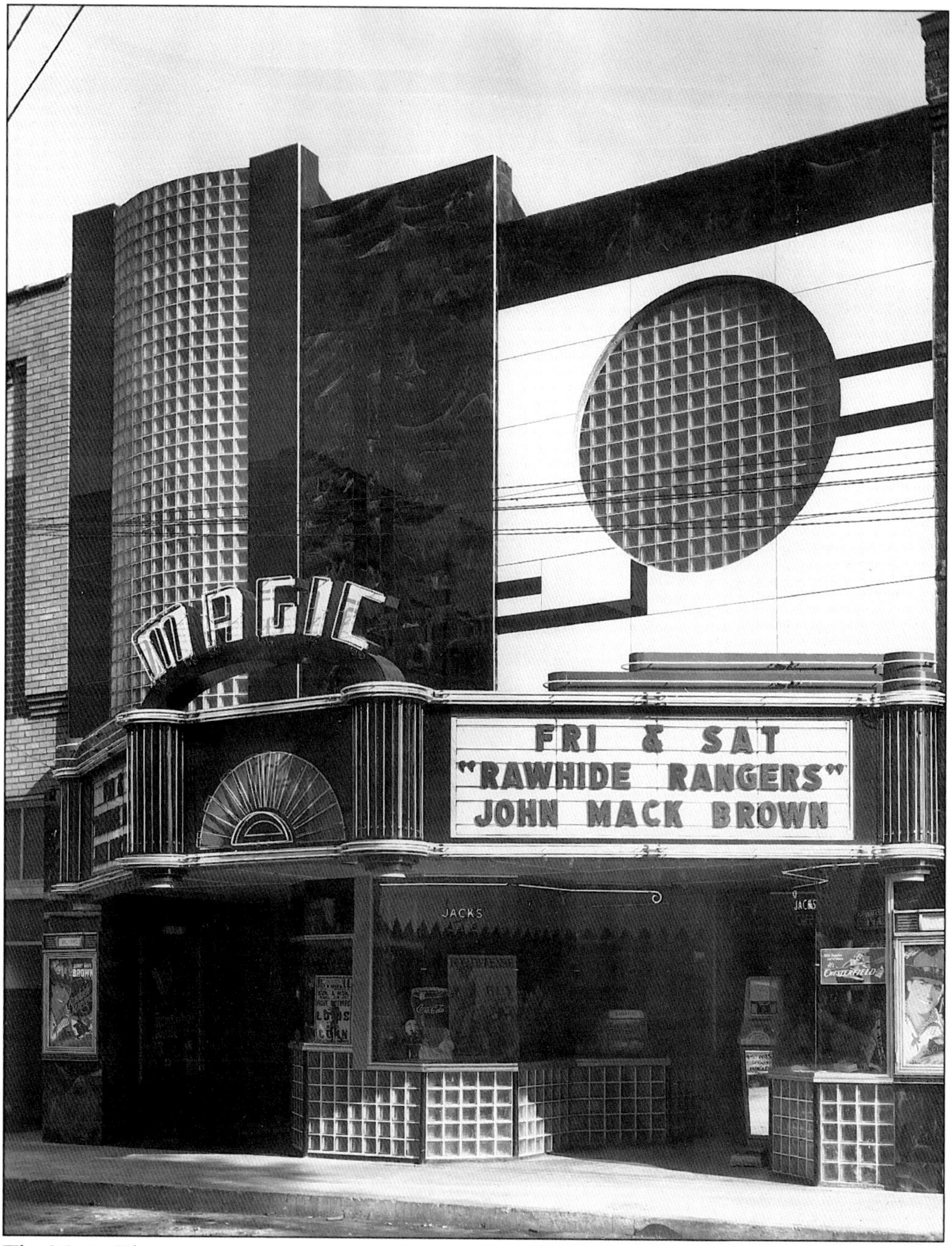

The Magic Theater was constructed in 1941 on Courthouse Square and closed in 1960.

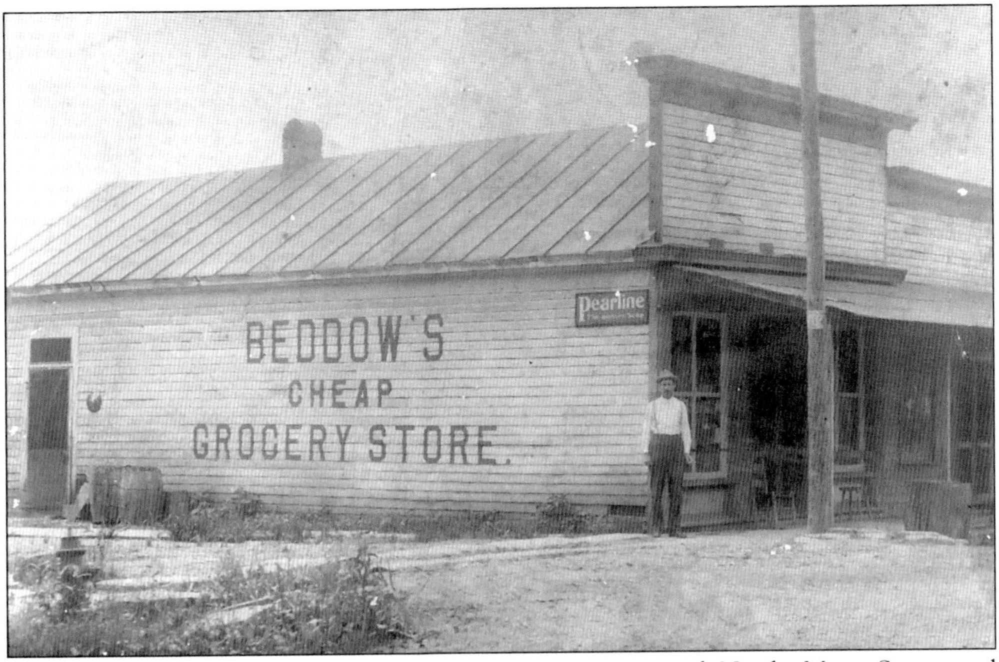

Beddow's Grocery Store was located at the intersection of North Main Street and Manchester Street.

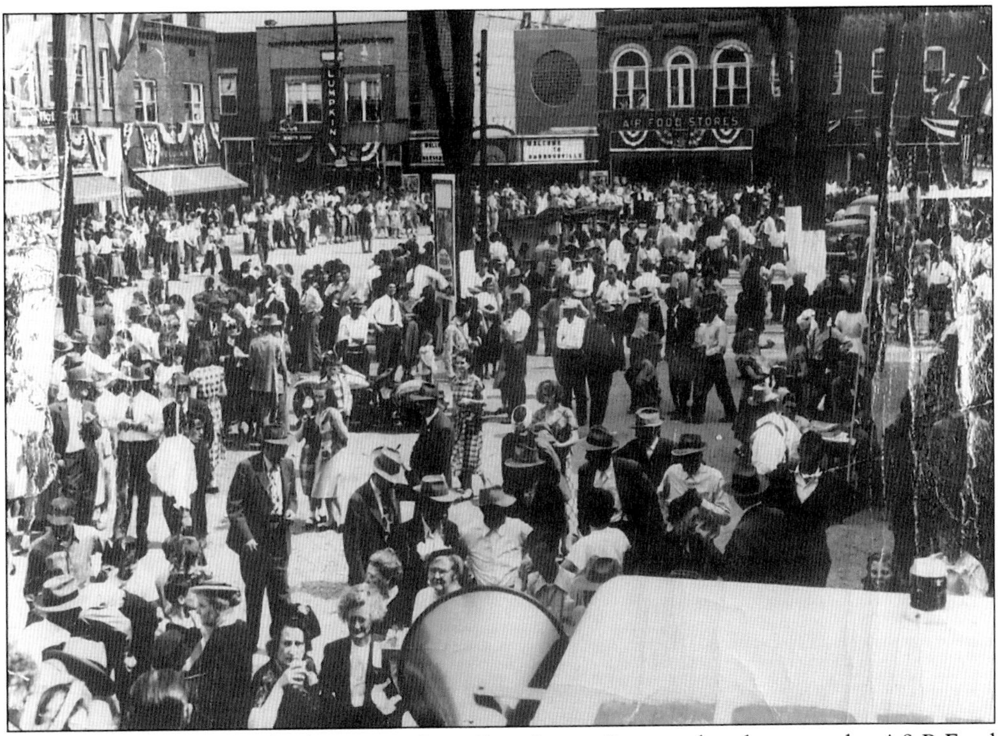

This 1950 photograph of a large crowd on Courthouse Square also shows us the A&P Food Store to the right of the Magic Theater. The banners are decoration, as the town is celebrating the bicentennial of Dr. Thomas Walker's exploration of the area.

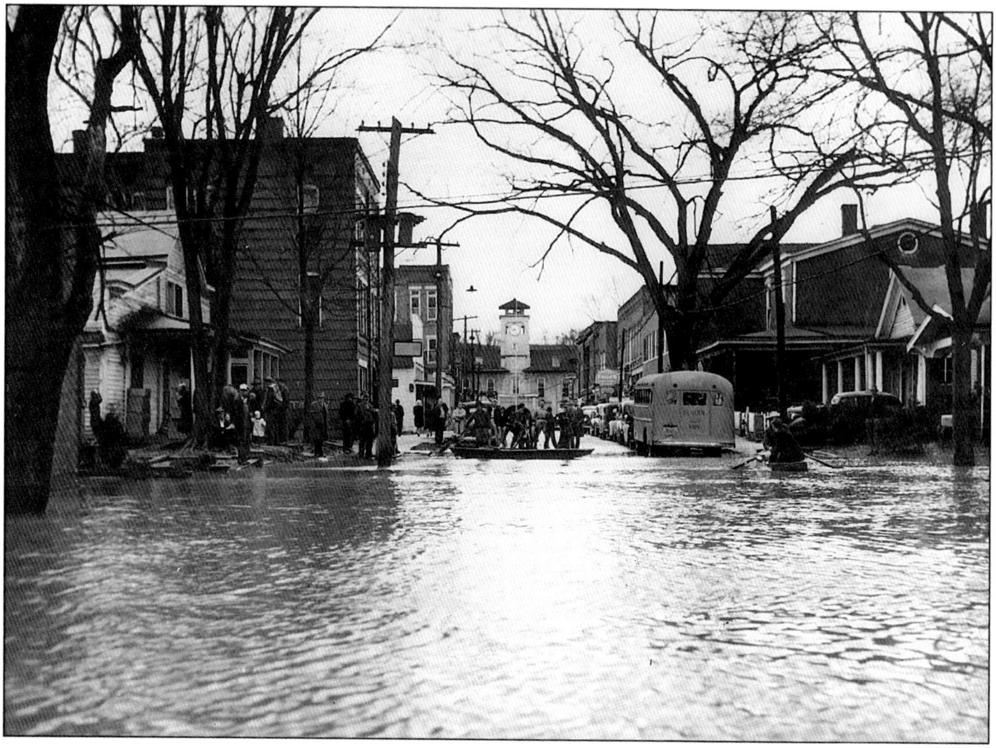

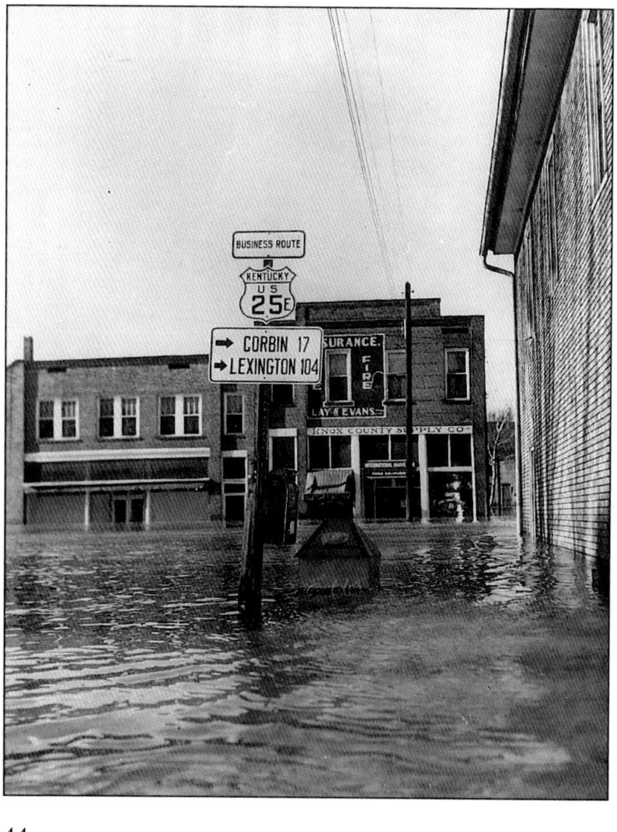

In 1946, Barbourville was devastated by a record flood. The old courthouse is visible in the background of this image of water halfway up Knox Street.

The flood waters also covered the northwest corner of Courthouse Square and entered businesses such as the Knox County Supply Store.

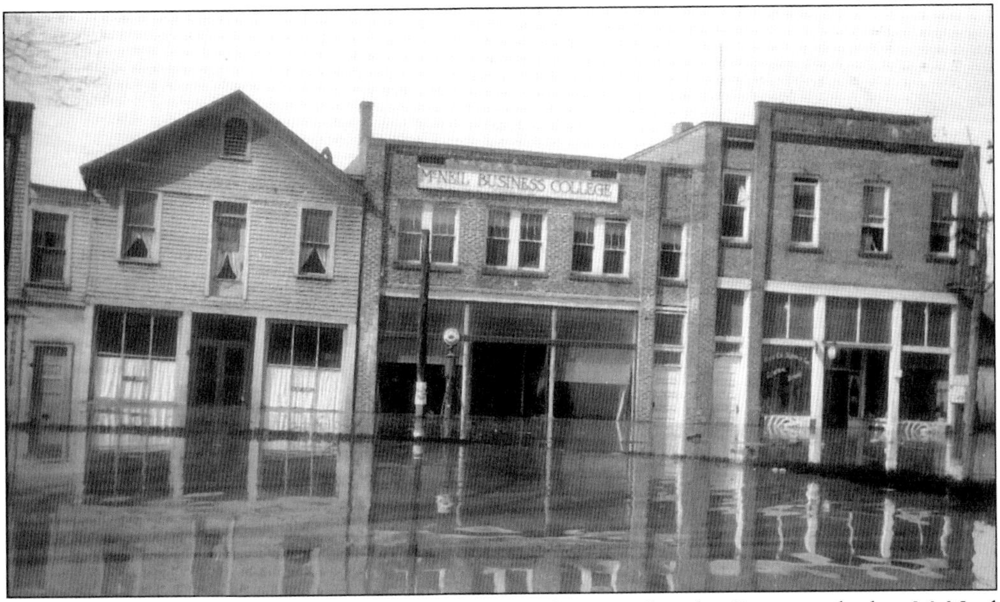

In the 1929 flood, water entered the Knox County Supply Store and the McNeal Business College.

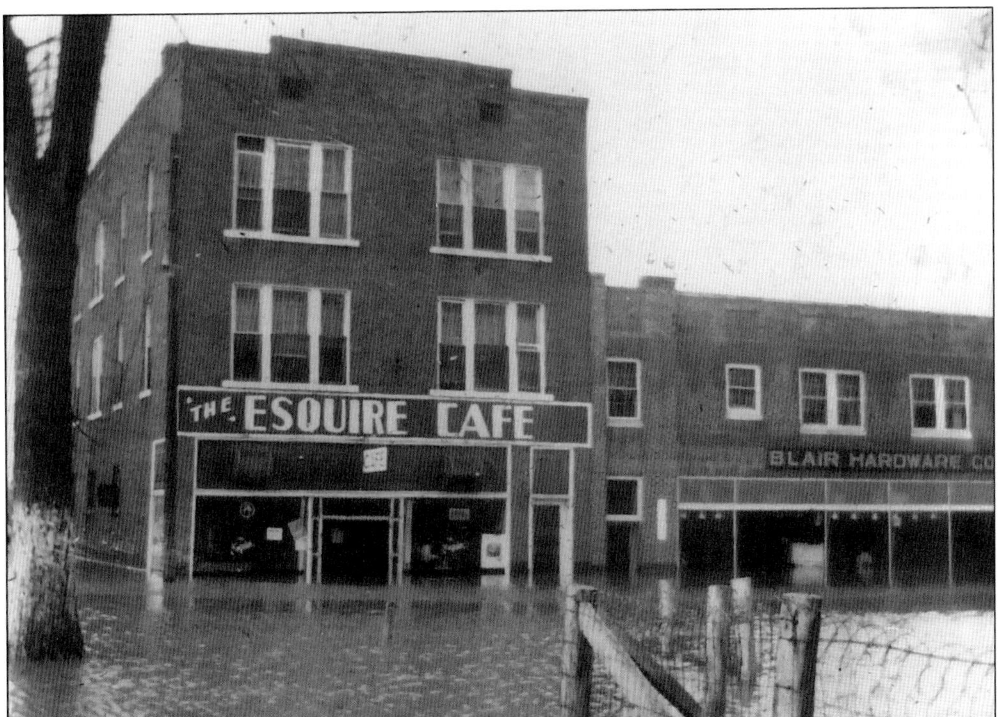

The Esquire Café and the Blair Hardware Company are shown here during the 1946 flood.

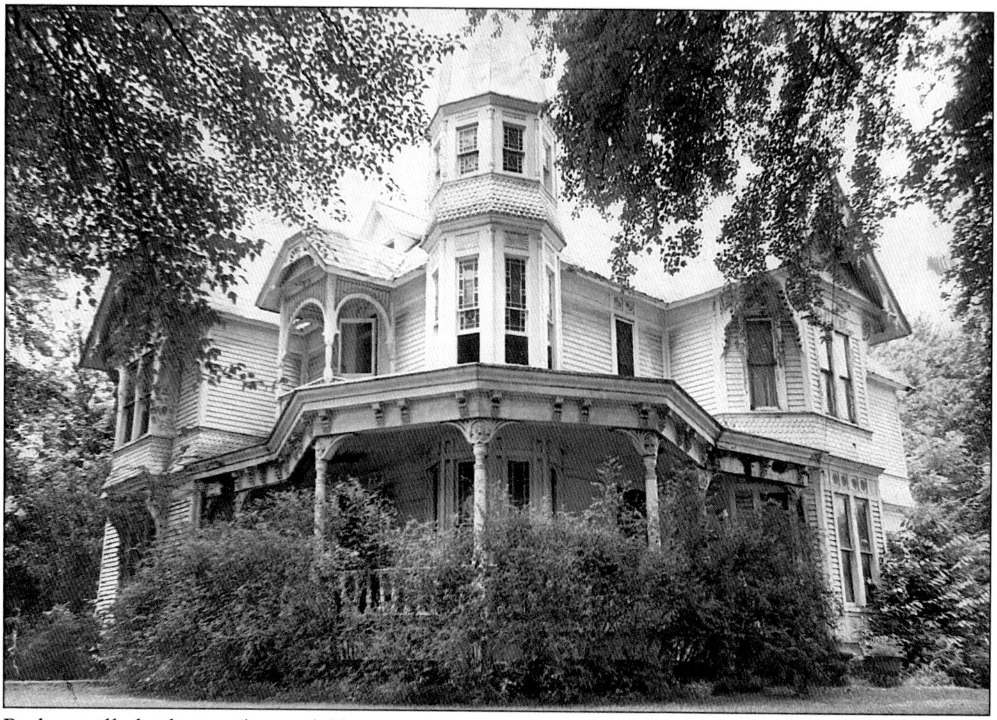

Barbourville had many beautiful houses at the turn of the 20th century, but none was as elegant as the old Owens Mansion. This Victorian beauty sat on Knox Street and was home to the J.A. Ownes family.

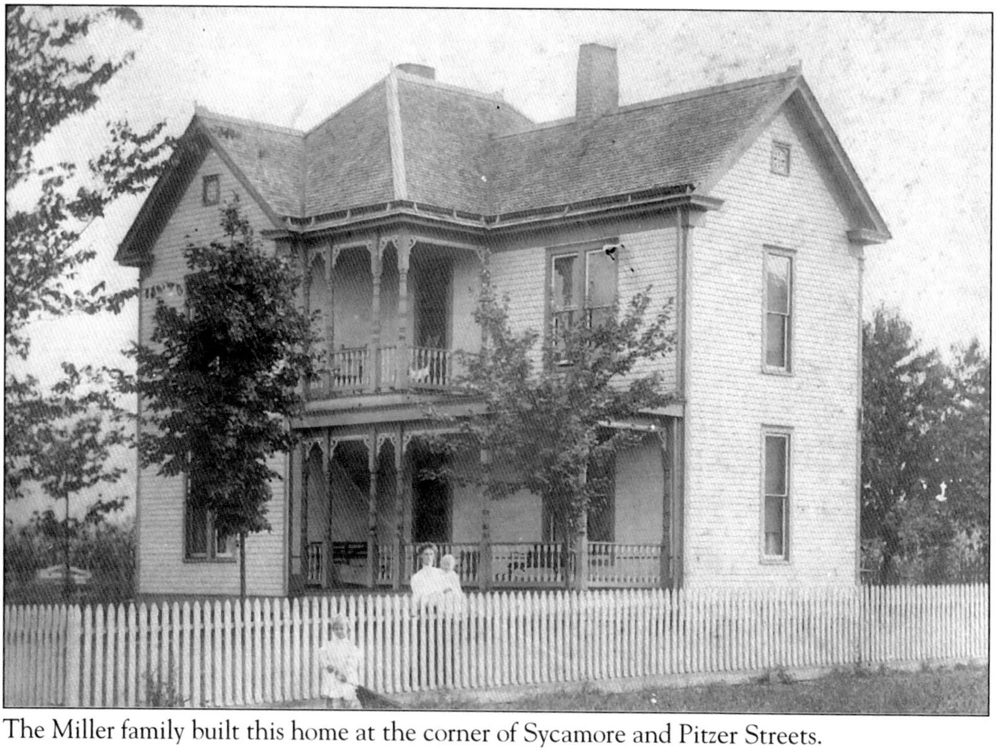

The Miller family built this home at the corner of Sycamore and Pitzer Streets.

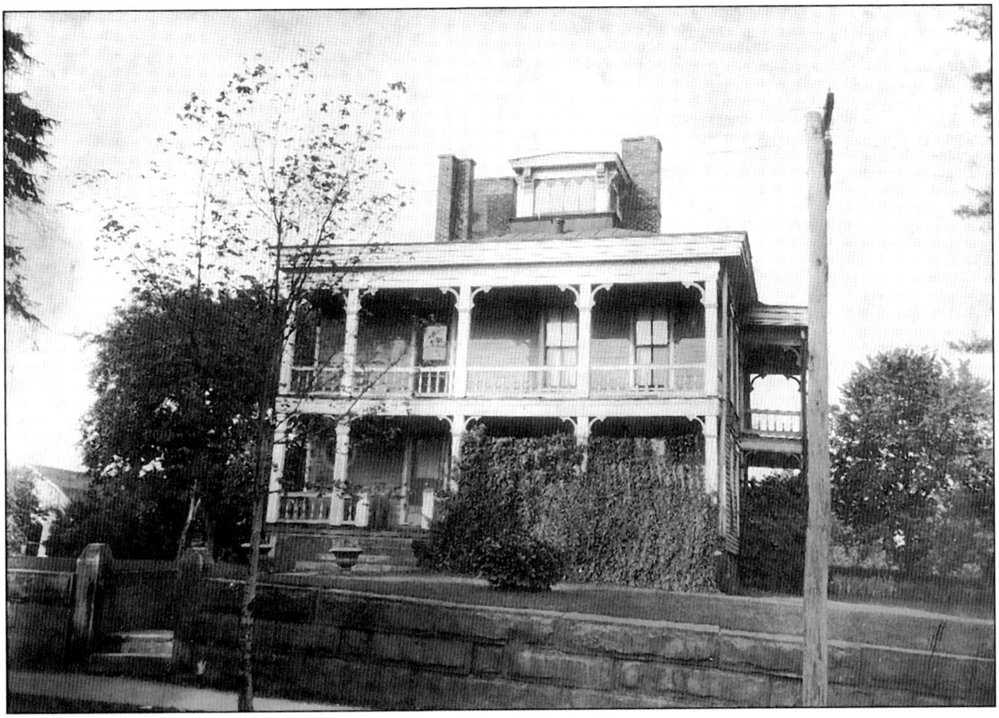

The Sawyers-Decker House was located on North Main Street.

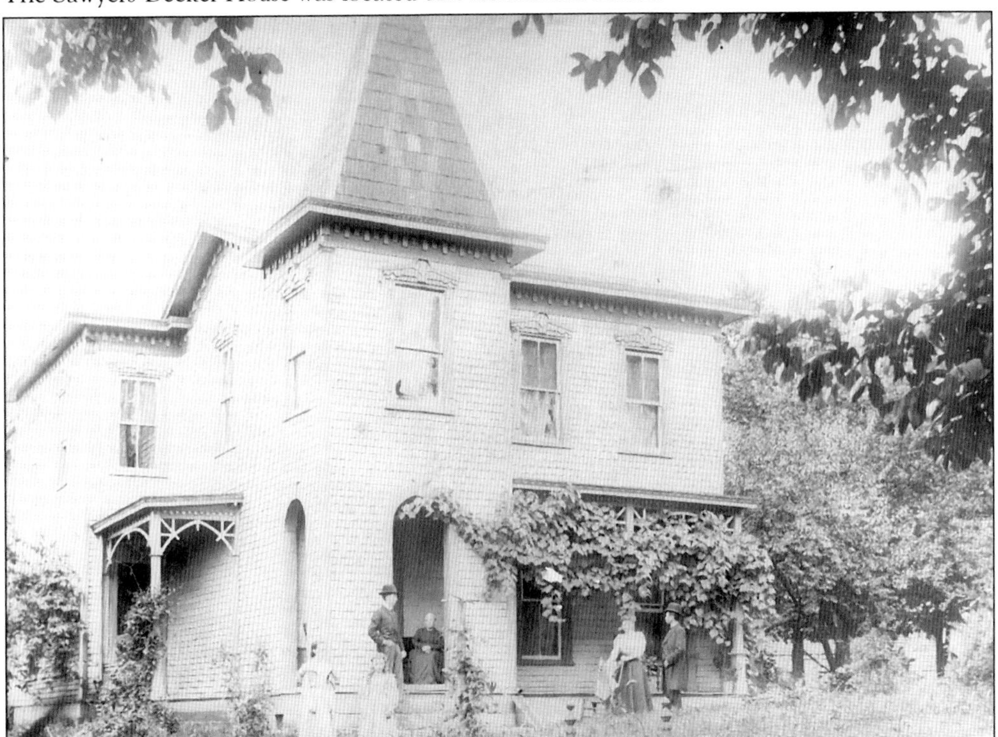

The T.J. Pitzer House was situated on the corner of North Main and High Street. It was razed to build the James D. Black residence. This is now the site of the Union National Bank.

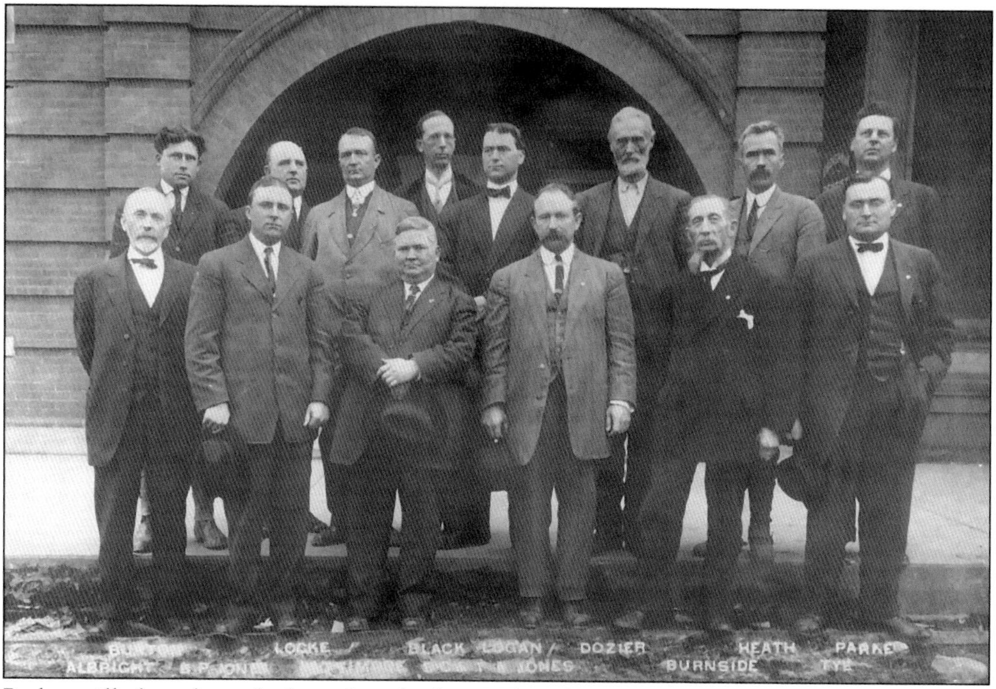

Barbourville has always had good medical providers. Here, in 1915, is a group photo in front of the First State Bank Building on Knox Street. Shown are the following, from left to right: (front row) Doctors Albright, B.P. Jones, S.C. Jones, T.N. Jones Burnside, and Tye; (back row) Doctors Burton, Locke, Lattimore, Black, Logan, Dozier, Heath, and Parker.

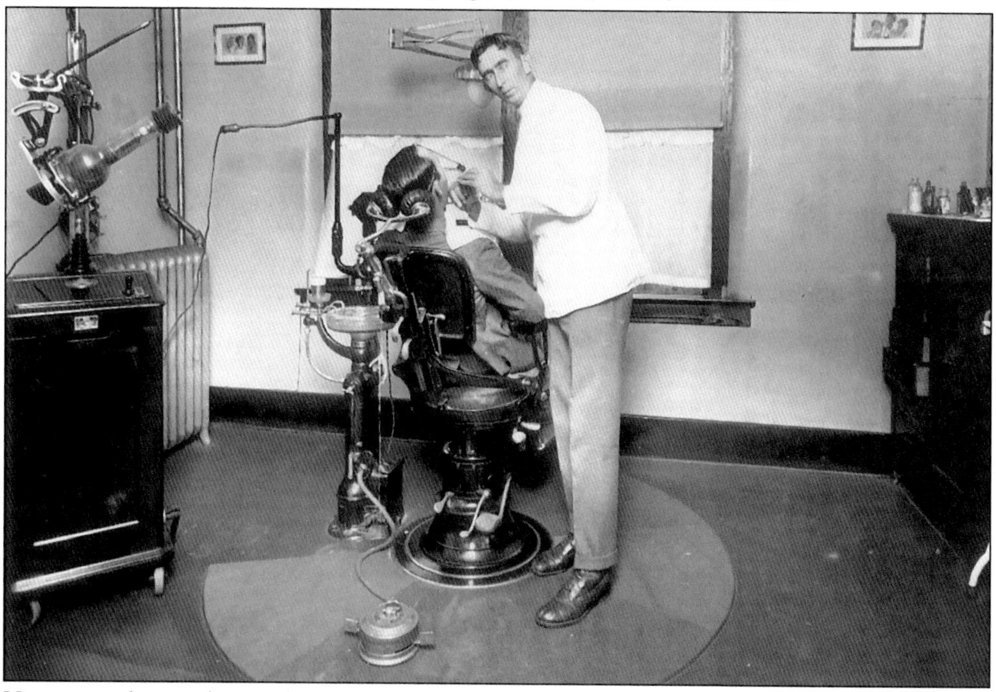

Here is a classic photo of an early 1900s dentist office. Doctor Faulkner was one of the city's finest.

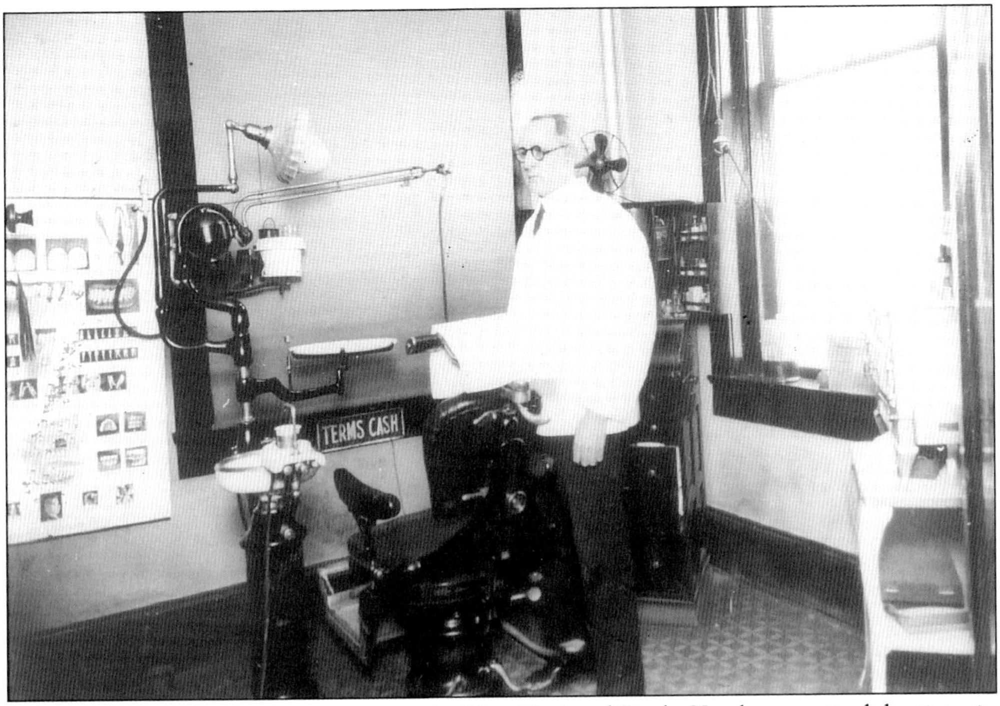

Doctor Parker's office was upstairs over the First National Bank. He also practiced dentistry in the early 1900s.

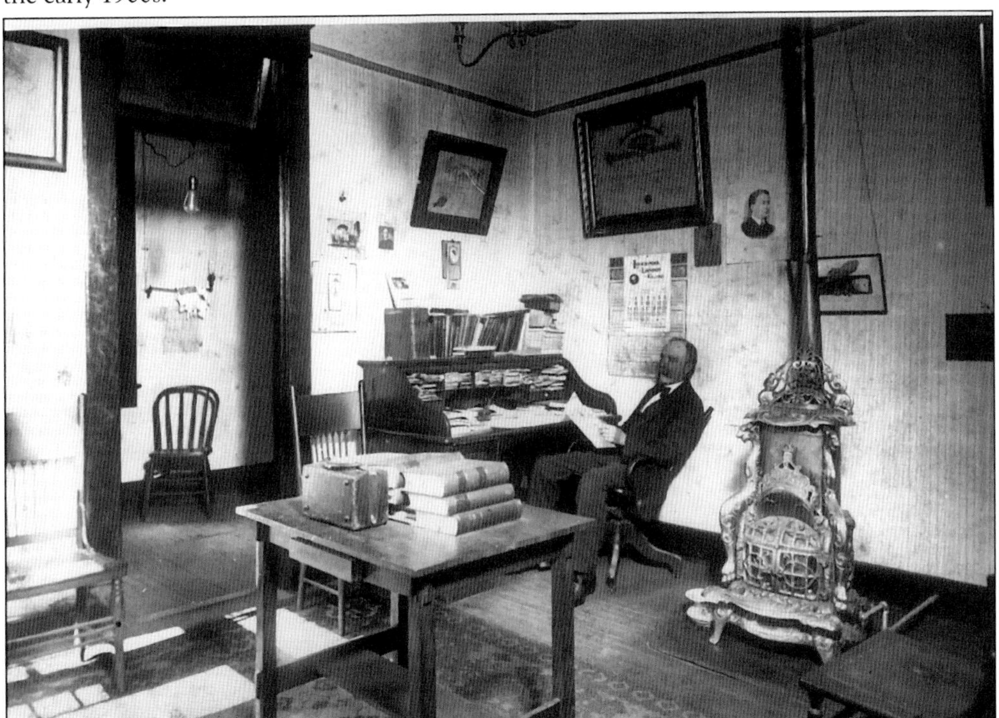

Here is Doctor Albright in his office at the rear of the old Corner Drug Store. This building was also known as the Albright Drug Company and the Costello Drug Store.

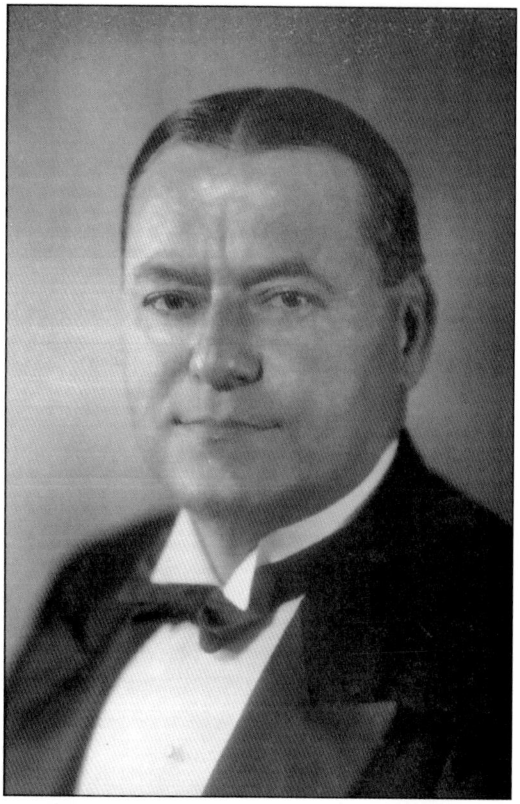

Doctor Leslie Logan built Knox County's first hospital in 1922. This building, now home to the office of David M. Mills, a local attorney, is located on the southwest corner of Courthouse Square.

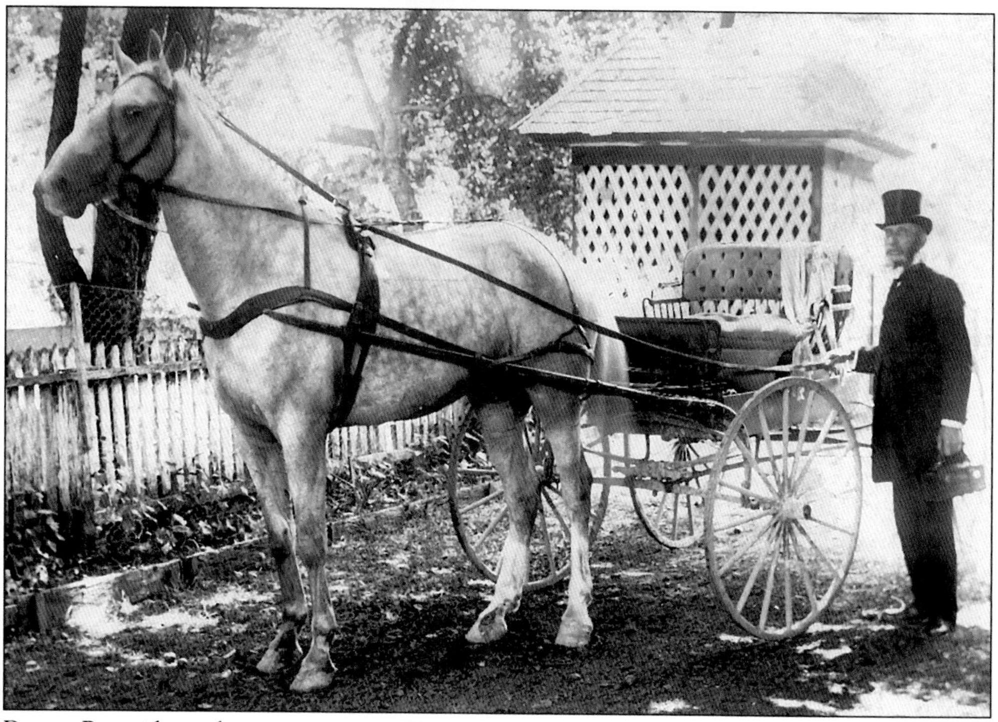

Doctor Burnside made many trips into Knox County to give medical assistance.

Three

THE COURTHOUSE SCENE

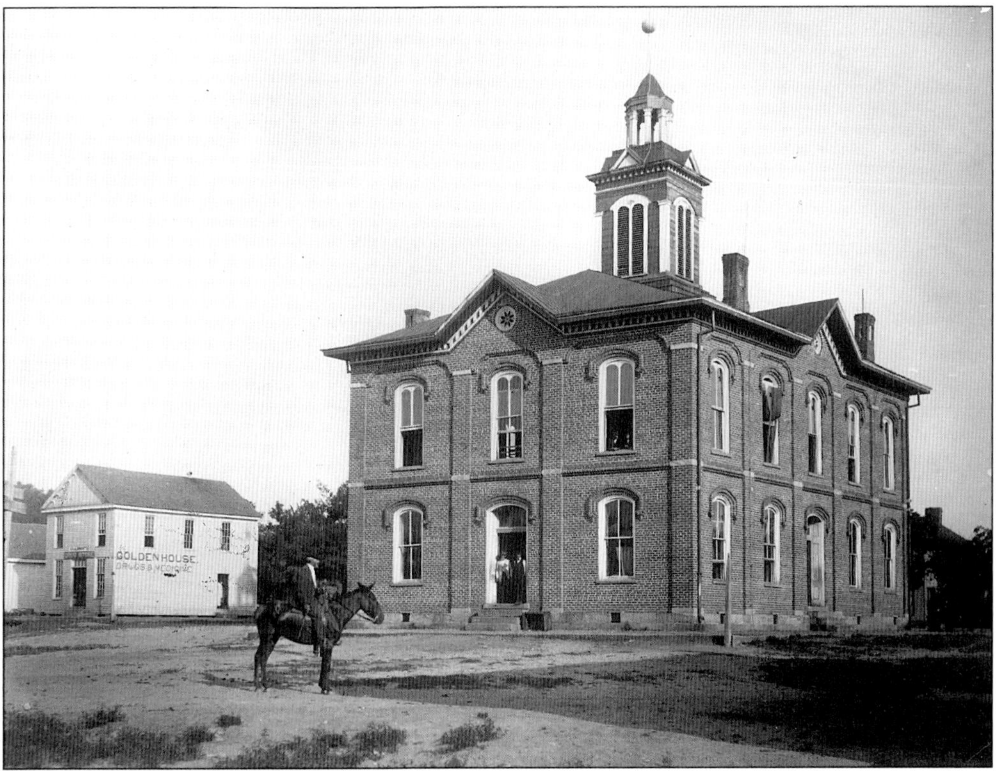

Knox County's first courthouse was built in Barbourville in 1802. From the beginning, it became the center attraction of the town. A second courthouse was built in 1811 and a third in 1831. No photographs could be made of the first three courthouses, but thanks to the Filson Club, a photo of the fourth courthouse was made and preserved. Shown here is the brick two-story courthouse that stood in Barbourville in 1875. One of the town's first buildings, a drug store, can also be seen at the entrance to Knox Street.

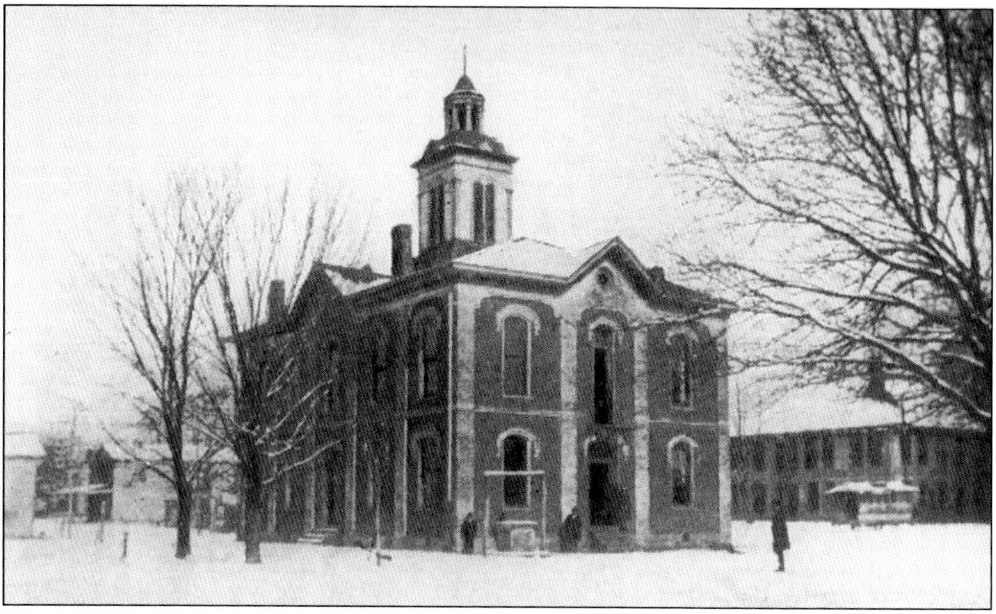

The 1875 courthouse is shown here during the winter of 1900.

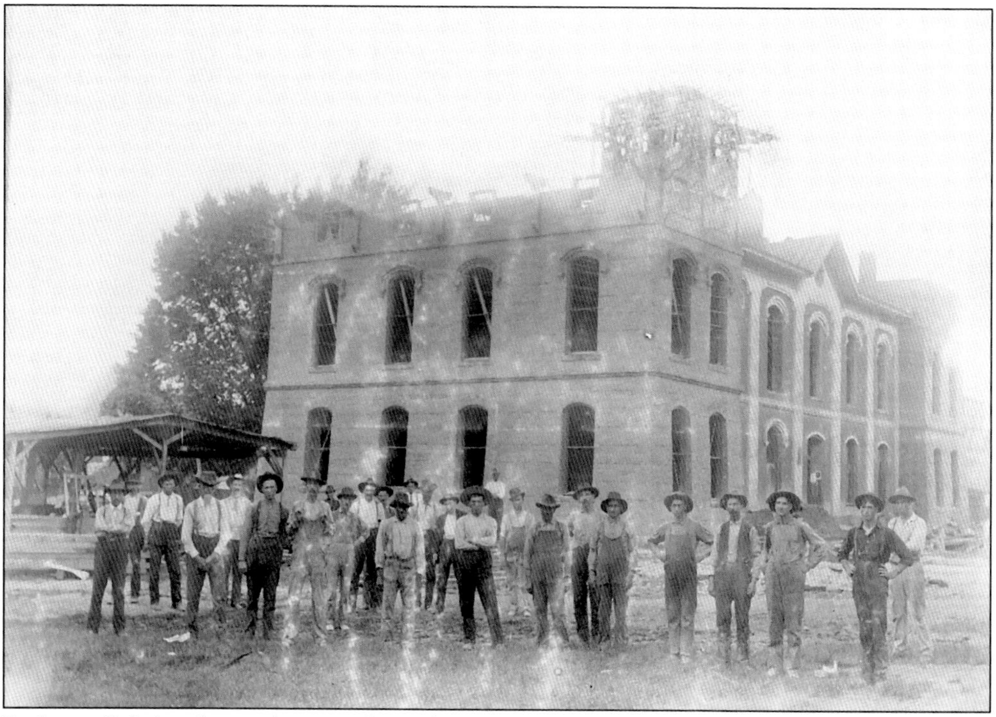

Barbourville's fourth courthouse is shown here in 1906 being remodeled into a Mission Revival–style building.

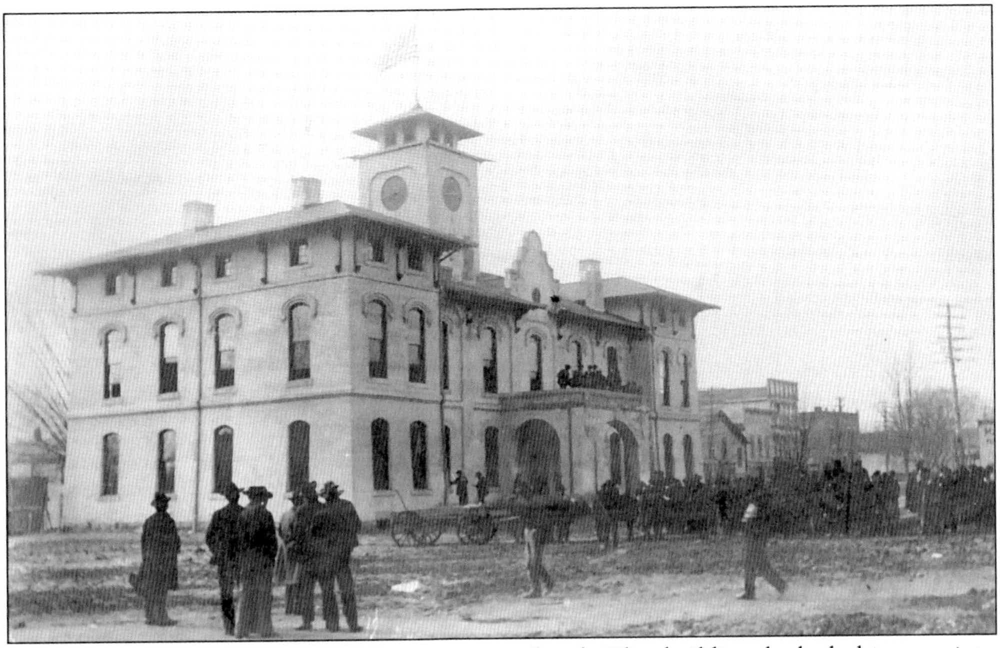

In 1908, the courthouse remodeling was completed. The building looked this way into the 1960s.

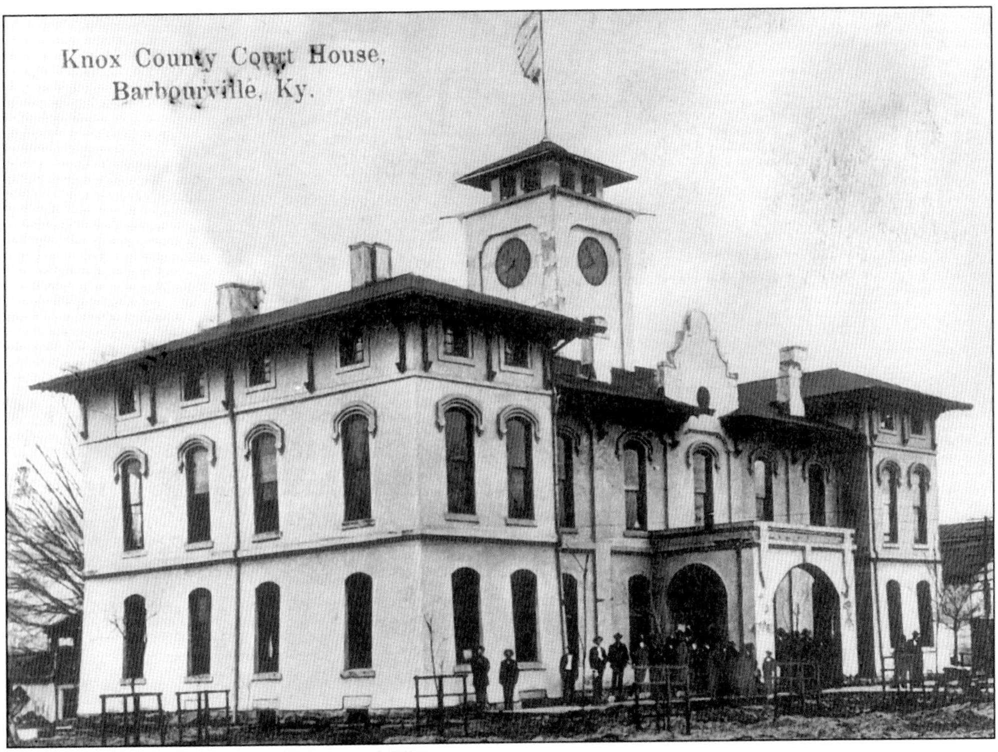

The courthouse is pictured here in 1909.

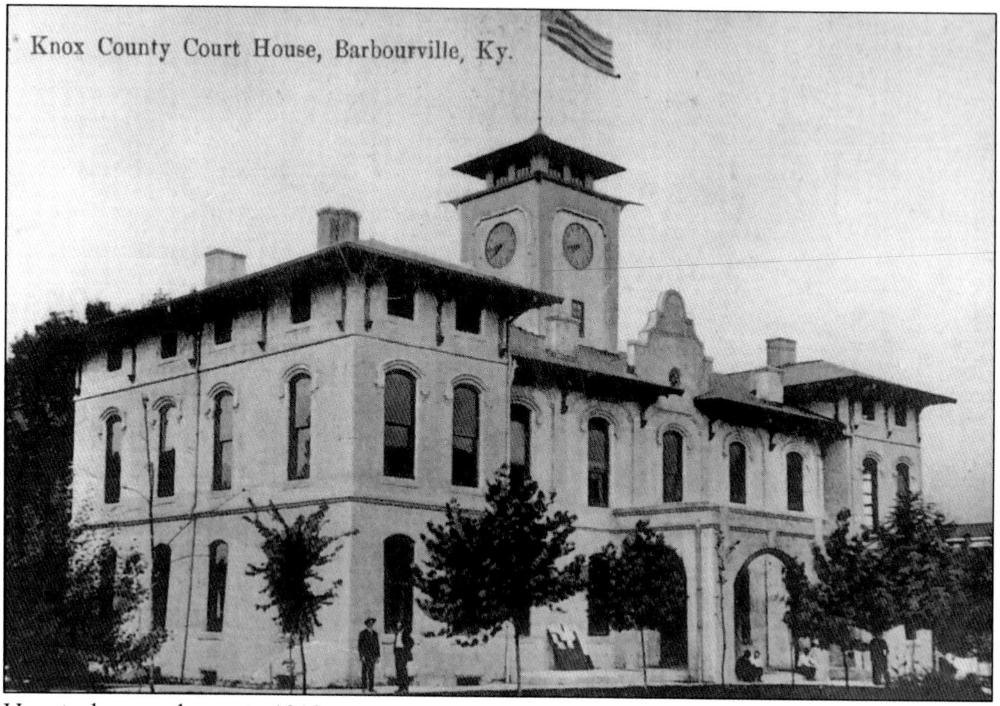

Here is the courthouse in 1910.

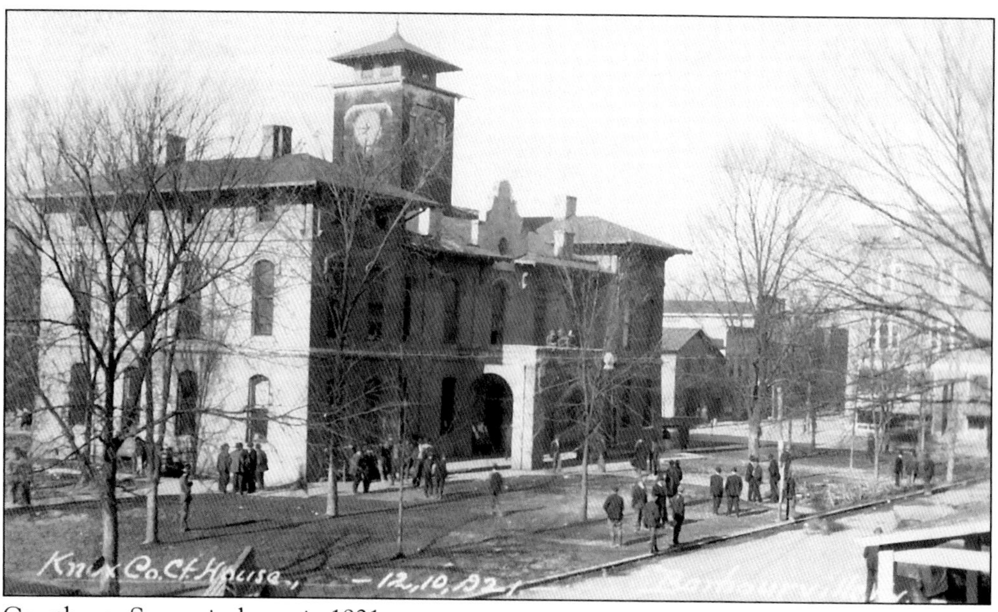

Courthouse Square is shown in 1921.

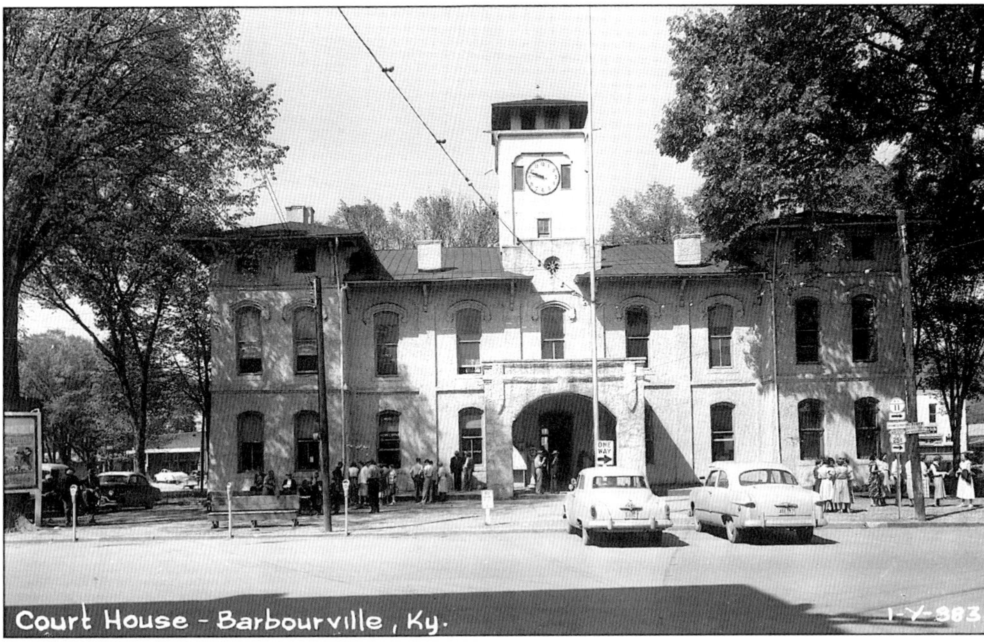

The courthouse is pictured in 1950.

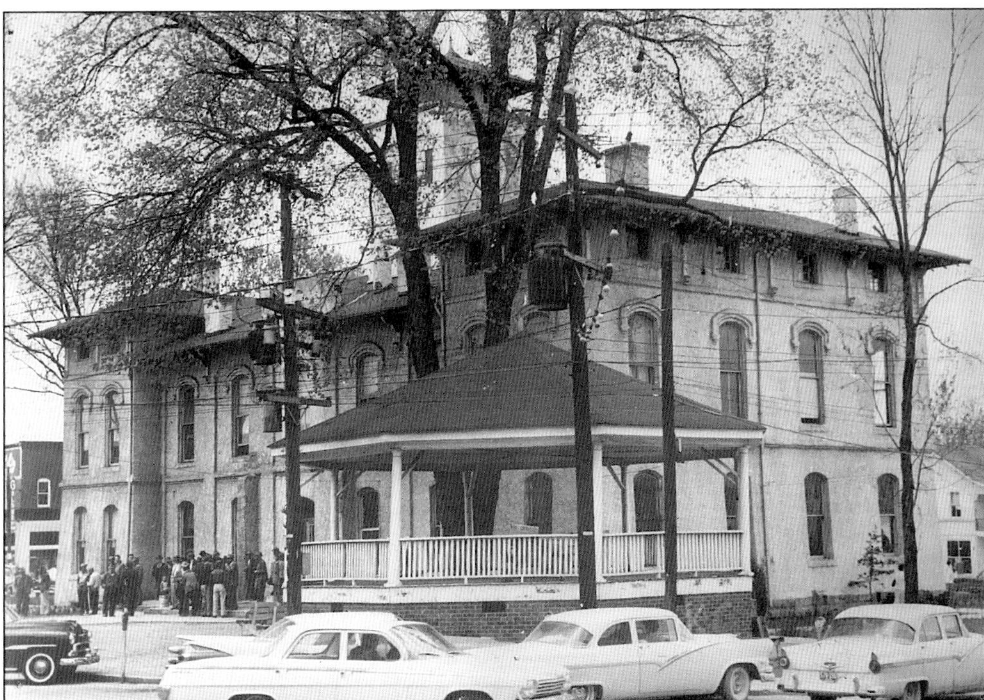
The courthouse is shown again in 1960.

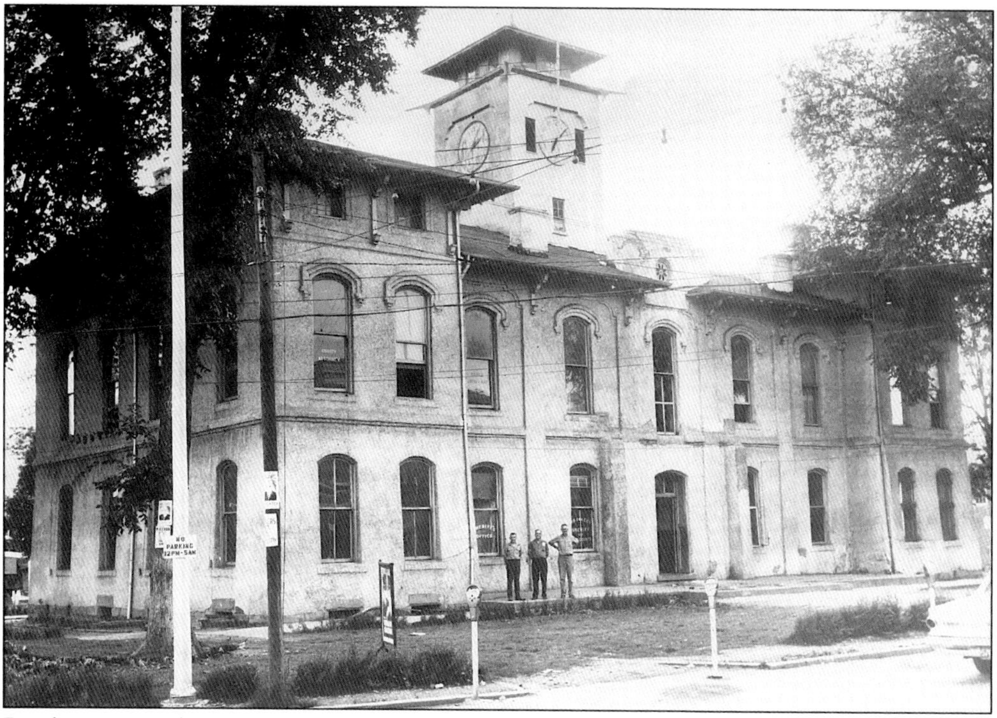

By the 1960s, the town's fourth courthouse had fallen into disrepair and was scheduled for demolition.

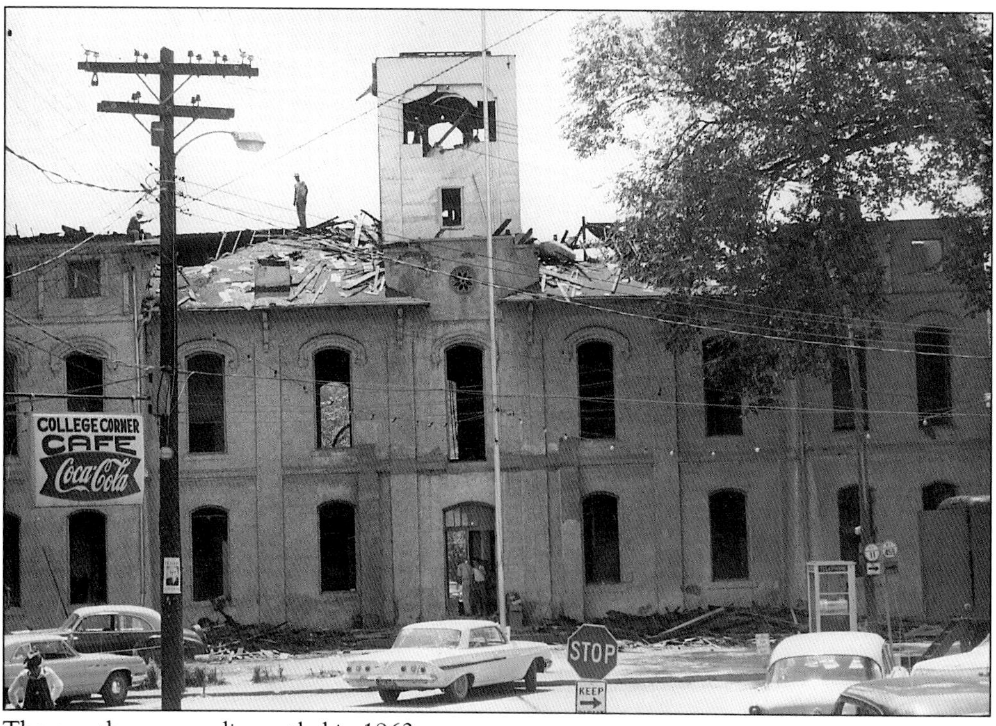

The courthouse was dismantled in 1963.

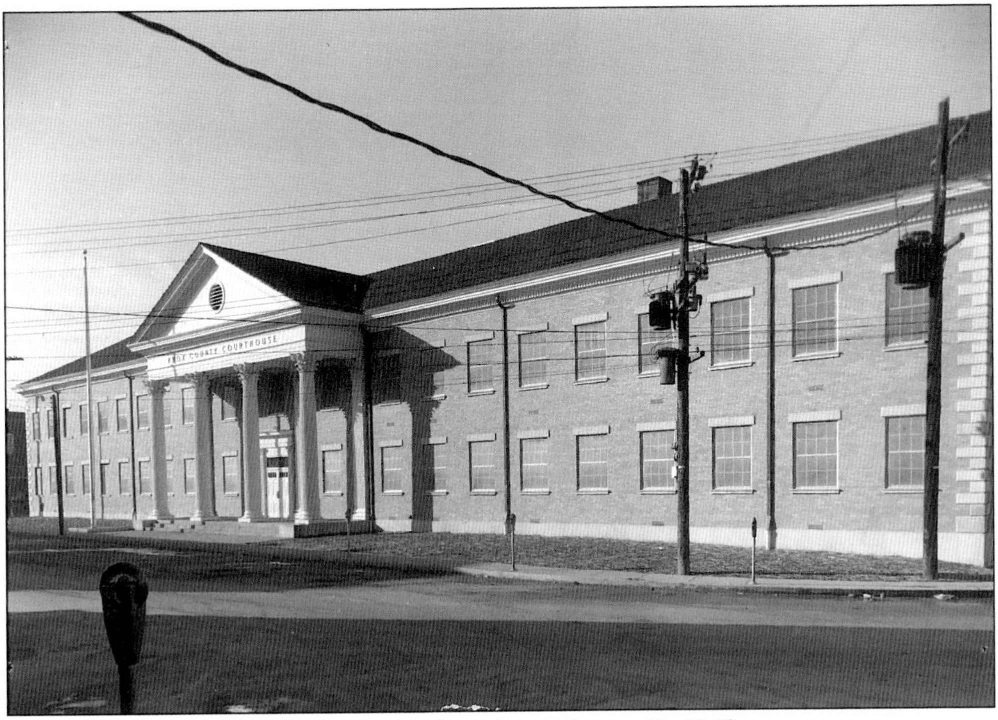

Barbourville's present courthouse was dedicated on February 20, 1965.

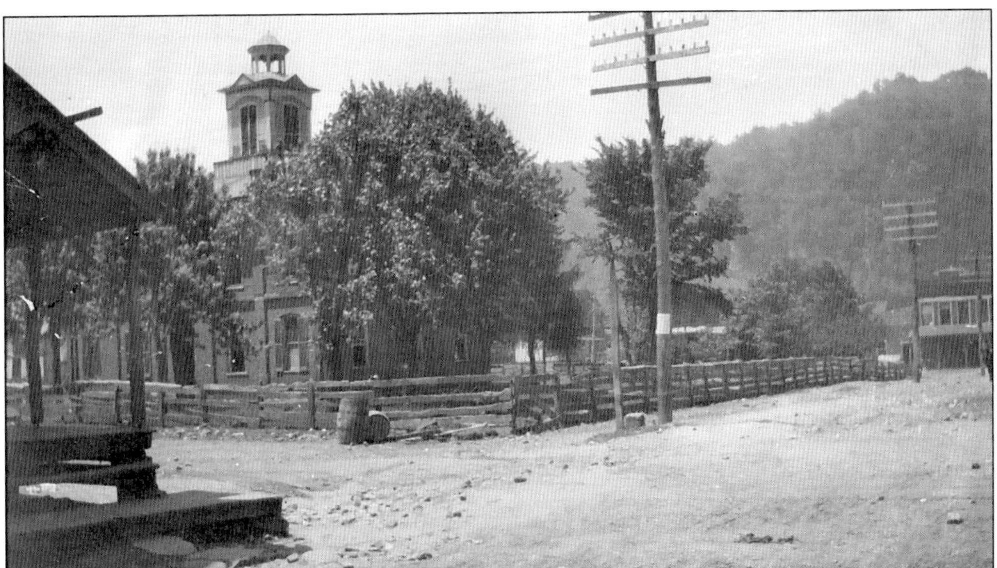

This parting view of Knox County's 1875 courthouse is a rare one. It shows an unpaved Courthouse Square and a rail fence encircling the courthouse lot.

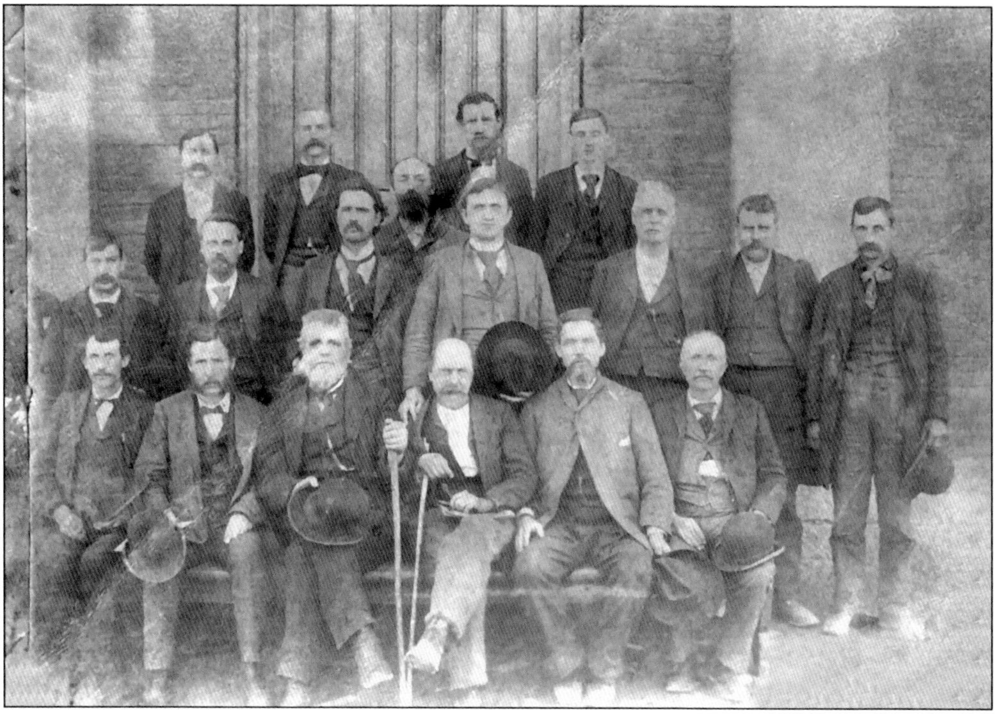

Knox County officials who worked in the courthouse from 1875 to 1906 are shown here. From left to right, they are as follows: (front row) Bud Bolin, Thomas J. Wyatt, Steven Golden, Tip Westerfield, Dan McDonald, and Frank Costellow; (middle row) James Jones, David Main, B.B. Golden, John G. Matthews, W.B. Anderson, William Byrley, and John Catron; (back row) W.W. Tinsley, James Black, Joshua Beams, William Black, and John Stivers.

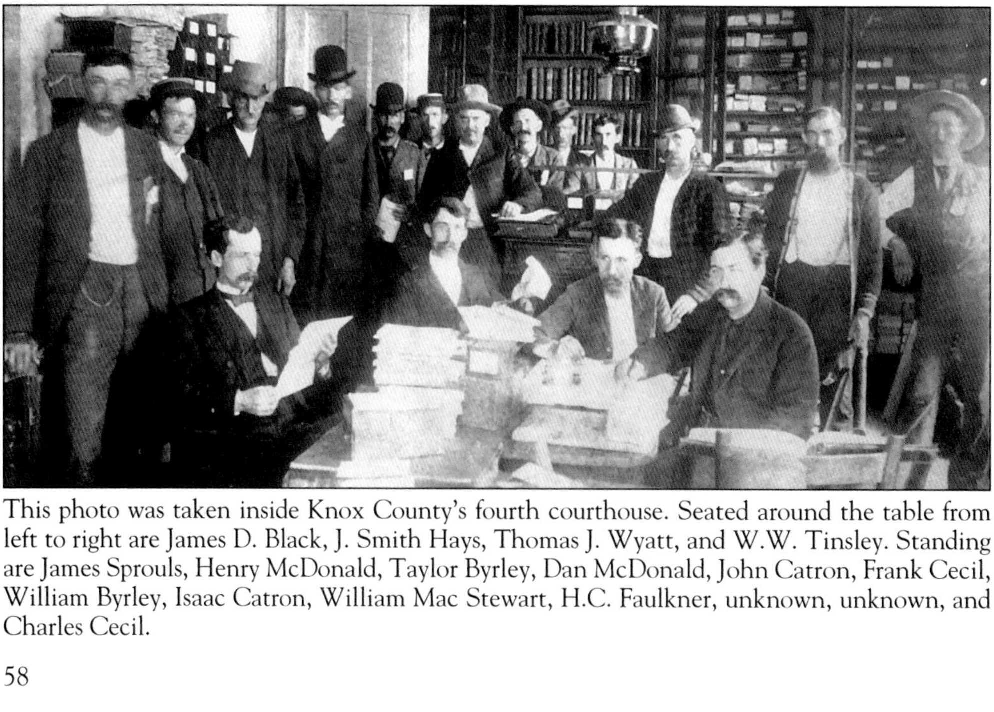

This photo was taken inside Knox County's fourth courthouse. Seated around the table from left to right are James D. Black, J. Smith Hays, Thomas J. Wyatt, and W.W. Tinsley. Standing are James Sprouls, Henry McDonald, Taylor Byrley, Dan McDonald, John Catron, Frank Cecil, William Byrley, Isaac Catron, William Mac Stewart, H.C. Faulkner, unknown, unknown, and Charles Cecil.

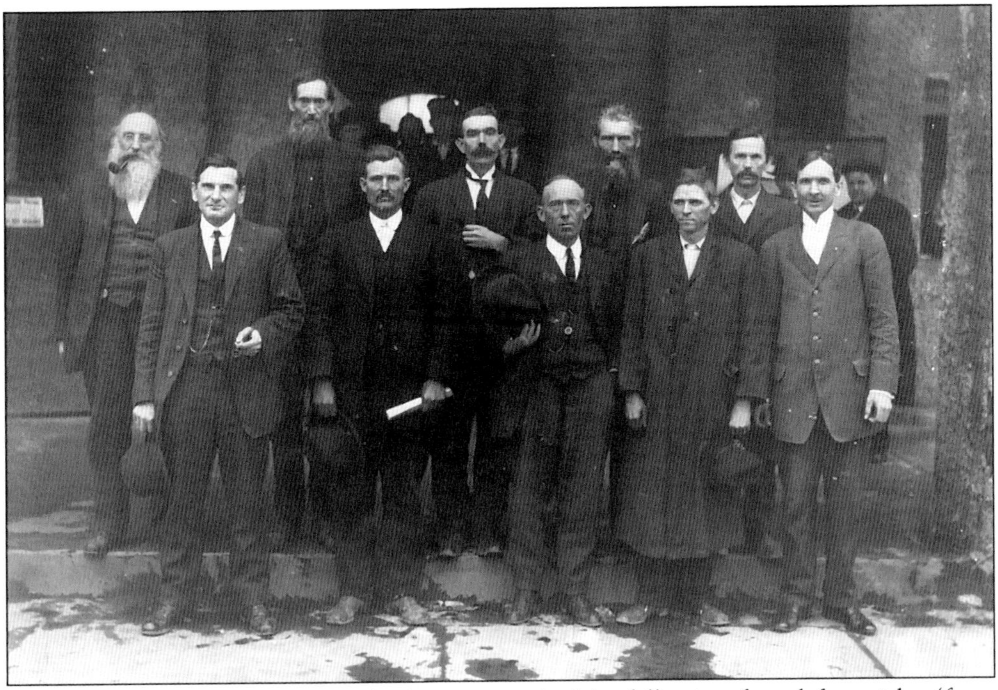

This group of early Knox County leaders consisted of the following, from left to right: (front row) ? Hubbard, unknown, Ben Golden, Frank Mitchell, and Reed P. Black; (back row) Judge Davis, unknown, Judge Stamper, unknown, and unknown.

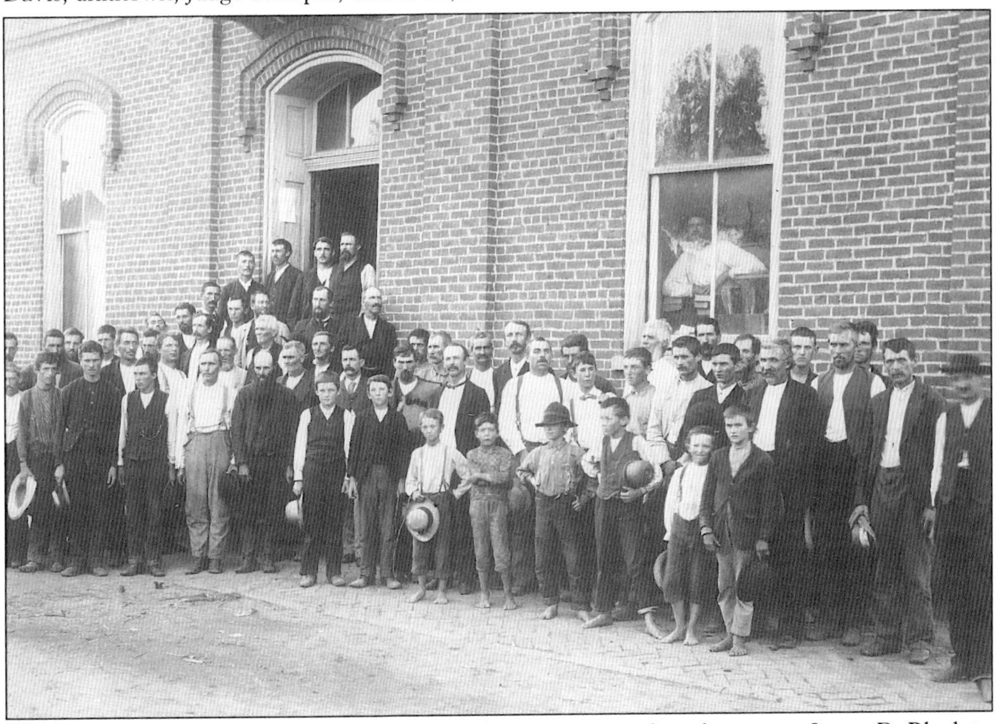

In this group photo in front of the 1875 courthouse, we can identify a young James D. Black in the center. He would later be governor of Kentucky.

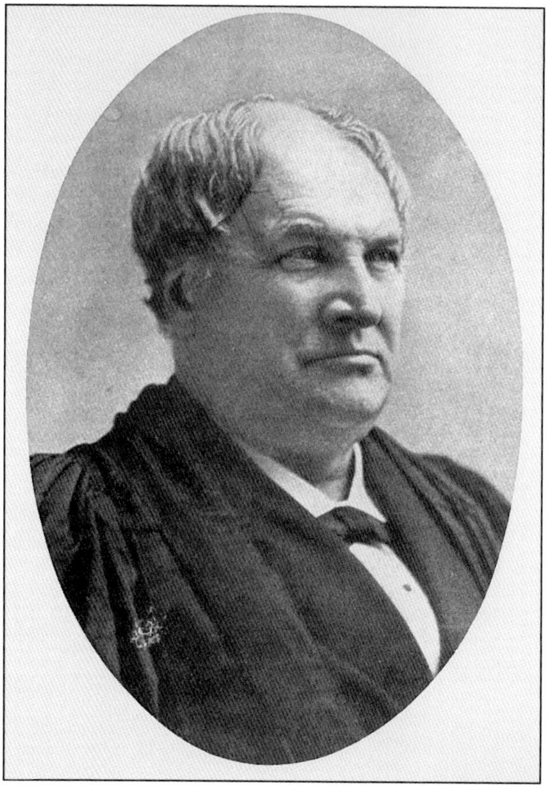

Samuel Miller moved to Barbourville in 1838 to practice medicine and law. He was admitted to the local bar in 1846. He later moved to Iowa and was appointed to the bench of the United States Supreme Court by President Abraham Lincoln.

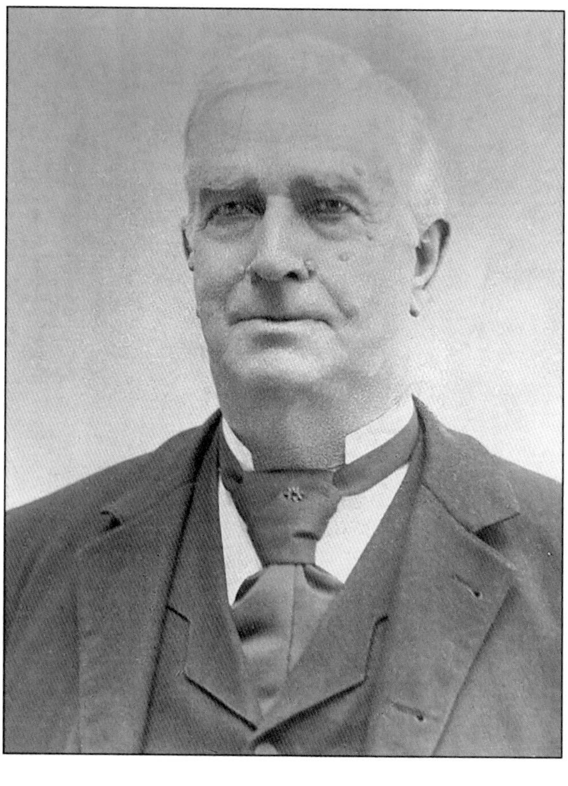

Silas Woodson was admitted to the local bar in 1839. He served Knox County as state representative, circuit attorney, and delegate to the Kentucky Constitutional Convention. After moving to Missouri, he was elected governor of that state in 1872. Woodson was the governor who posted a $2,000 reward on the outlaw Jesse James.

James D. Black was elected state representative in 1875. He was the superintendent of Knox County schools in 1884, was president of Union College in 1901, and became governor of Kentucky in 1919.

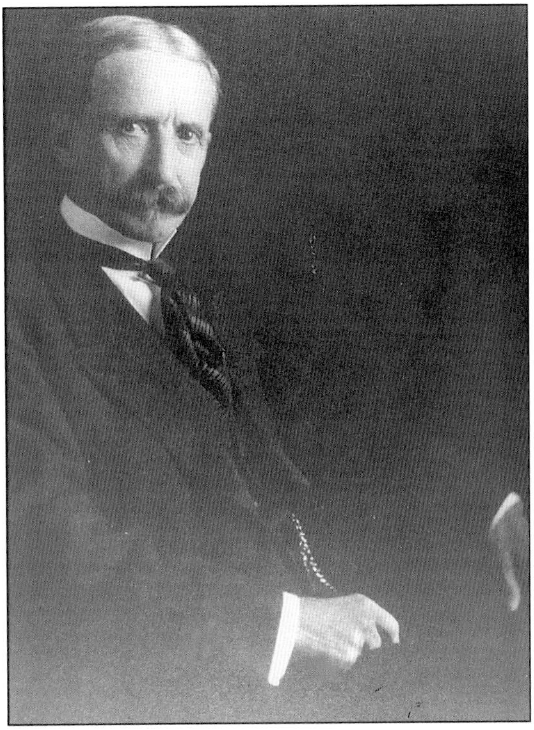

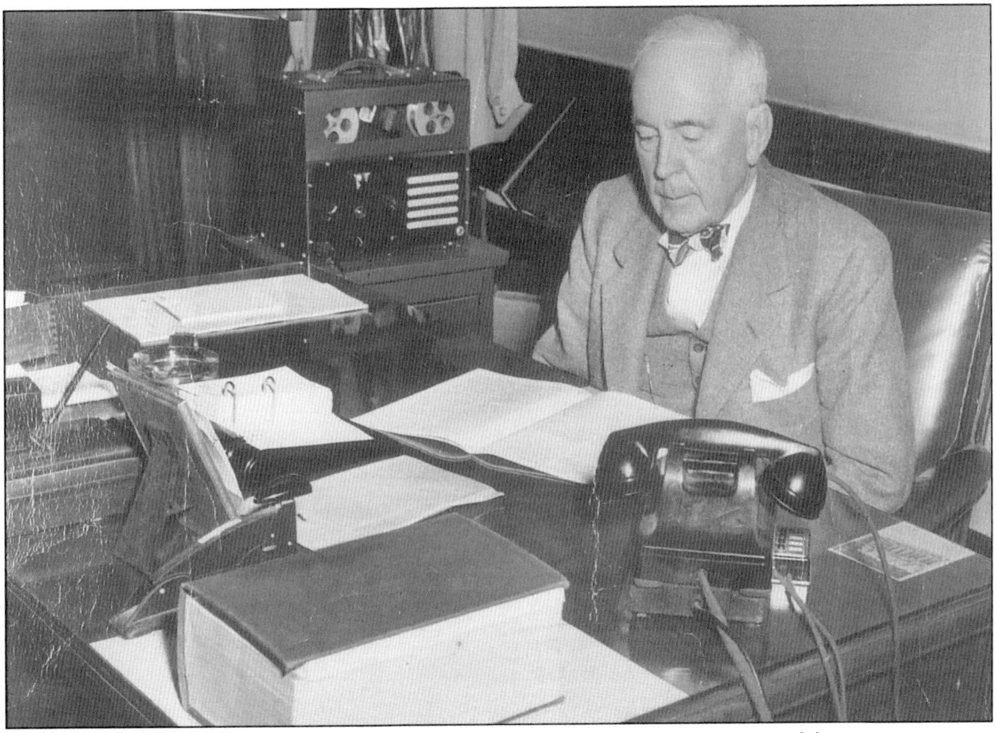

Flem D. Sampson was elected to the State Court of Appeals in 1916 and became governor of Kentucky in 1927. As governor, he led the fight to supply free textbooks to children in public schools.

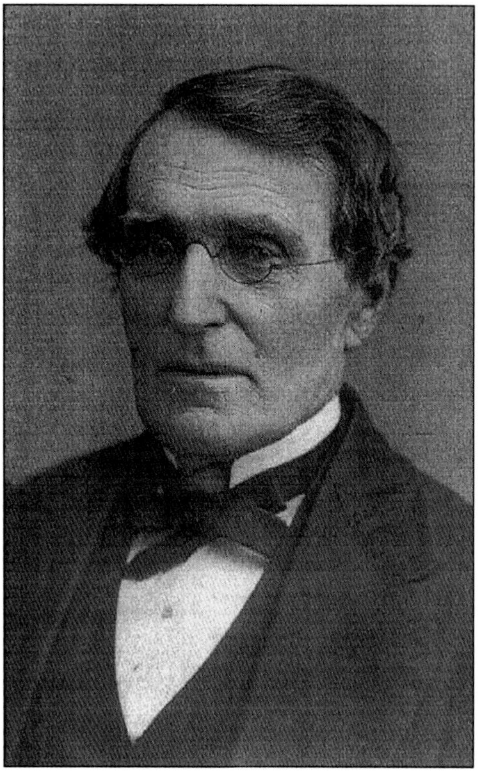

Six Knox County lawyers have served in Congress. The first was James Love (1795–1874). He served in the War of 1812, was a member of the state house of representatives from 1819 to 1831, and was elected to Congress in 1833. (Photo courtesy of the Library of Congress.)

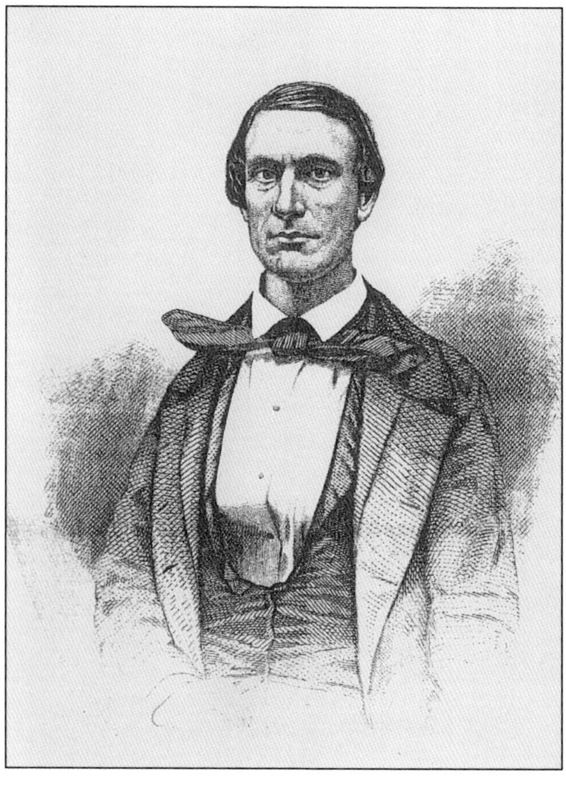

Green Adams (1812–1884) was a member of the state house of representatives in 1839. He was elected to Congress in 1847. (Photo courtesy of the Library of Congress.)

George Madison Adams (1837–1920) was clerk to the Circuit Court in 1859. He was elected to Congress on March 4, 1867. (Photo courtesy of the Library of Congress.)

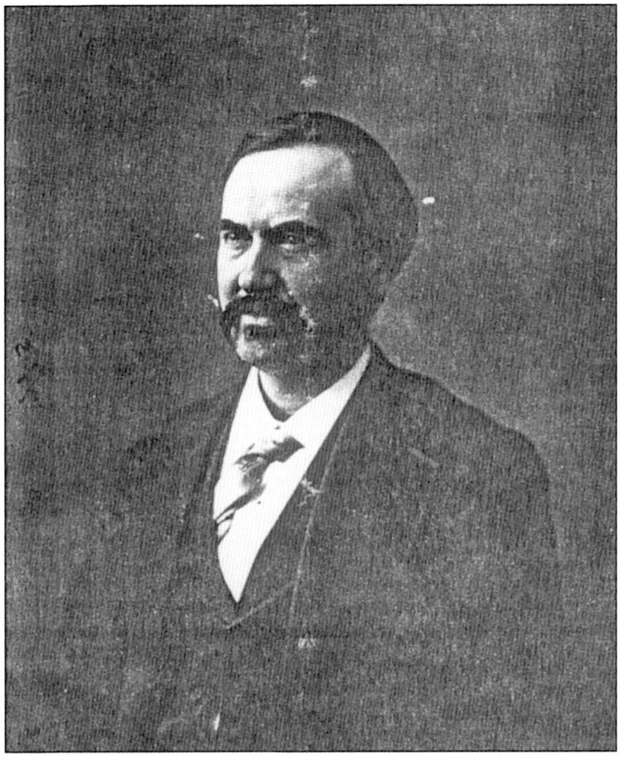

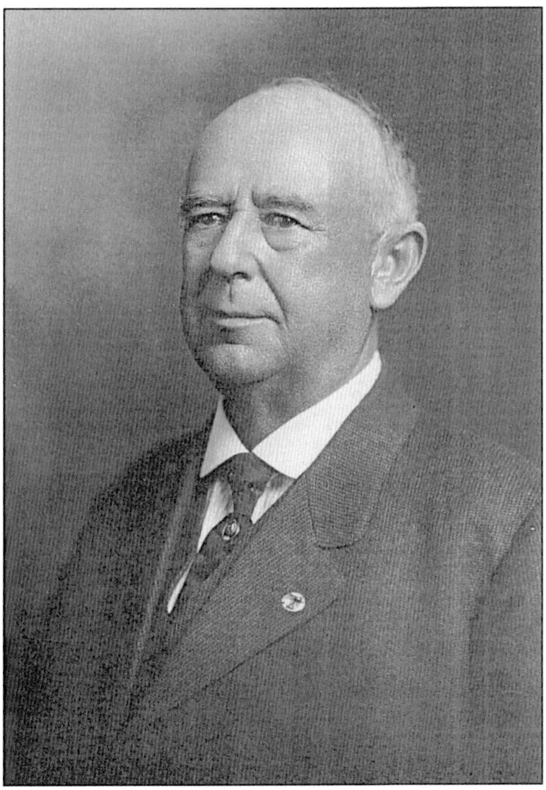

John Henry Wilson (1846–1923), a Barbourville lawyer, was a member of the state senate in 1883 and was elected to Congress on March 4, 1889. (Photo courtesy of the Library of Congress.)

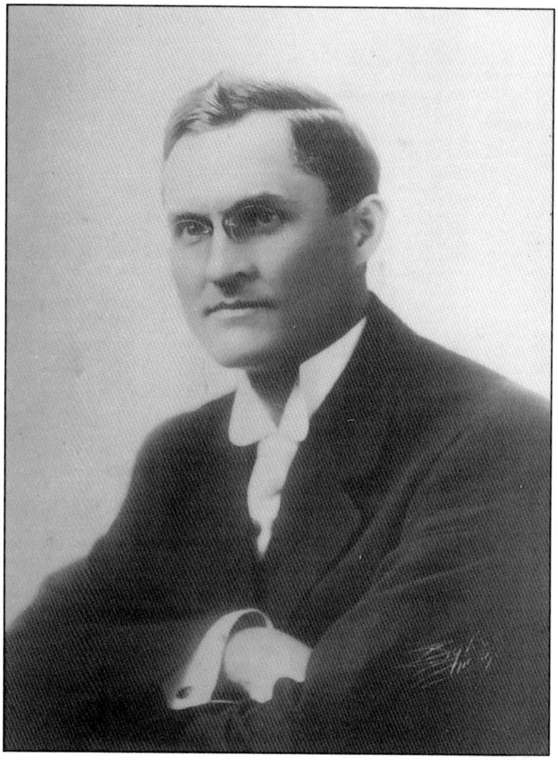

Caleb Powers (1869–1932) practiced law in Barbourville. He was superintendent of Knox County schools in 1894, was elected secretary of state in 1899, and was elected to Congress on March 4, 1911.

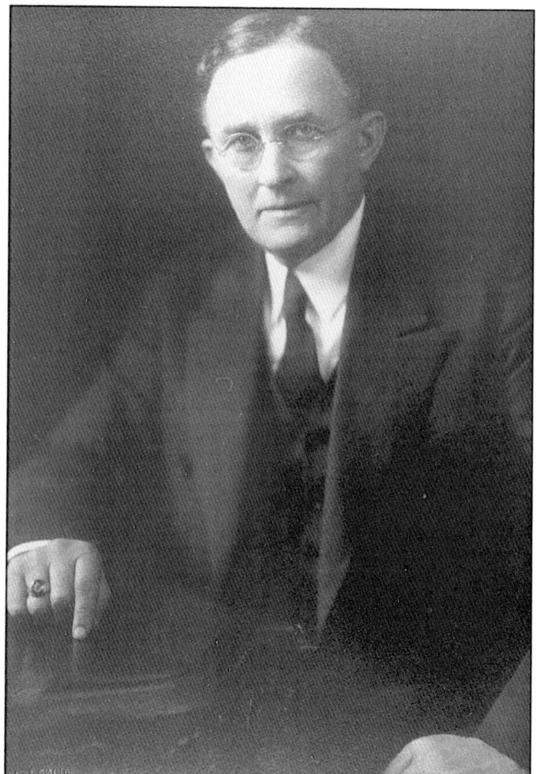

John M. Robsion (1873–1948) was president of Barbourville's old First National Bank. He was elected to Congress on March 4, 1919.

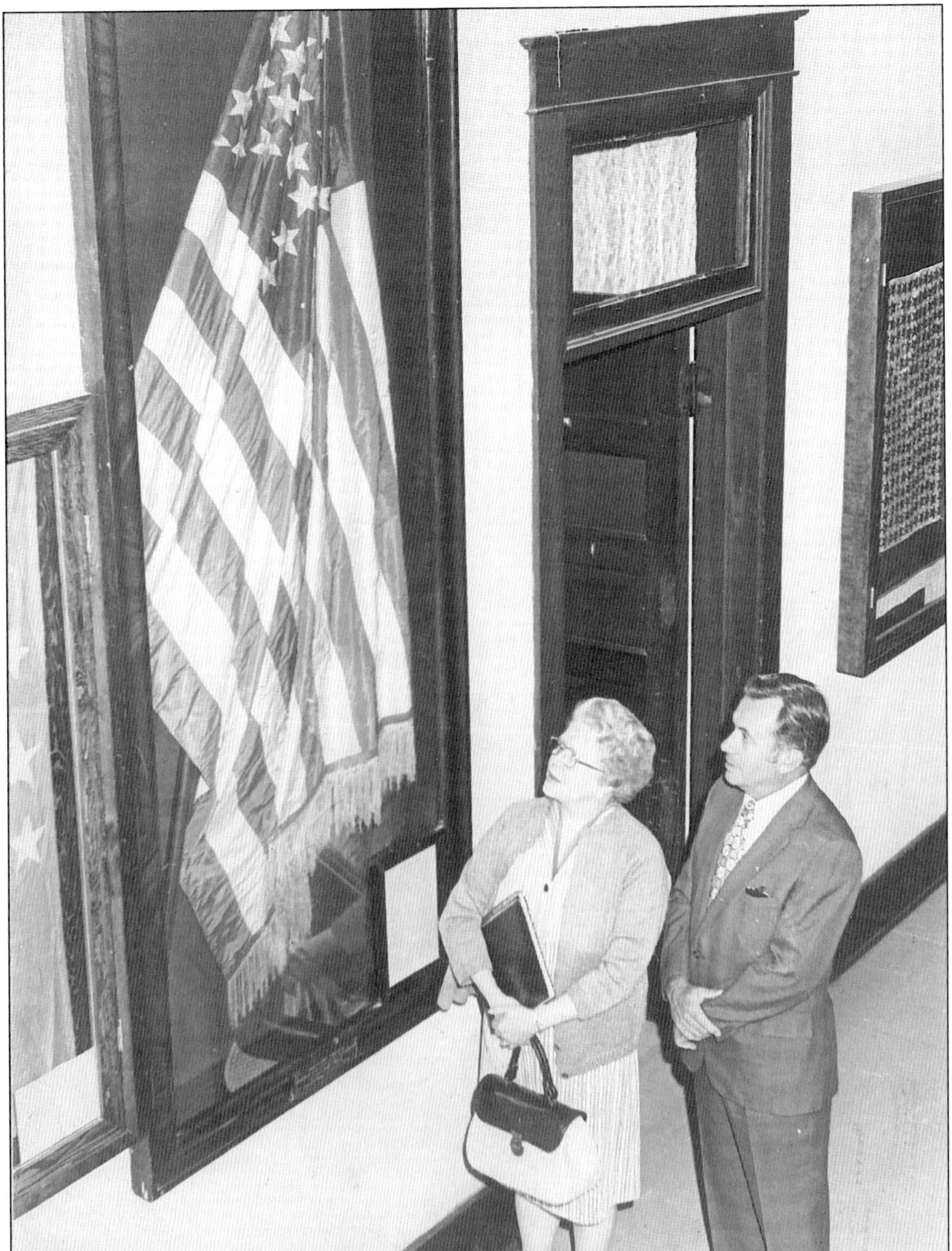

During the first days of the Civil War, Barbourville became the site of the first armed conflict on Kentucky soil. On September 19, 1861, Confederate forces entered Barbourville. These troops were resisted by the home guards of the city. This battle happened at the Barbourville Bridge, which is now the intersection of Cumberland Avenue and Daniel Boone Drive. Barbourville was occupied by both the Union and Confederate armies during the early years of the war. Many local residents are descendants of Civil War soldiers. Charles D. Black was a descendant of Captain Isaac J. Black.

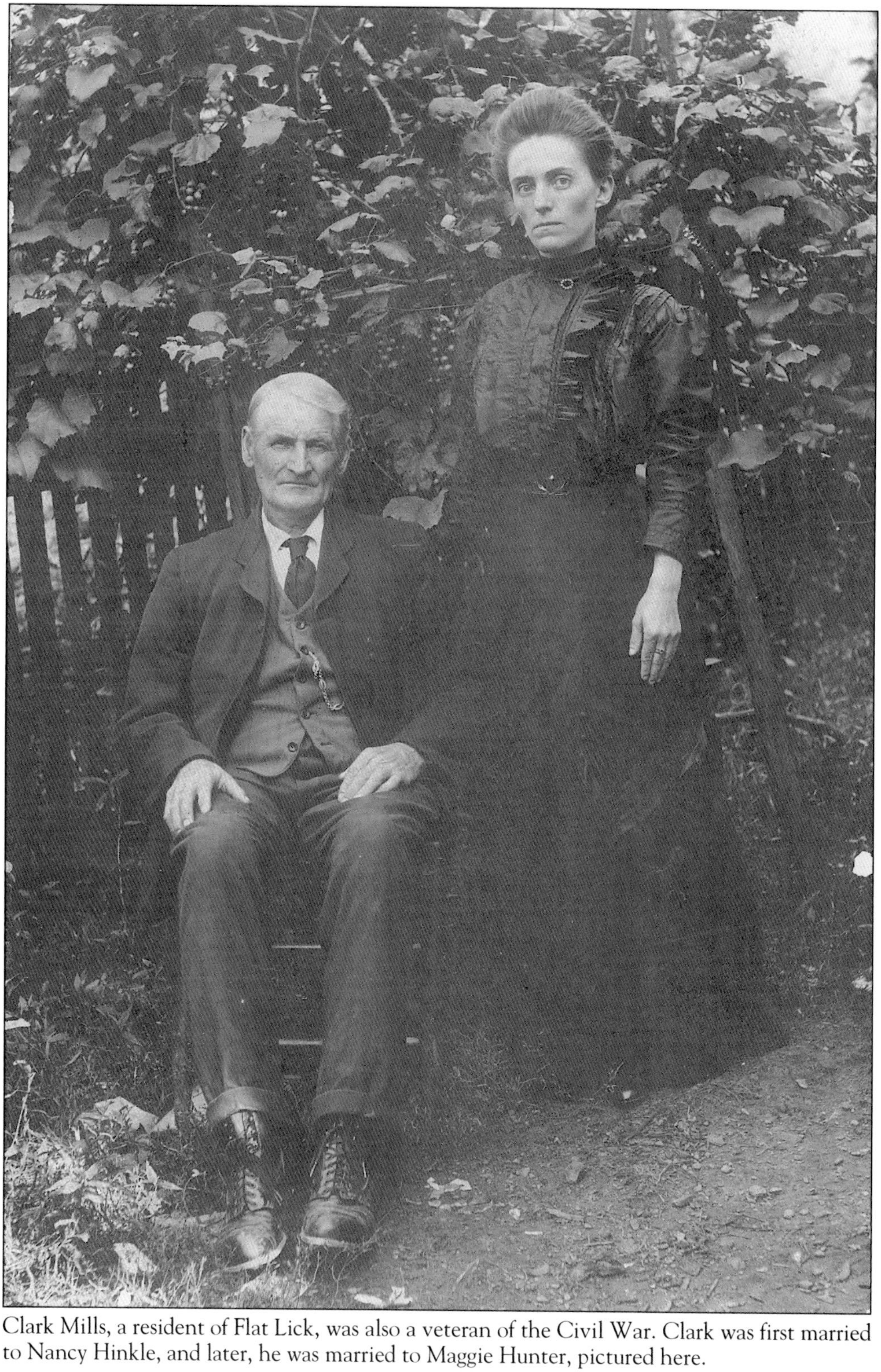

Clark Mills, a resident of Flat Lick, was also a veteran of the Civil War. Clark was first married to Nancy Hinkle, and later, he was married to Maggie Hunter, pictured here.

Four

Early Transportation

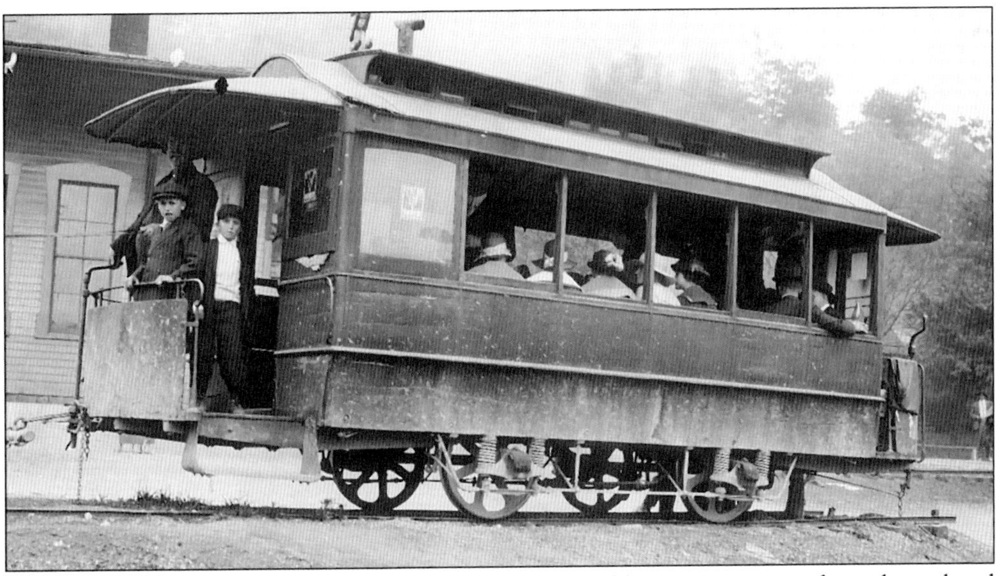

In 1890, Barbourville businessmen wanted to provide public transportation from the railroad depot to the town square. They built a one-mile track and purchased a horse-drawn streetcar, thus beginning the Barbourville street railway system, which operated from 1890 until 1919. Here we see the streetcar at the depot on Cumberland Avenue, ready to make a trip to the town square.

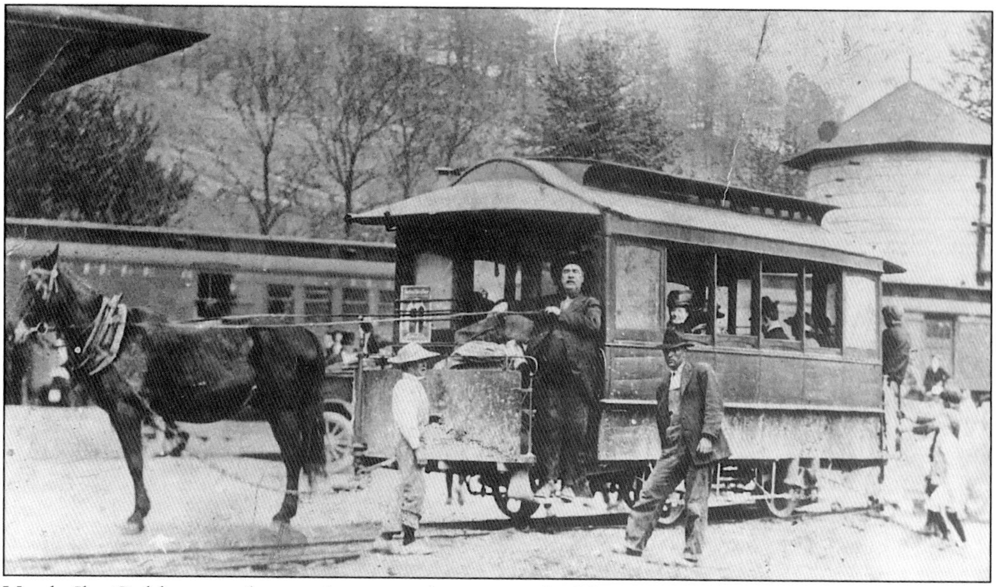

Uncle Ike Golden was the conductor as this car readied for a trip to town.

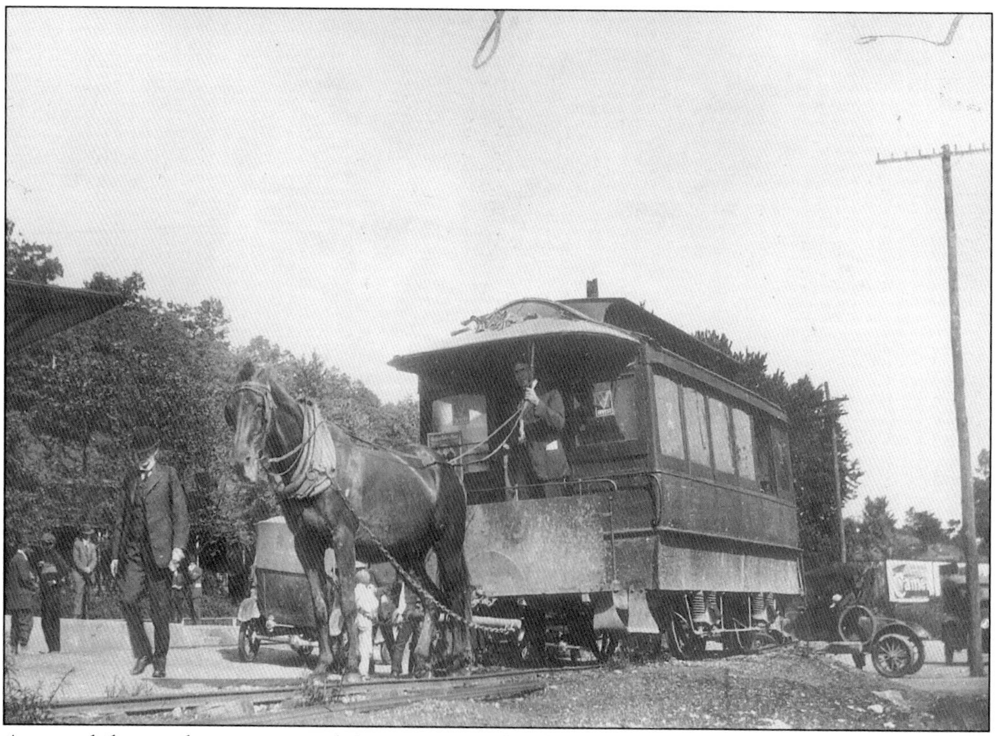

Automobiles can be seen around this streetcar; the days of the streetcars were numbered.

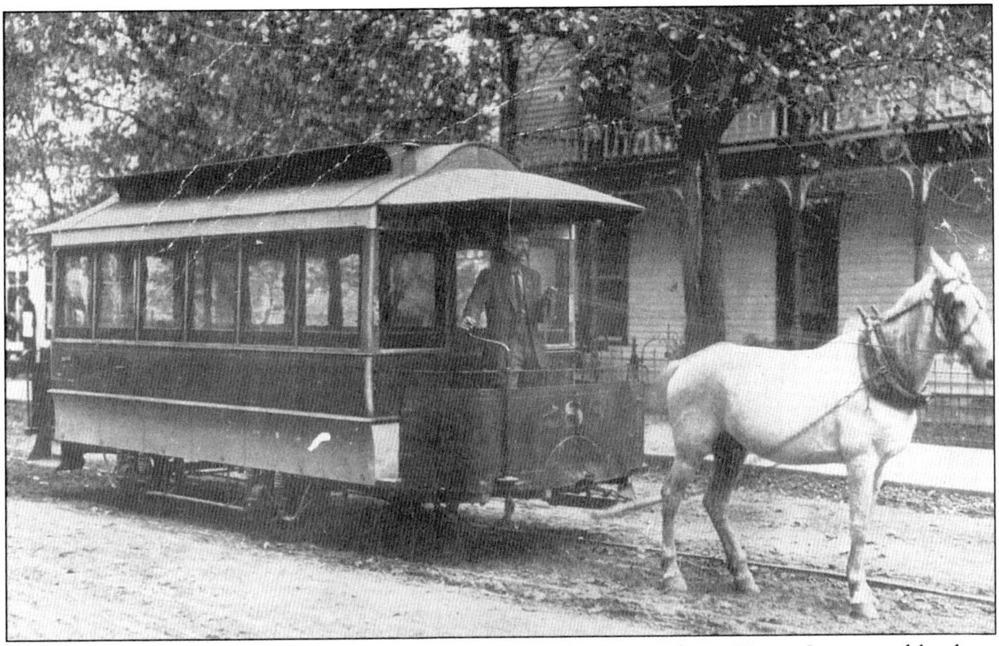

A.J. Mitchell was the conductor as this streetcar made its way down Knox Street and back to the depot.

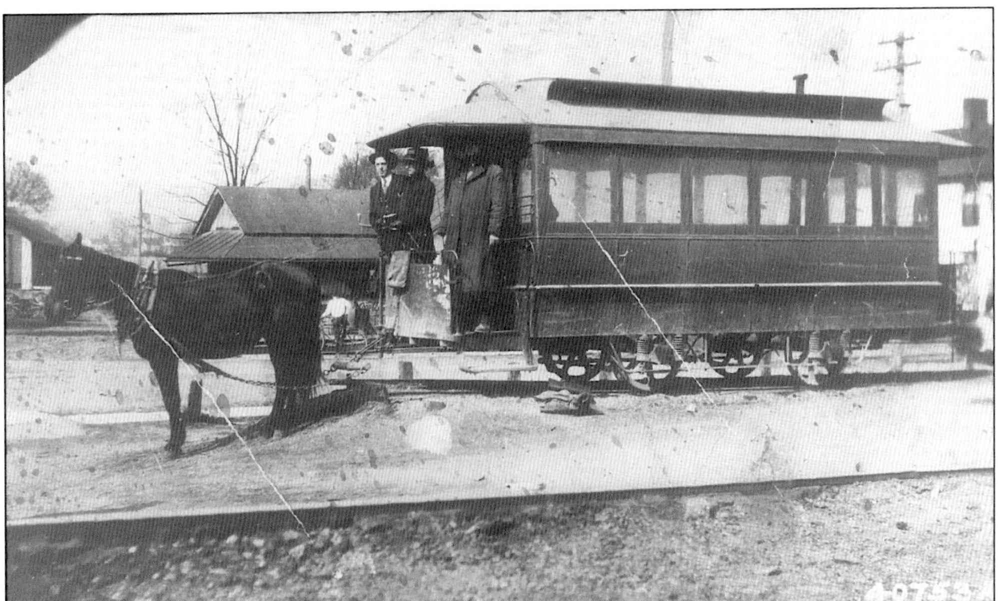

This streetcar is seen at its tracks end. Many postcard images were made over the years of the Barbourville streetcars.

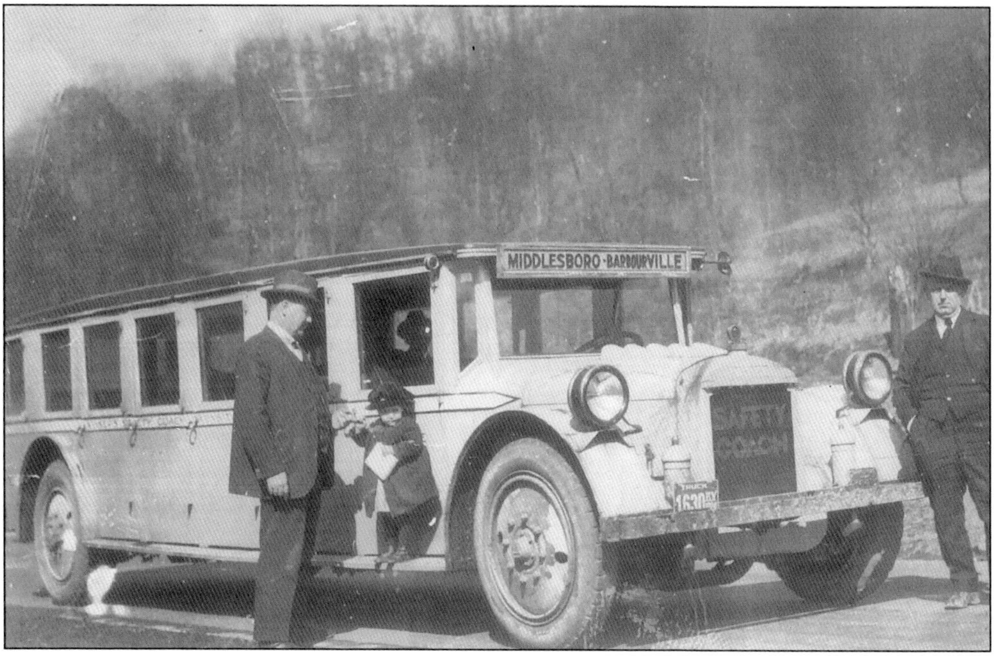

After the streetcar days were over in Barbourville, bus lines sprang up all over the mountains. In this picture, the Barbourville-Middlesboro bus is seen in 1924. The owner was Robert Johnson. His daughter, Maxine, stands by the door, and bystander Walter Disney stands at the front of the bus.

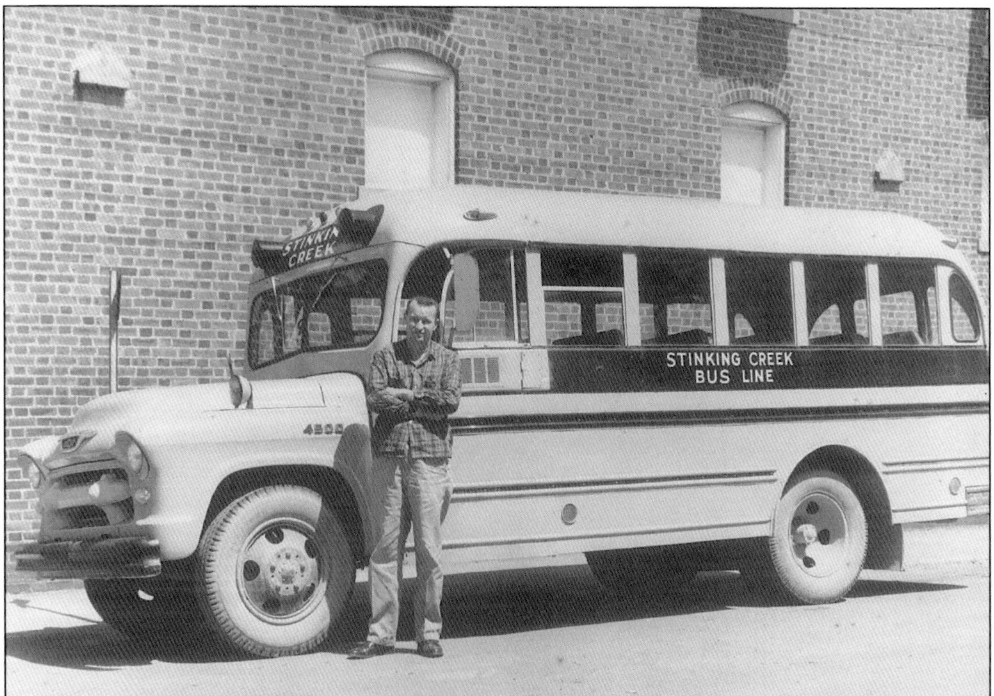

In the 1950s, a very popular bus was the Stinking Creek bus. The driver here is Mitchell Carnes.

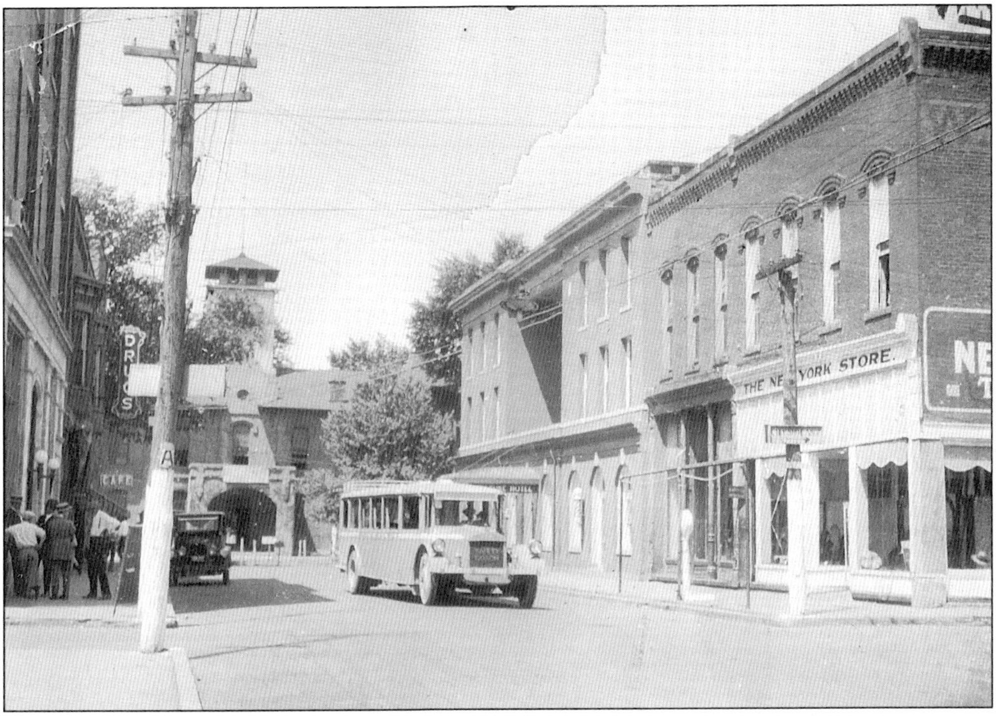

This bus, sometimes called the "Blue Goose," is leaving Courthouse Square down Knox Street and heading to Corbin.

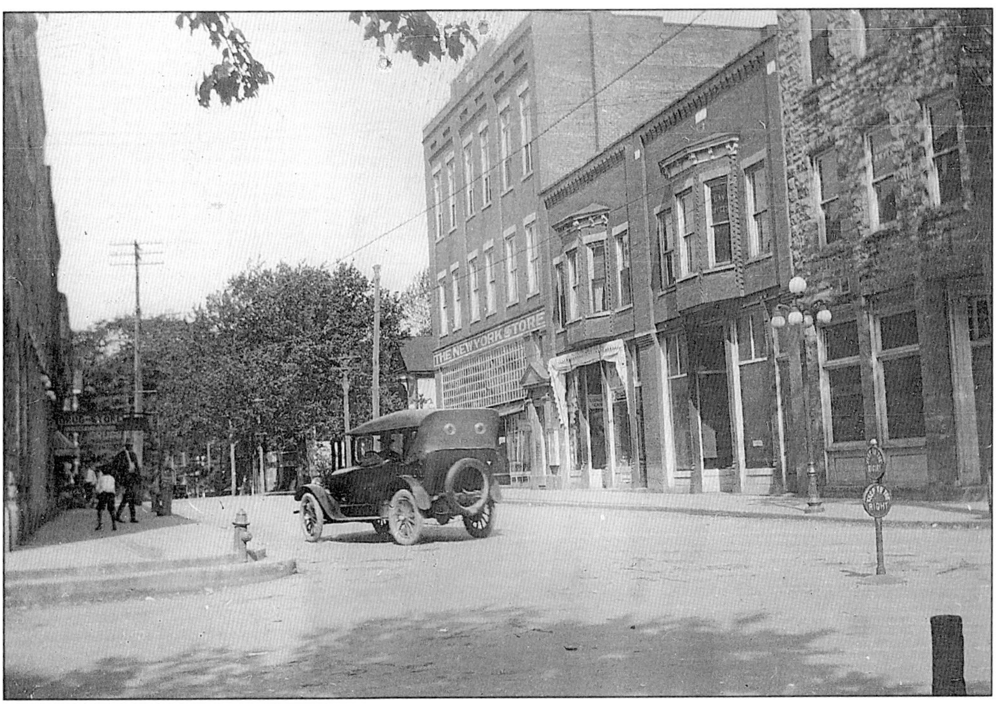

Here, the passenger car is leaving Courthouse Square by way of Knox Street in the 1920s.

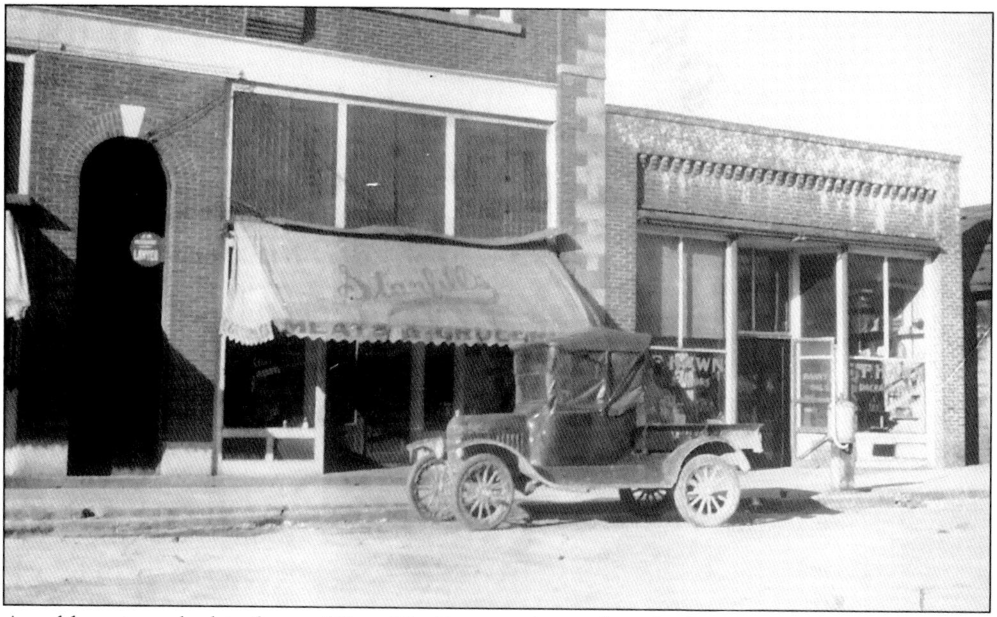

An old car is parked in front of Stanfills Grocery, located in the Lawson Building. The Hawn Drug Store is to the right.

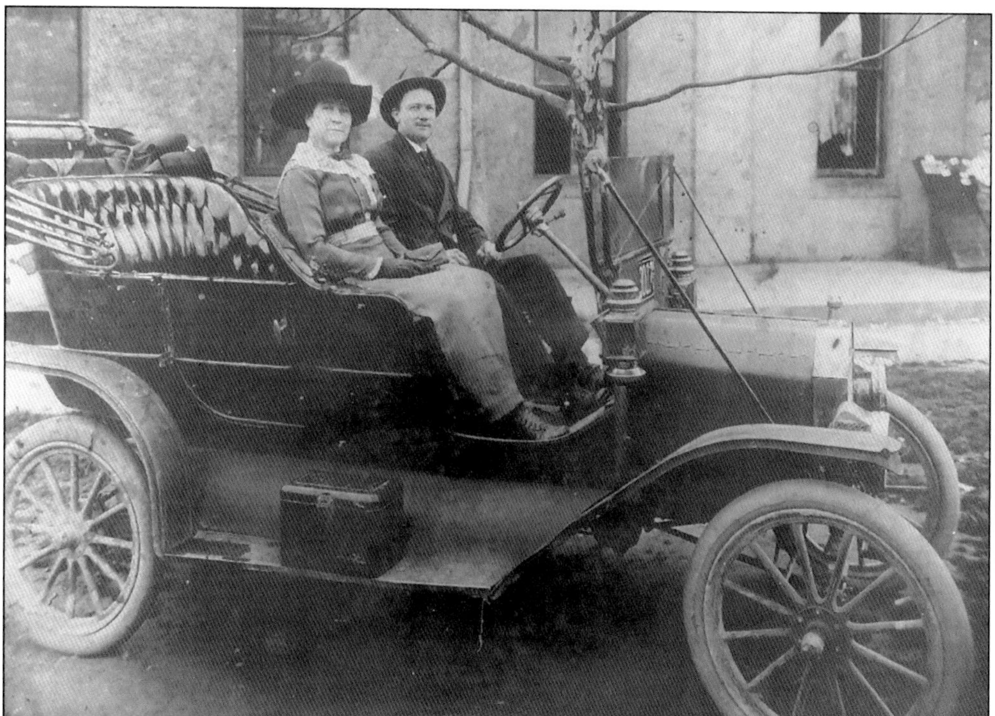

Mr. and Mrs. Henry McDonald owned one of Barbourville's first passenger cars.

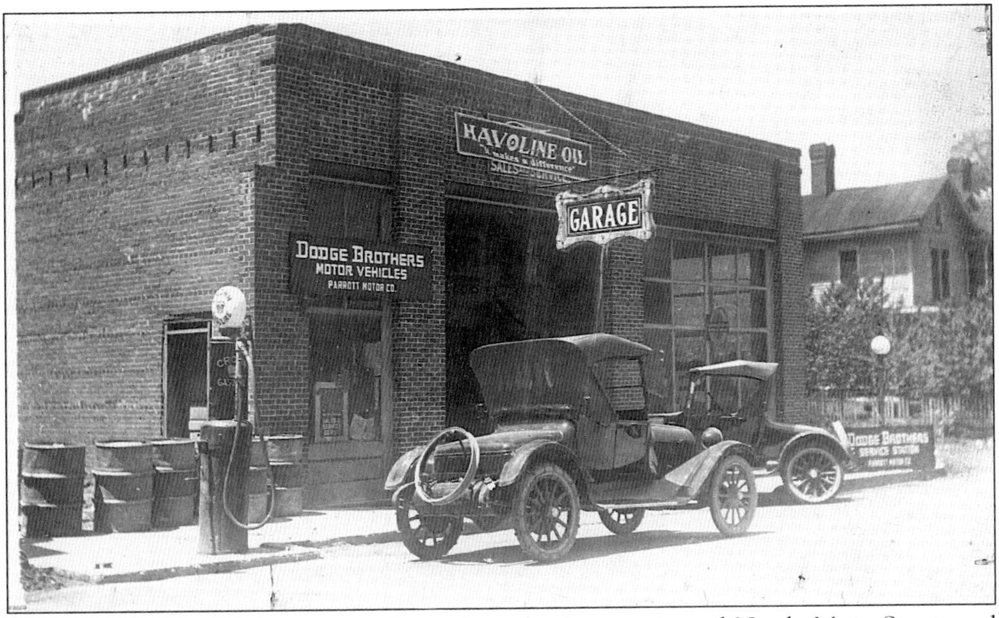

The Parrott Motor Company was located at the intersection of North Main Street and Wall Street.

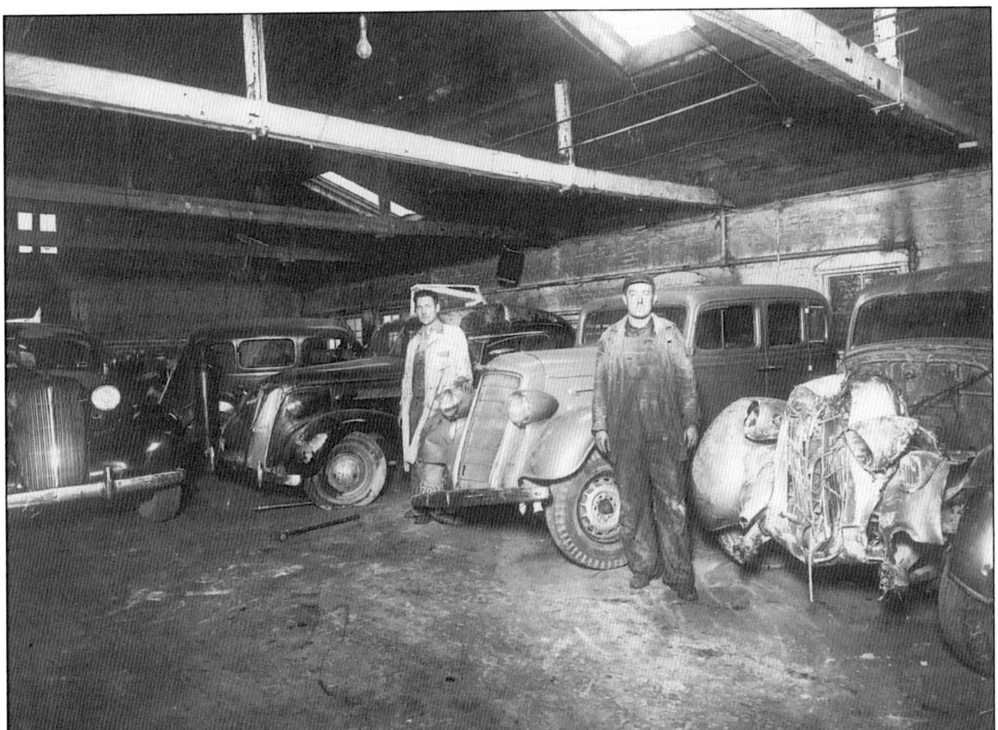
The Hutton Garage was located at the corner of Cumberland Avenue and Dishman Street in the 1940s.

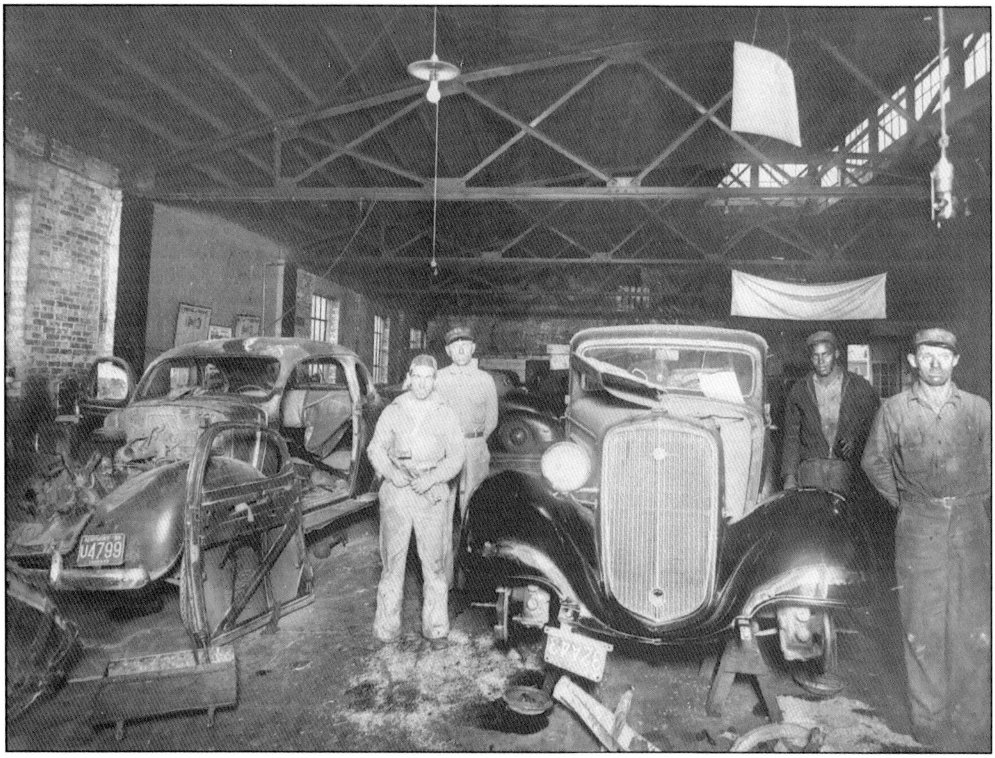

The Universal Garage was located at the corner of Knox Street and College Street.

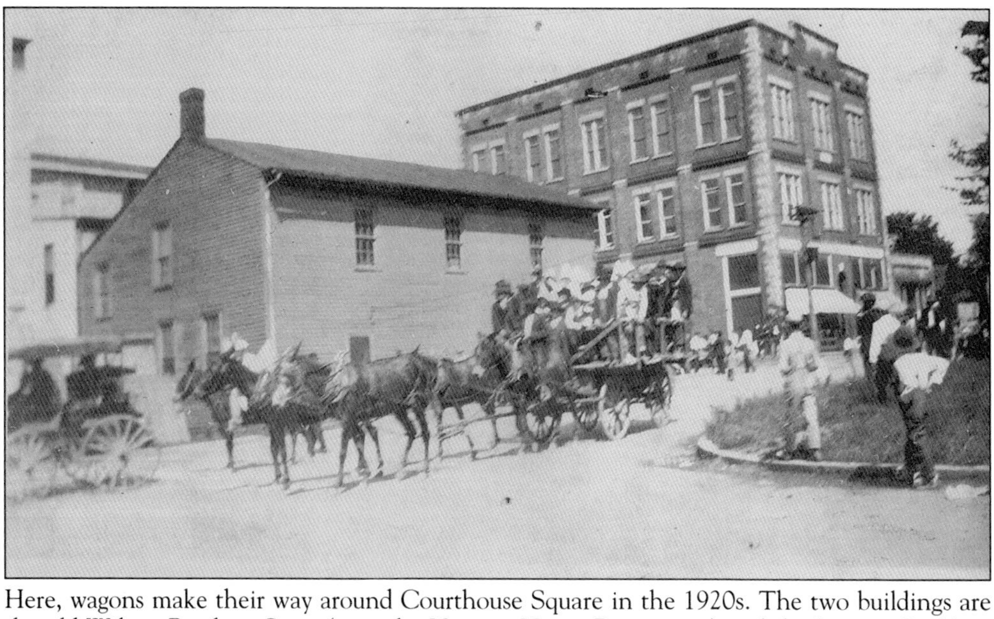

Here, wagons make their way around Courthouse Square in the 1920s. The two buildings are the old Wilson Brothers Store (now the Vintage House Restaurant) and the Lawson Building (at right).

Five

Crime and Punishment

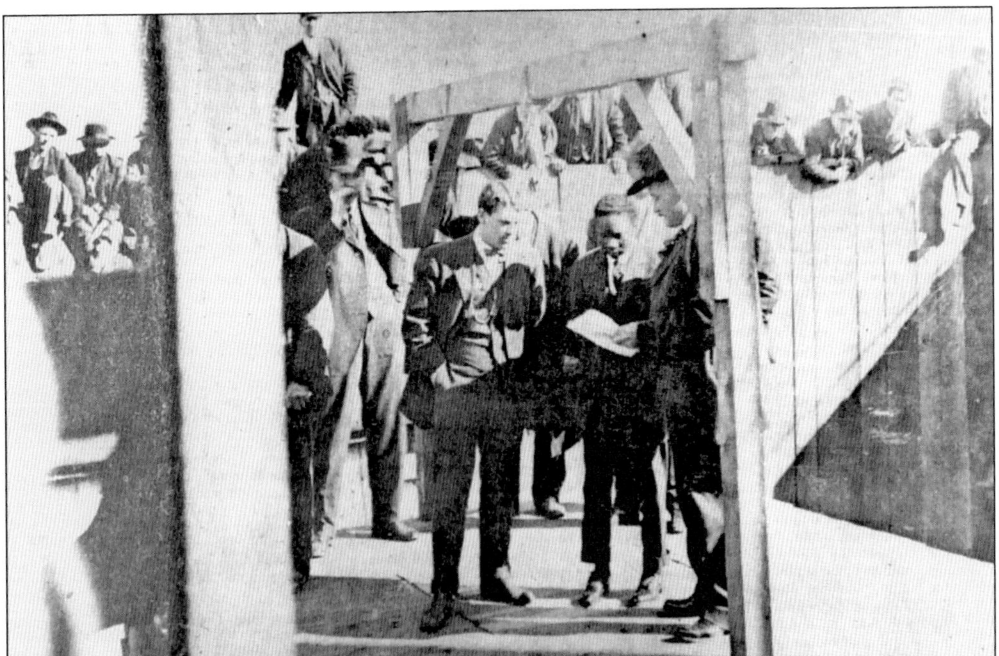

The last public hanging in Knox County took place in February 1907, when Jesse Fitzgerald was convicted of the killing of Martha Broughton. Several photos survive to tell this story. In this photo, Deputy Sheriff George Tinsley reads Jesse his sentence as he stands on the trap door alongside Sheriff Dan Williams.

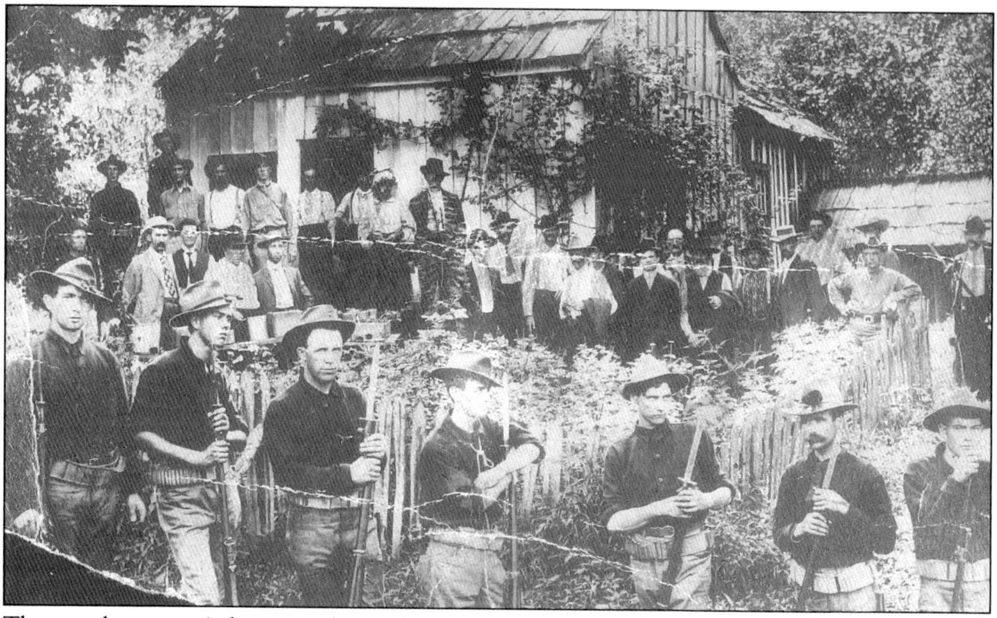

The murder victim's home is shown here, just hours after the crime. Local guardsmen have secured the area.

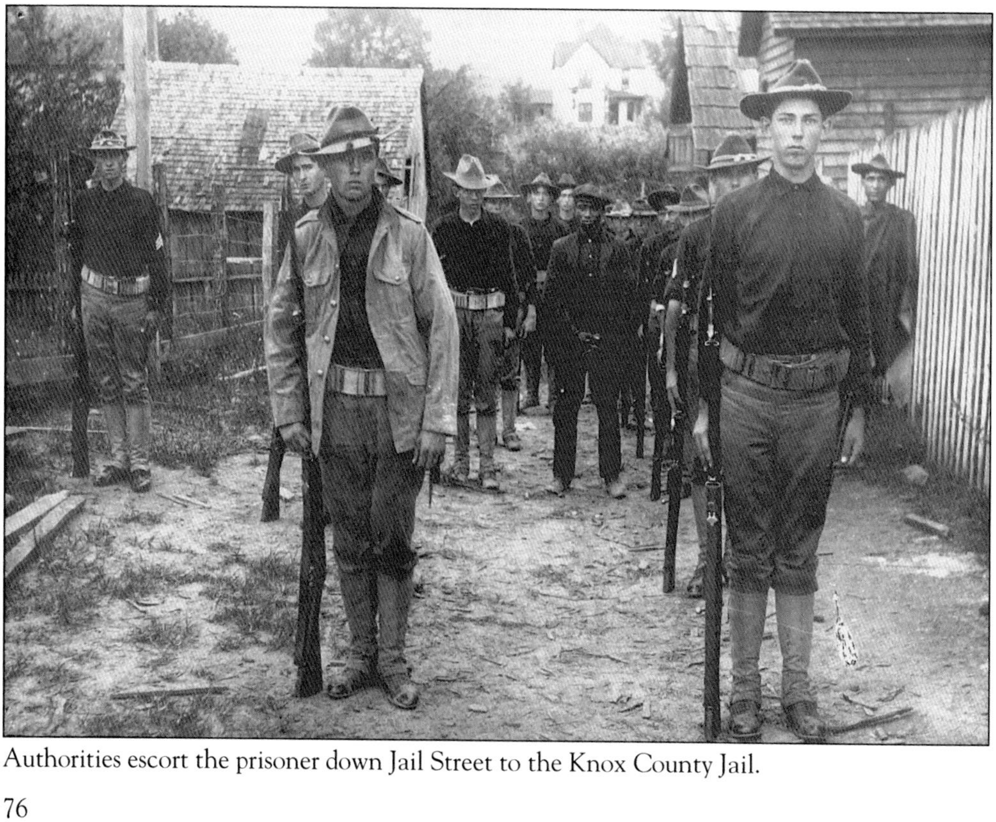

Authorities escort the prisoner down Jail Street to the Knox County Jail.

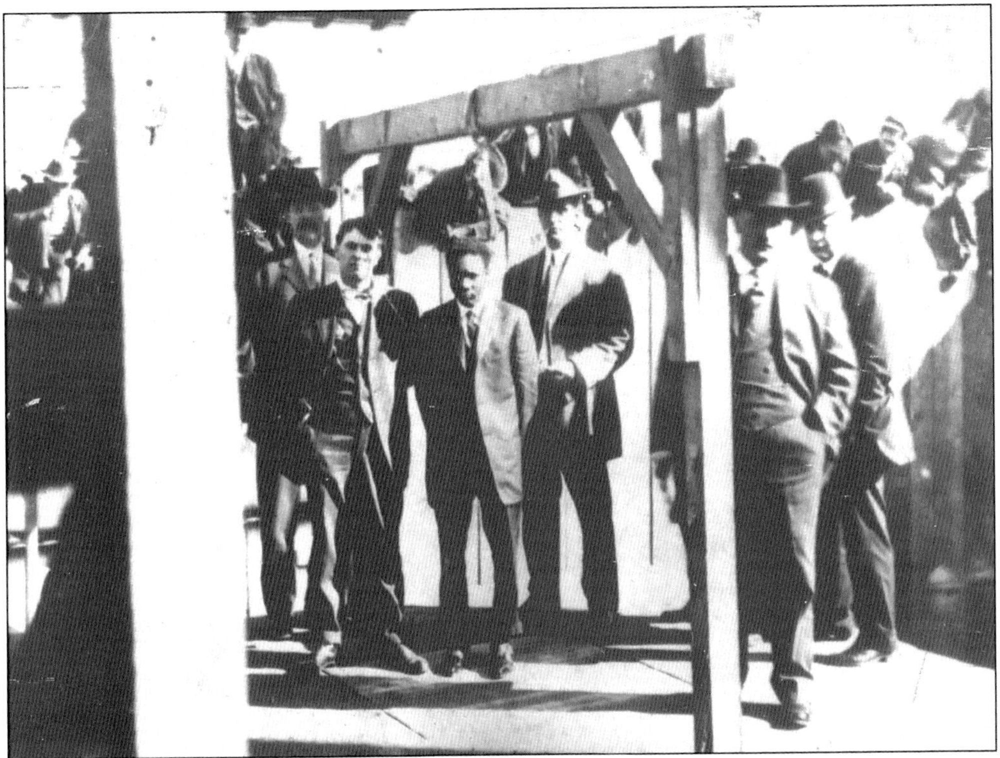

Here is the most frequently found photograph of the hanging. Jesse and the county officials appear to be posing for the photographer.

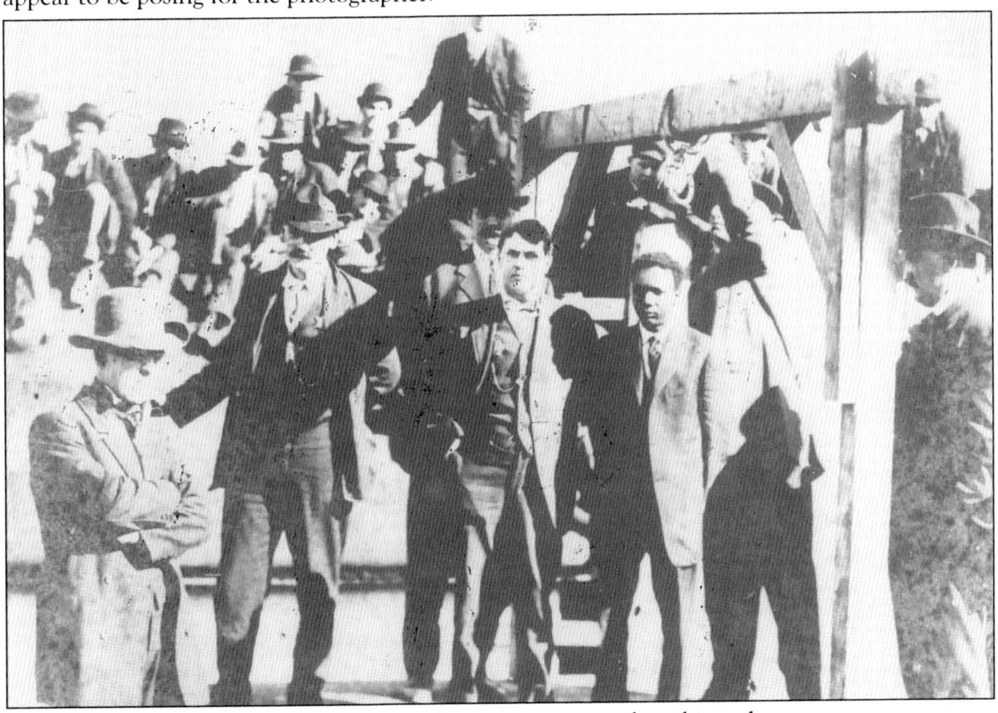

In this photo, the grim task of adjusting the noose seems to be taking place.

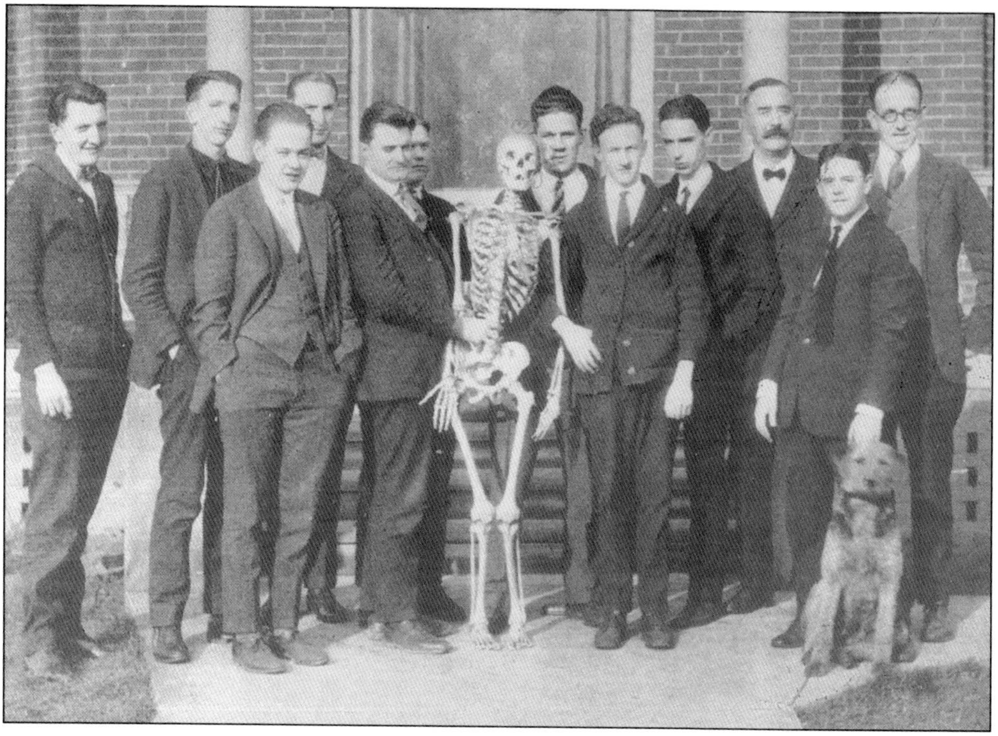

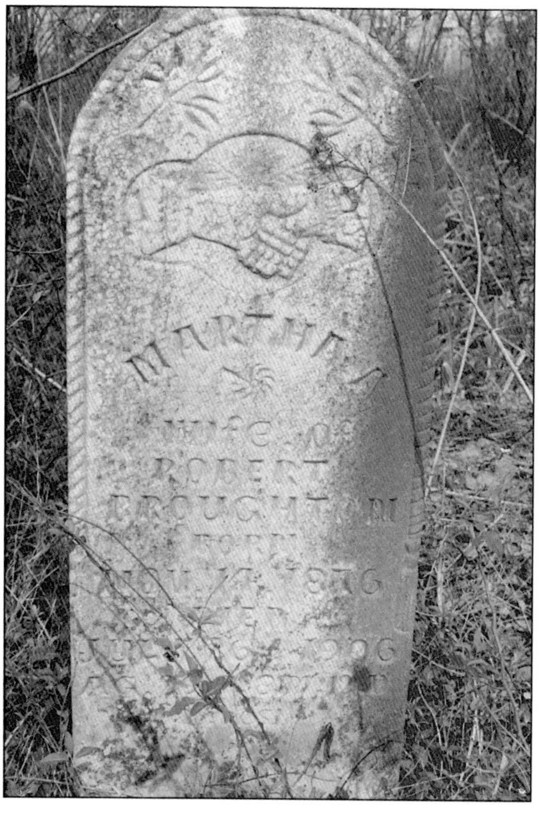

Legend has it that Jesse Fitzgerald's skeletal remains were preserved and used for biological studies in medical classes.

Jesse's victim, Martha Broughton, is buried in a local cemetery near the new Knox County Hospital. An account of this and six other public hangings can be found in the Knox County Historical Museum's quarterly magazine, *The Knox Countian*.

In March of 1885, John Sexton was hanged behind the old jail in Barbourville. The victim was George Routen; the charge was robbery and murder. An account of this hanging can be found in the files of the *Barbourville Mountain Advocate* as well as the Knox County Historical Museum.

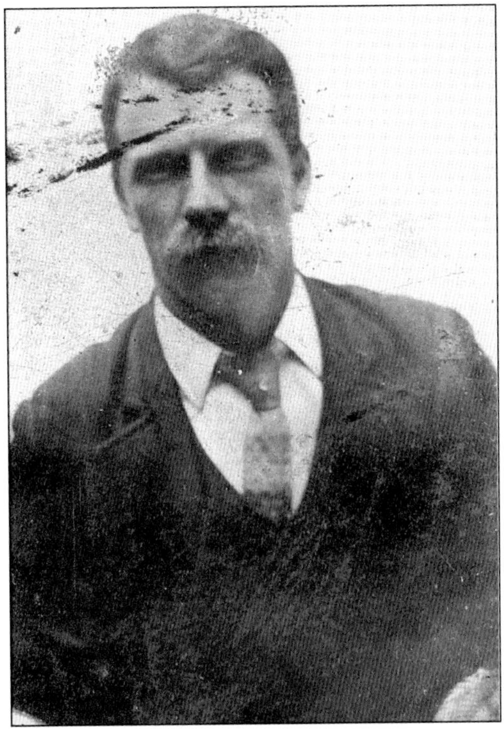

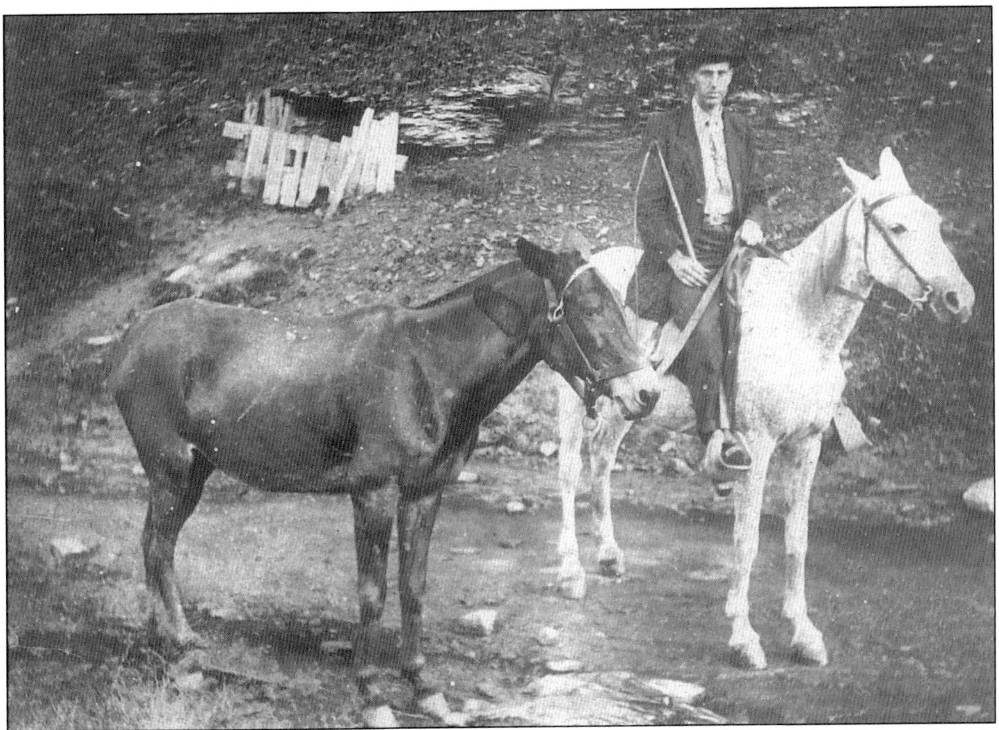

In September of 1920, Levi Lee, a merchant farmer, stockman, and deputy sheriff, was shot to death on the public square. His murderer was captured and was himself killed while awaiting trial in a nearby town.

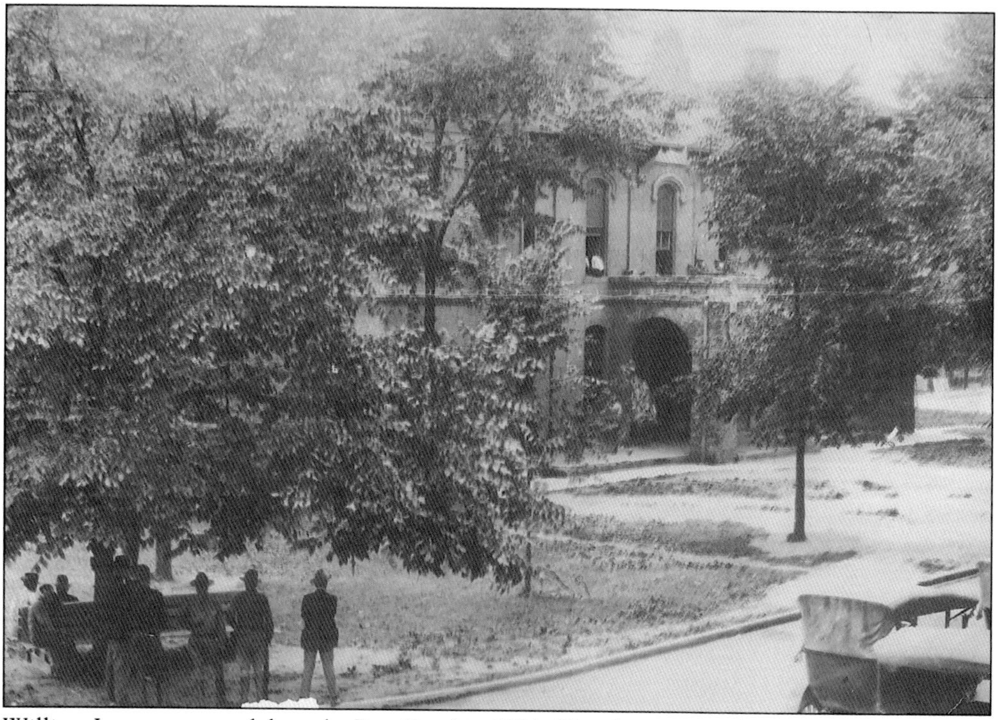

William Lee was gunned down by Bart Reed in 1921. The shooting took place on Barbourville's North Main Street. The trial was held in the Knox County Courthouse. Notice that the building is heavily guarded, both on the grounds and the courthouse porch.

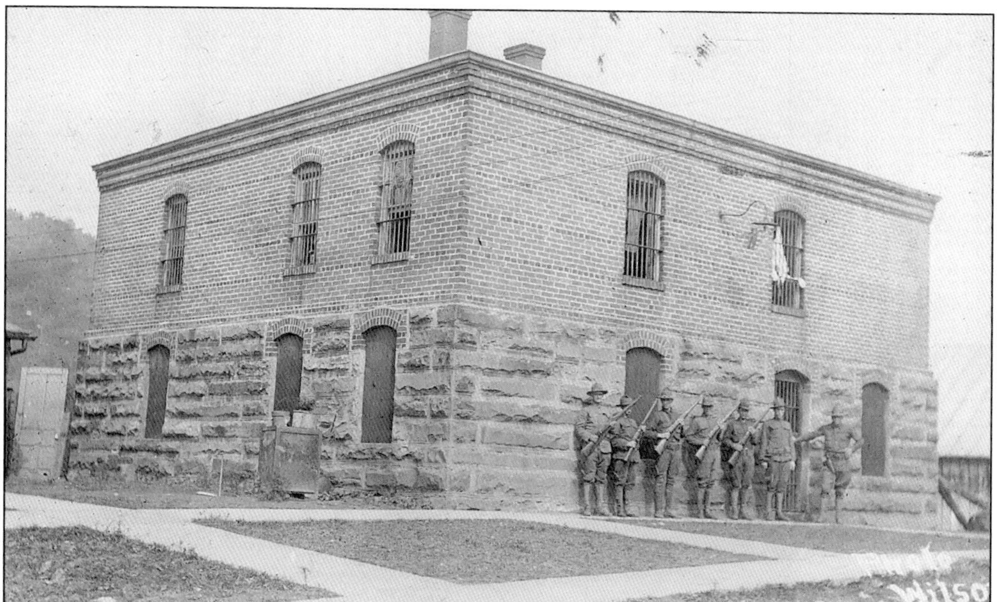

This is the old Knox County Jail in 1906. Here, guards stand watch after Jesse Fitzgerald was captured and charged with murder.

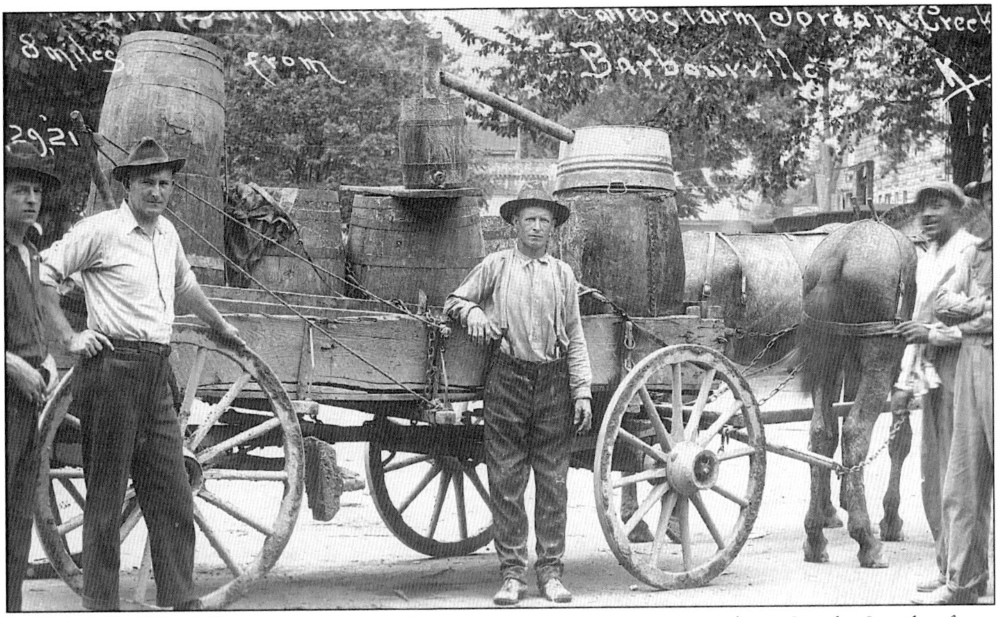

This moonshine still was confiscated from the Callebs' farm on Jordans Creek, 8 miles from Barbourville, on June 29, 1921.

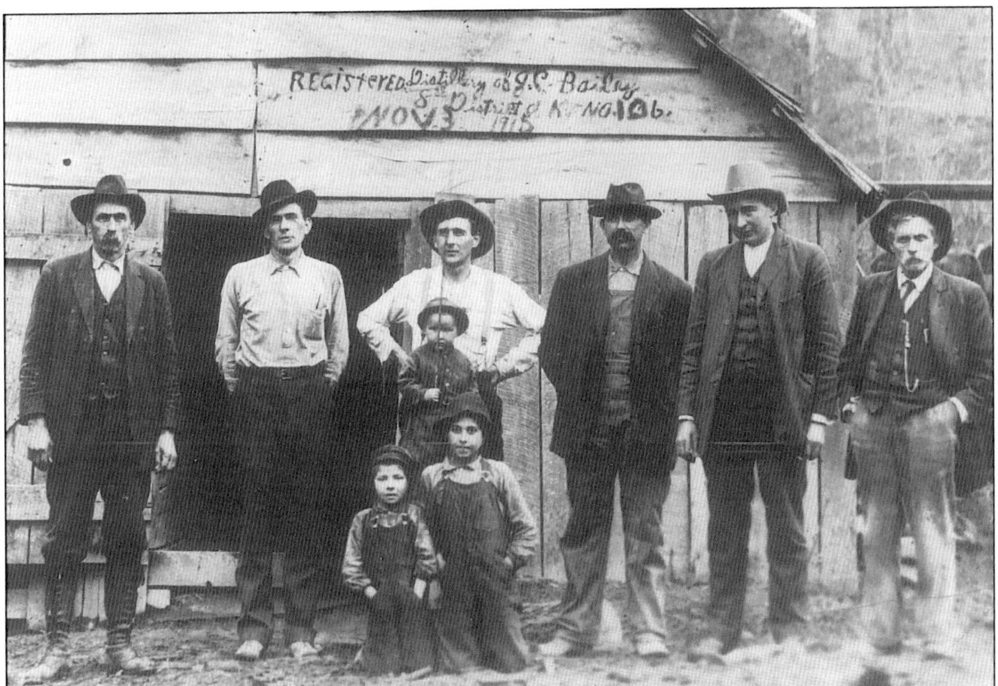

This distillery was located on Highway 11 between Barbourville and Manchester in 1910. Pictured from left to right are Bill Bailey, John Bailey, Beverly Bailey, unknown, James Bailey, and the U.S. whiskey gauger.

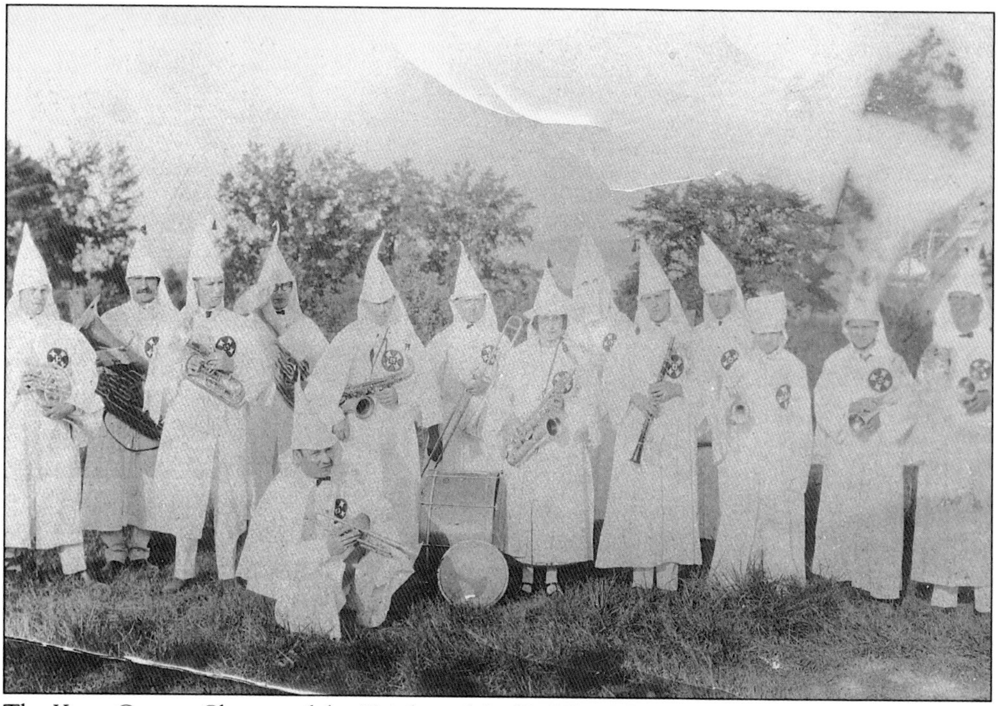

The Knox County Chapter of the Knights of the Ku Klux Klan Band is shown here.

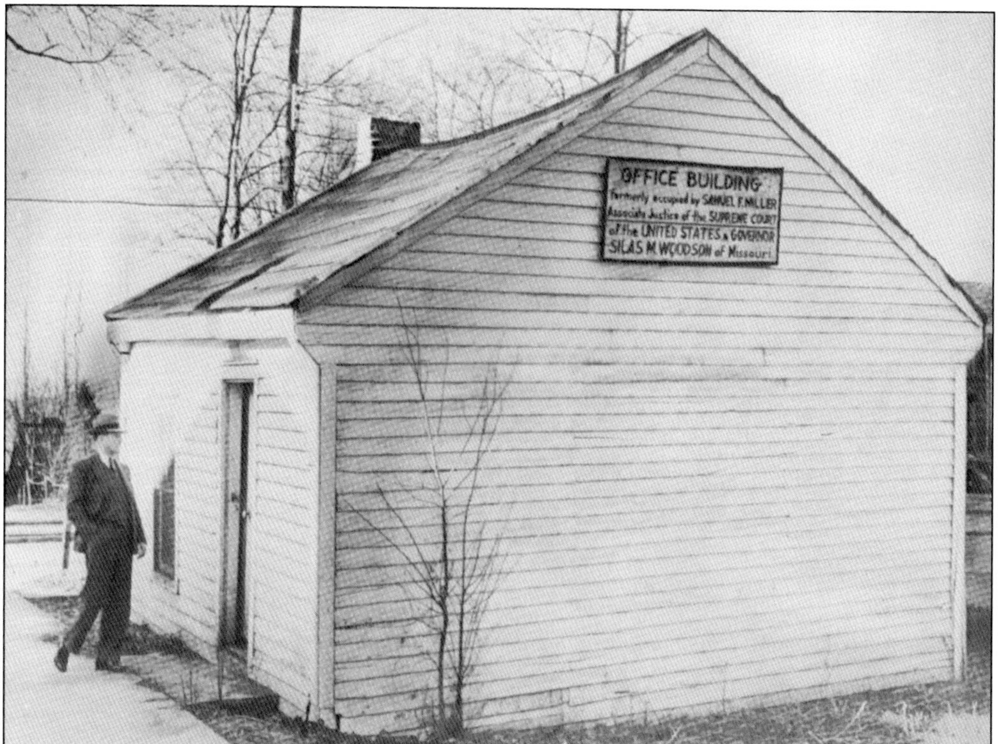

This law office was occupied by two of Knox County's most famous lawyers, Samuel Miller (who became a Supreme Court justice) and Silas Woodson (who was governor of Missouri).

Six

EDUCATION

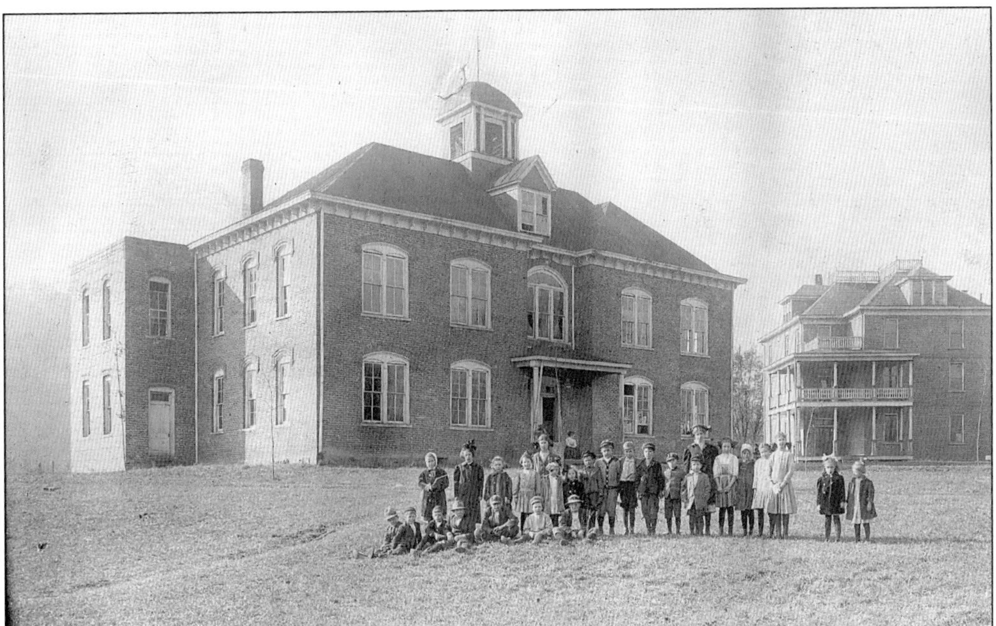

BARBOURVILLE BAPTIST INSTITUTE. Knox County has a rich history when it comes to educational institutions. Union College was founded by the citizens of Barbourville in 1879, and soon after, in 1899, the Barbourville Baptist Institute was established. The Barbourville school system traces its beginnings back to c. 1888. Knox Central High School was started in 1935 on the grounds of the old B.B.I. school. Lynn Camp High School was started in 1922, and like Boone School, it consisted of grades 1 through 12. Boone School was established in 1928, and Rosenwald High School was created in 1930. Pictured here is the early campus of the Barbourville Baptist Institute.

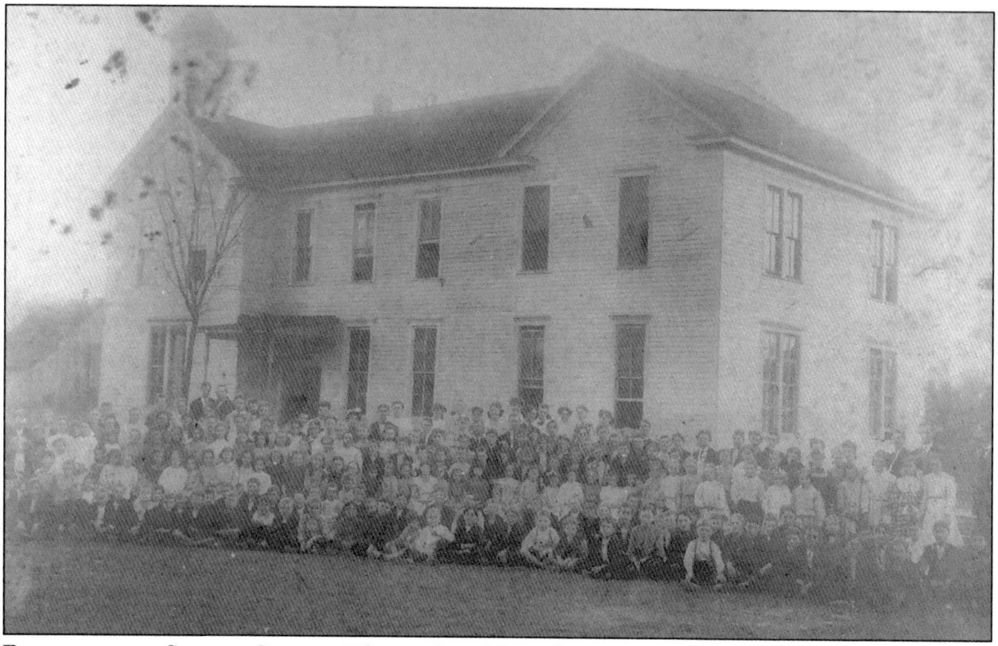

Barbourville School System. This is the oldest photo in existence of the old Barbourville school system in the 1890s. A grade school was established in 1890 and a high school in 1914.

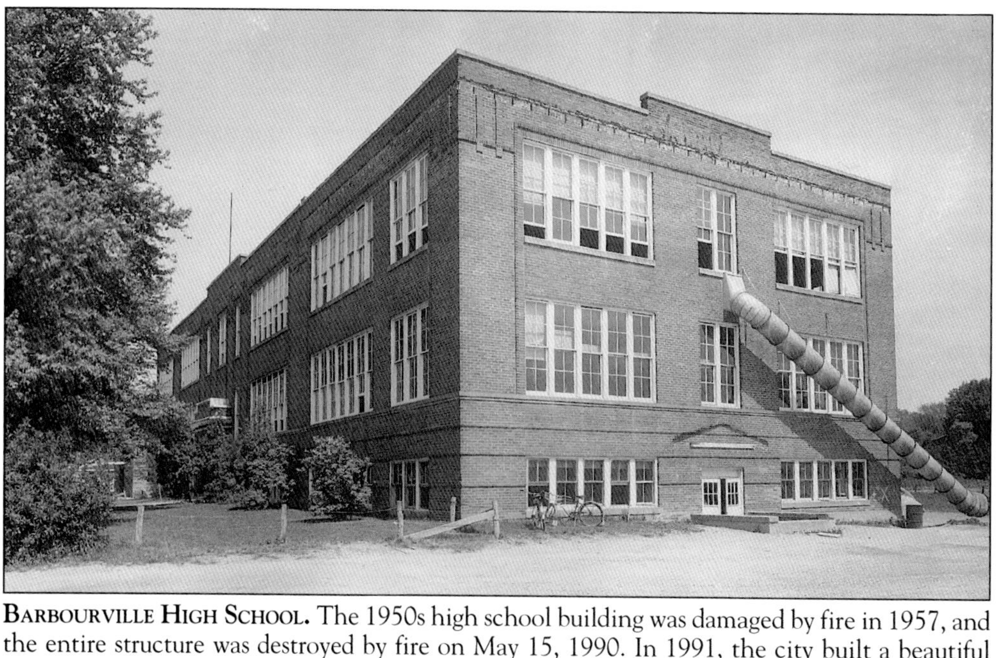

Barbourville High School. The 1950s high school building was damaged by fire in 1957, and the entire structure was destroyed by fire on May 15, 1990. In 1991, the city built a beautiful new high school.

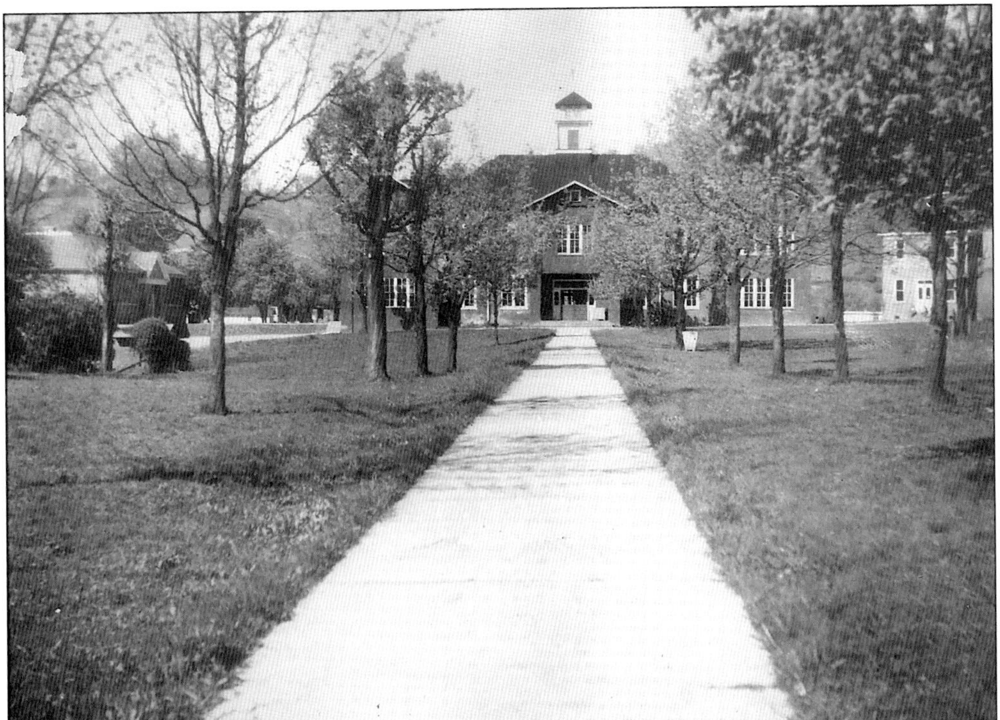

Knox Central High School. This school was built on the grounds of the old Barbourville Baptist Institute and used this old classroom building in 1935.

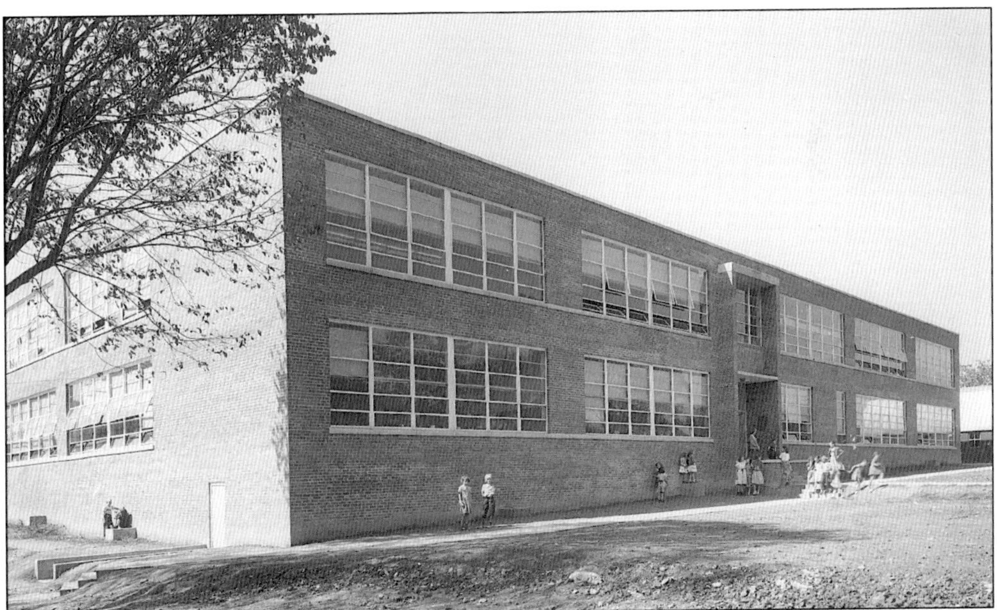

Knox Central, 1950s. This school serves all of Eastern Knox County's high school population.

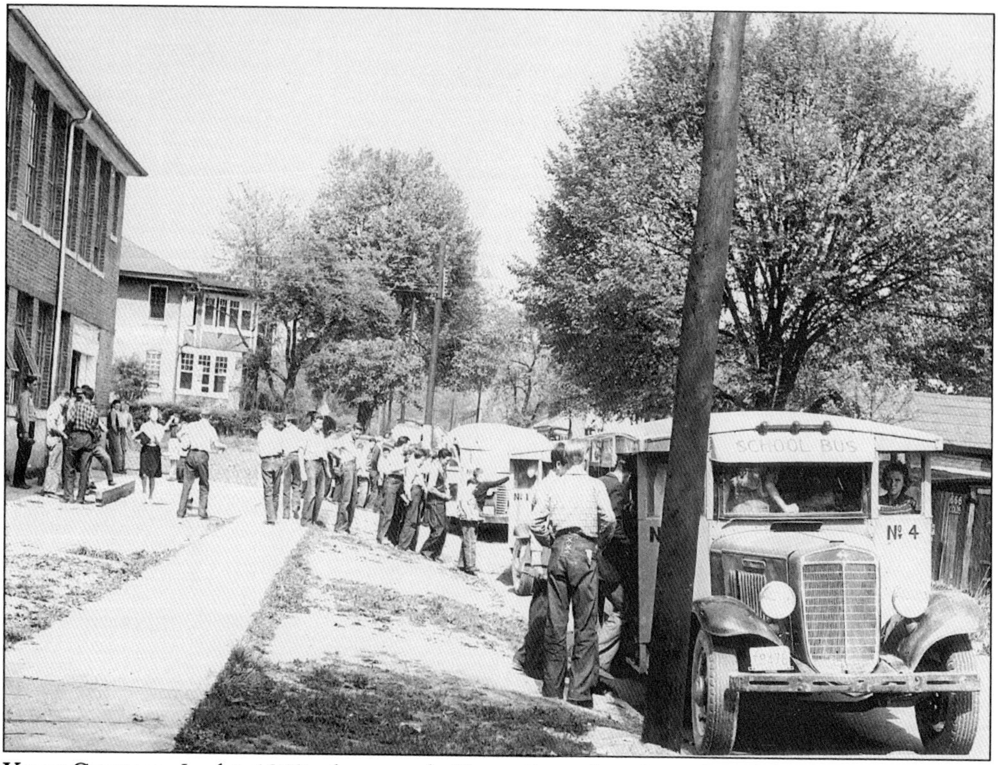

KNOX CENTRAL. In this 1940s photograph, Knox Central students board the buses for the long trip home.

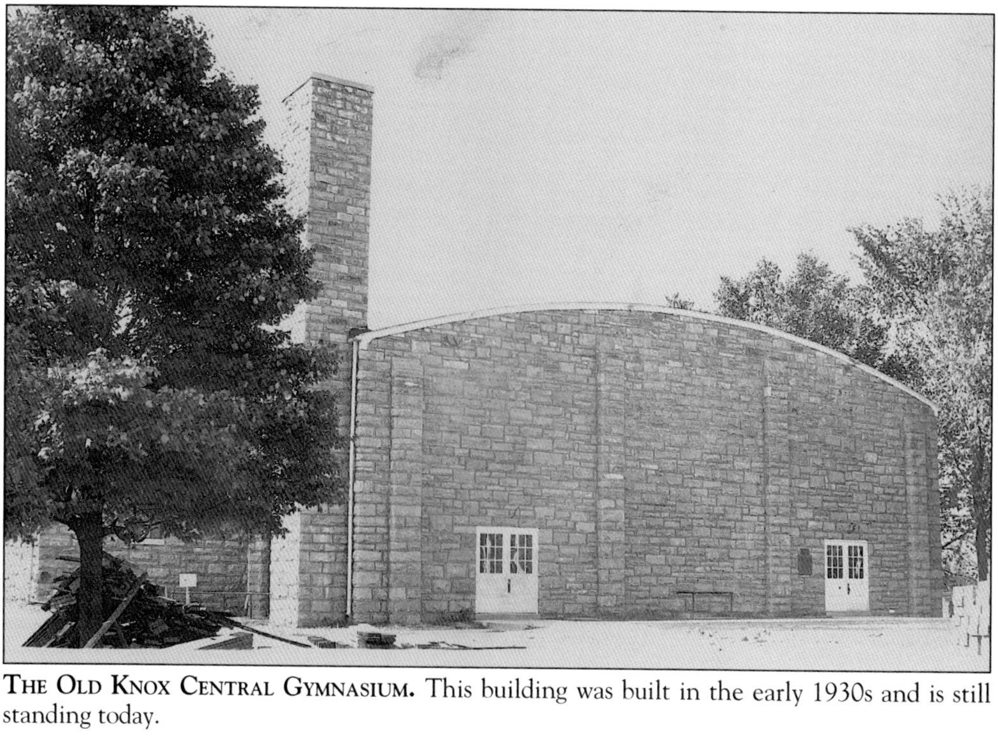

THE OLD KNOX CENTRAL GYMNASIUM. This building was built in the early 1930s and is still standing today.

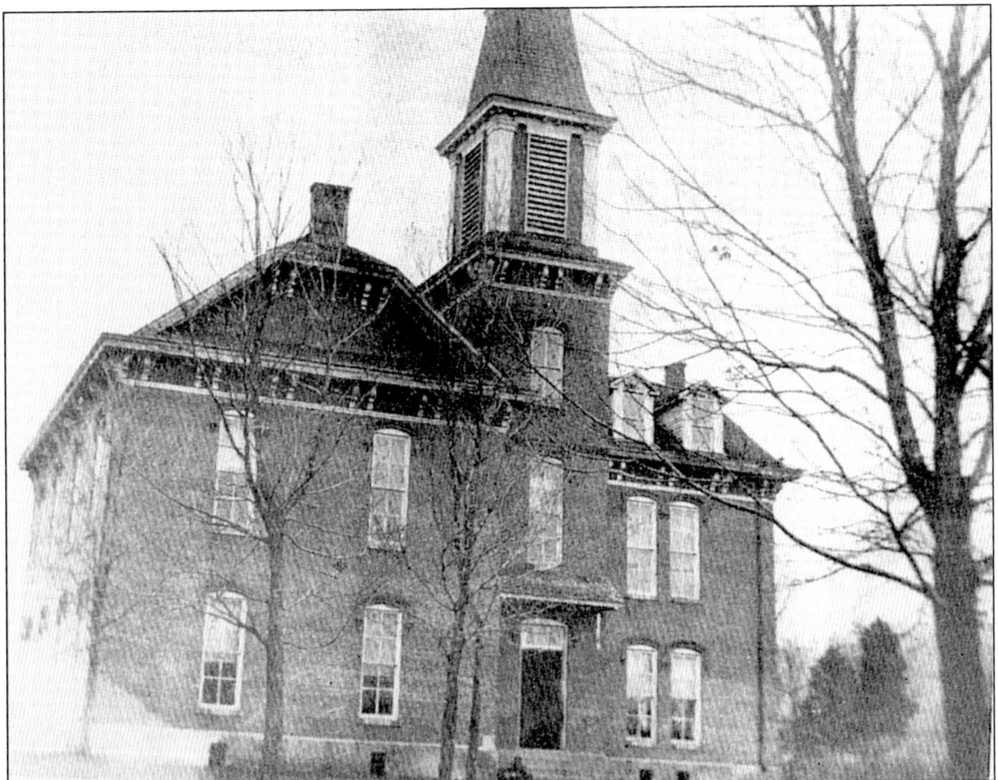

UNION COLLEGE. This is Union College's first building. It served the college until 1906, when it was destroyed by fire. The oldest building on Union's campus today is Speed Hall, built some time after 1897.

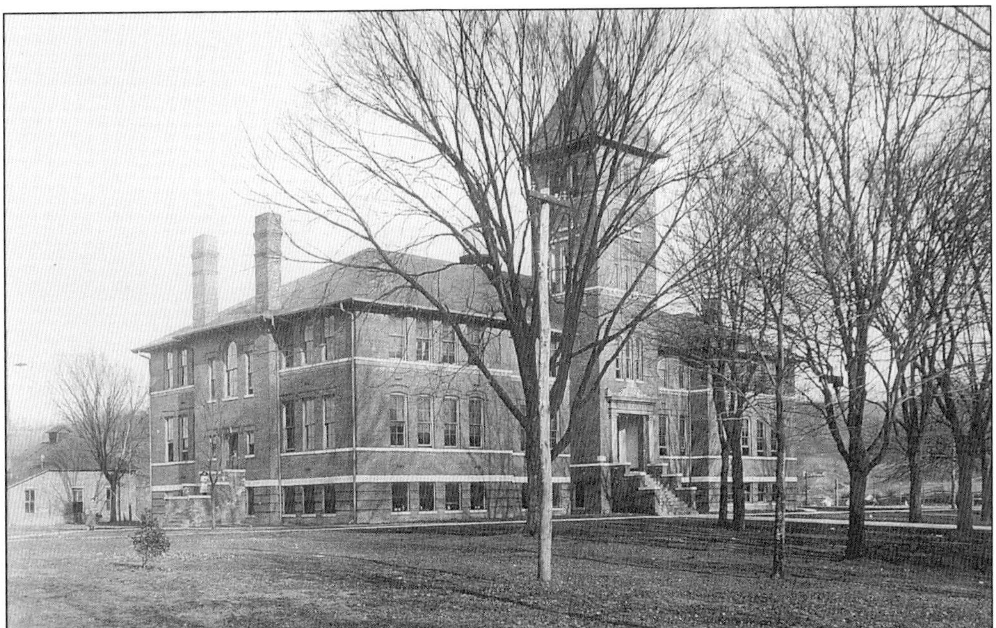

CENTENNIAL HALL. This classroom building was erected in 1907.

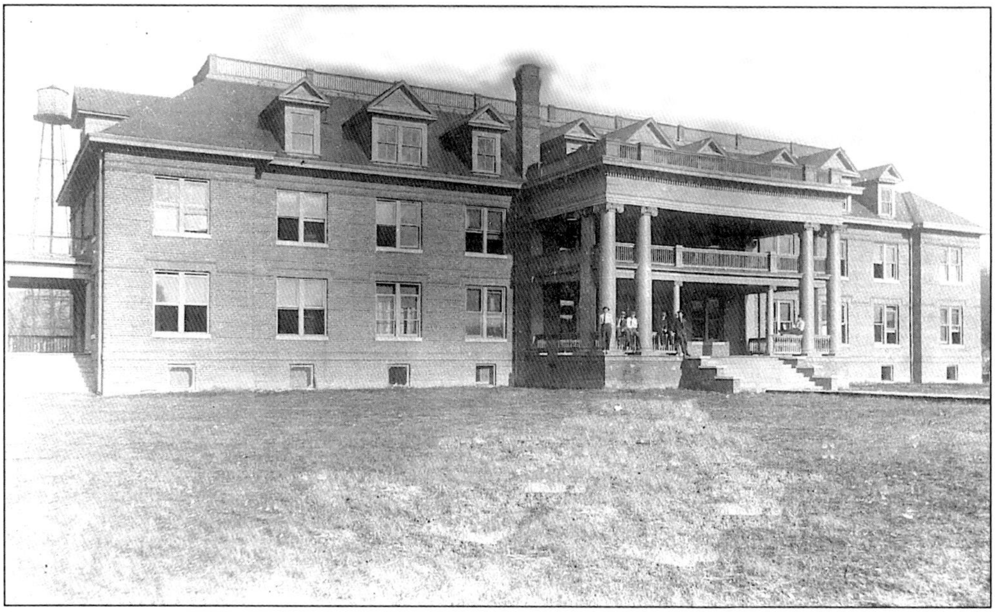

Stevenson Hall. This was the dormitory for men until 1999, when it was renovated to become the Academic Center.

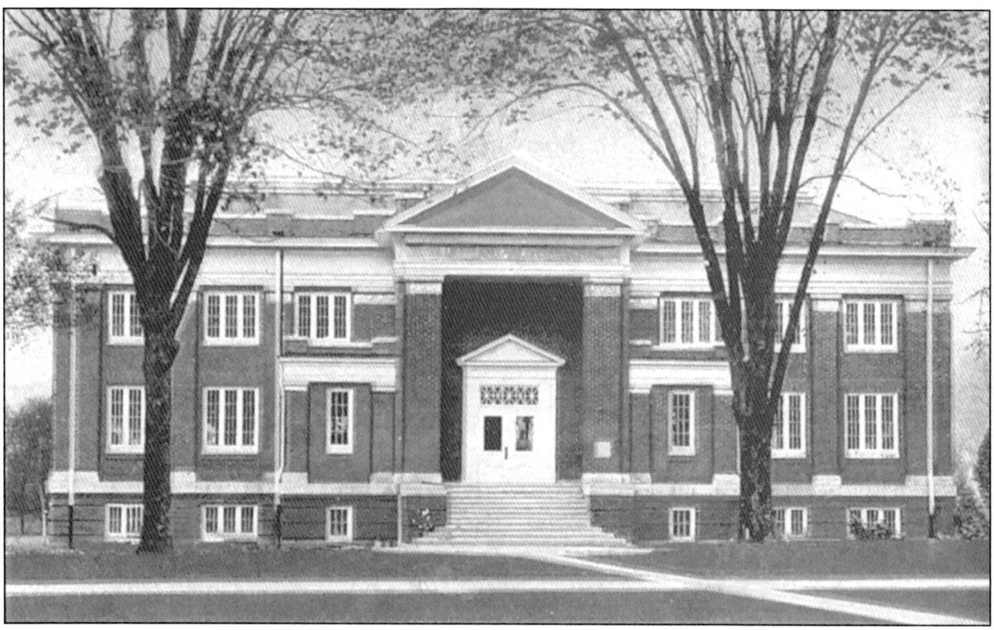

The Soldiers and Sailors Gymnasium. This building was constructed in 1919.

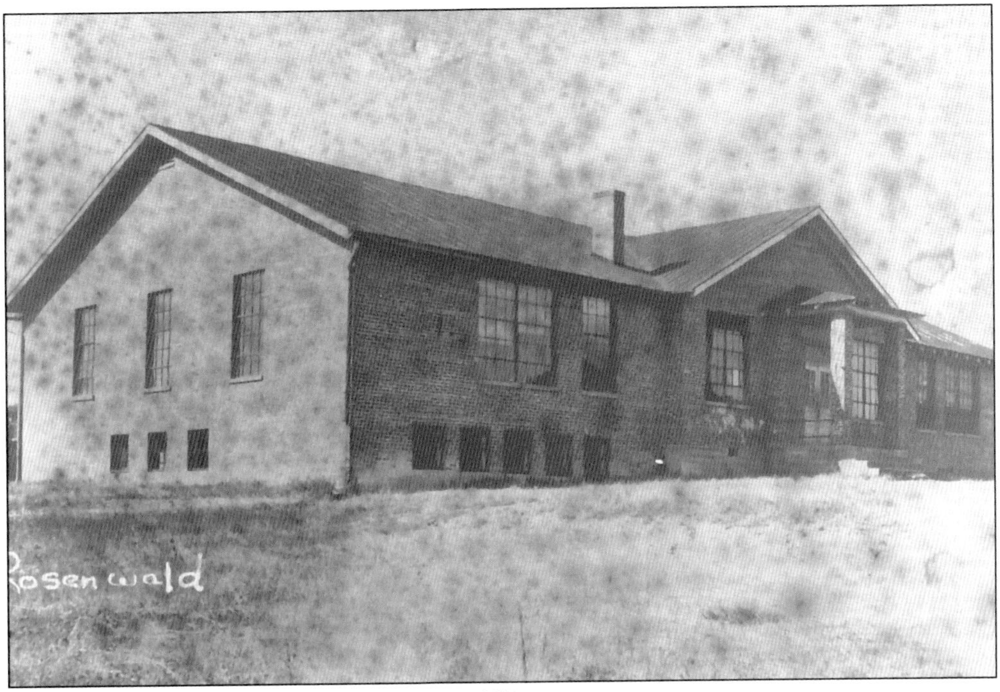

THE ROSENWALD HIGH SCHOOL BUILDING, 1950S.

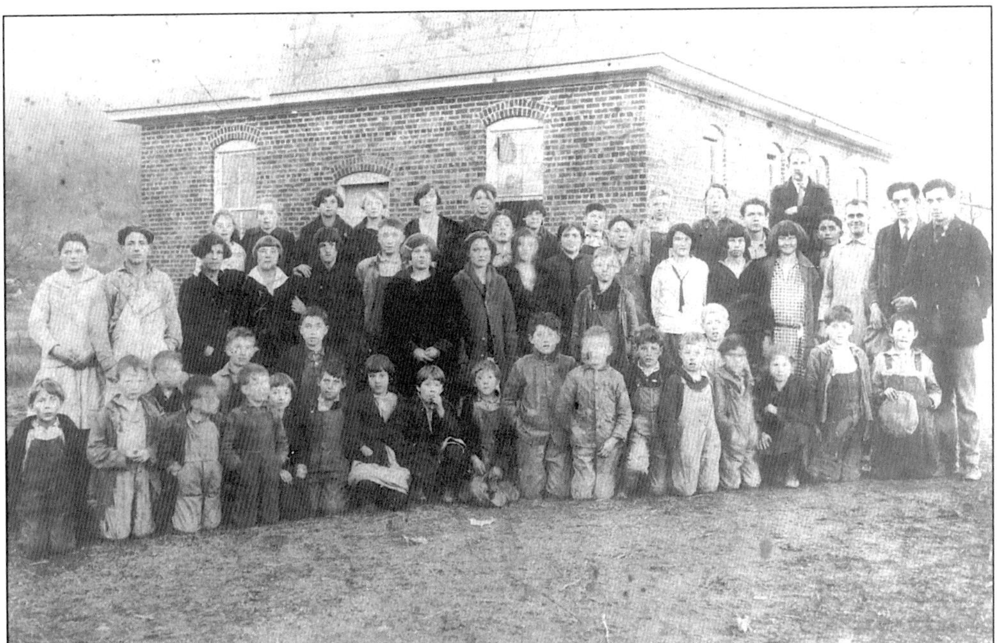

SWANPOND SCHOOL. In 1867, the Knox County school system had 78 school districts, which meant there were at least 78 rural schools to serve these communities throughout the last part of the 19th century. Here we see the old Swanpond School in 1924.

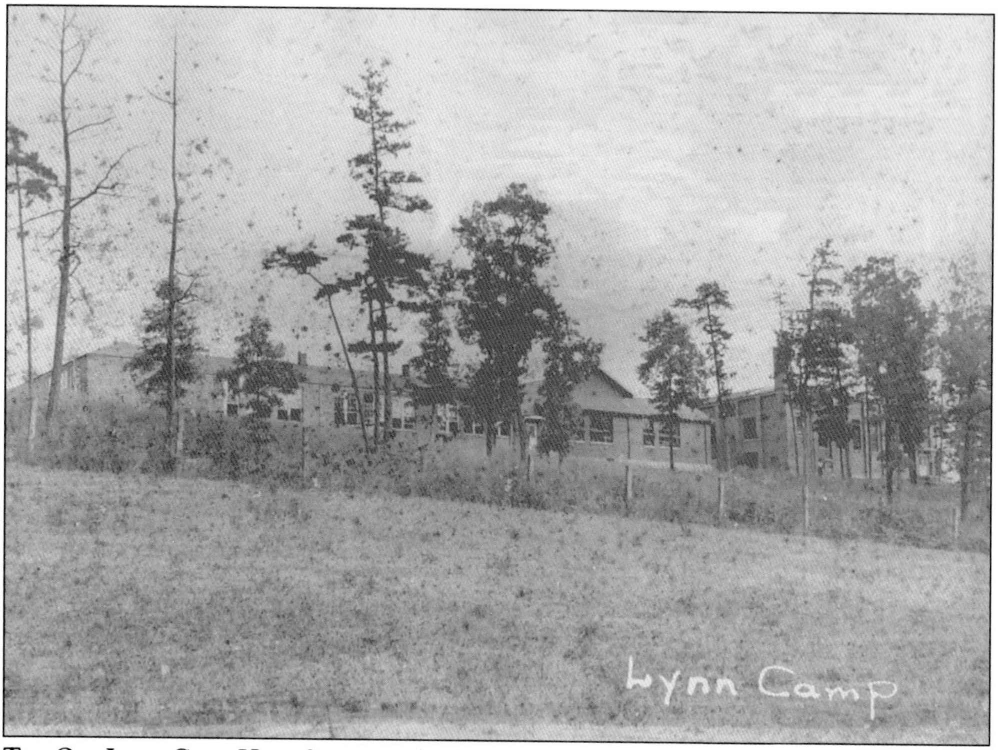

THE OLD LYNN CAMP HIGH SCHOOL. This building and gymnasium served the western part of Knox County until 1999.

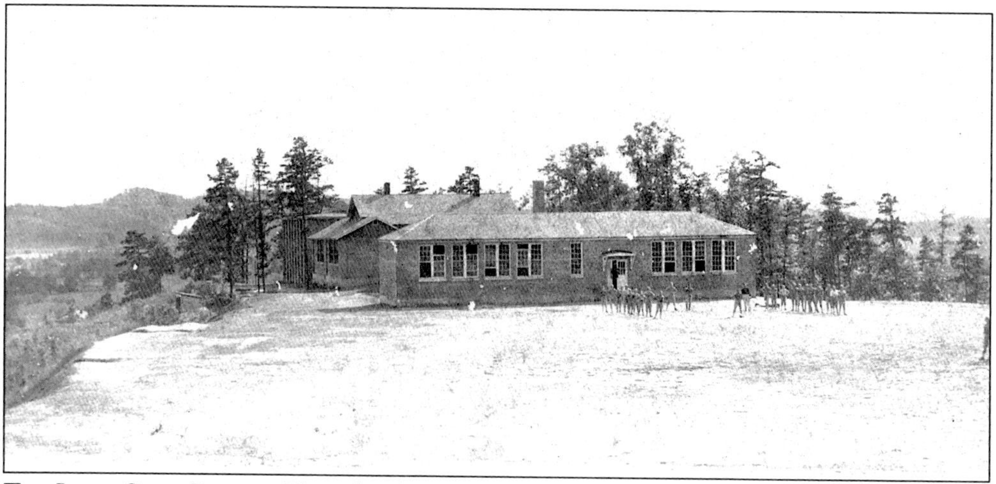

THE LYNN CAMP SCHOOL. The school is shown as it looked in its early days. It was given the name Lynn Camp in 1922.

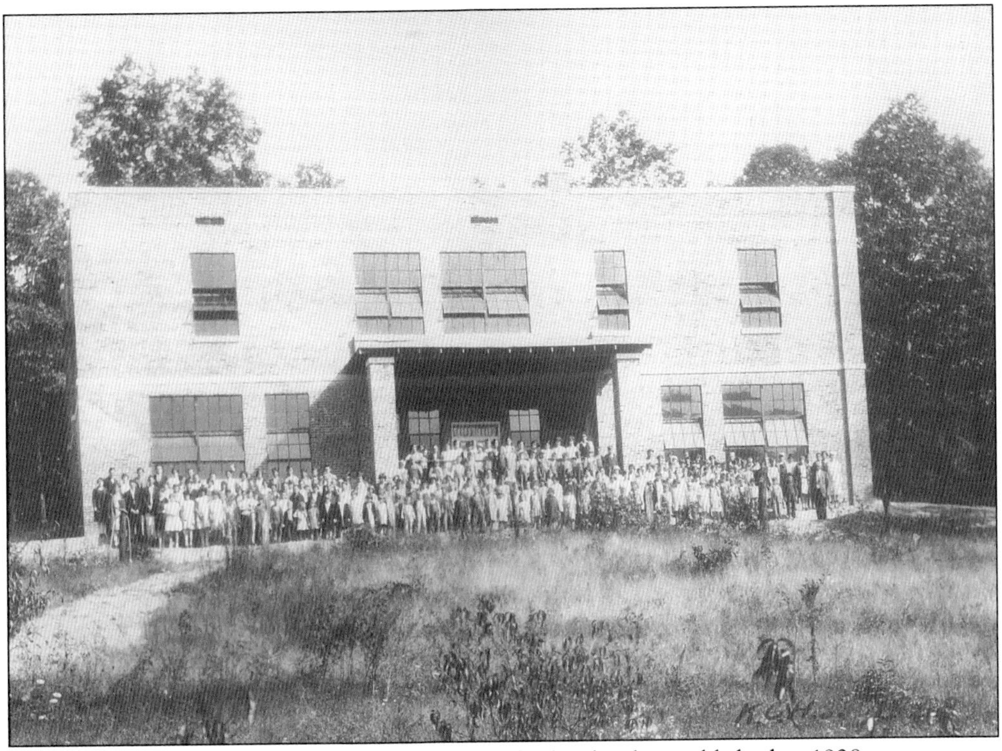

Boone School. This was one of Knox County's high schools, established in 1928.

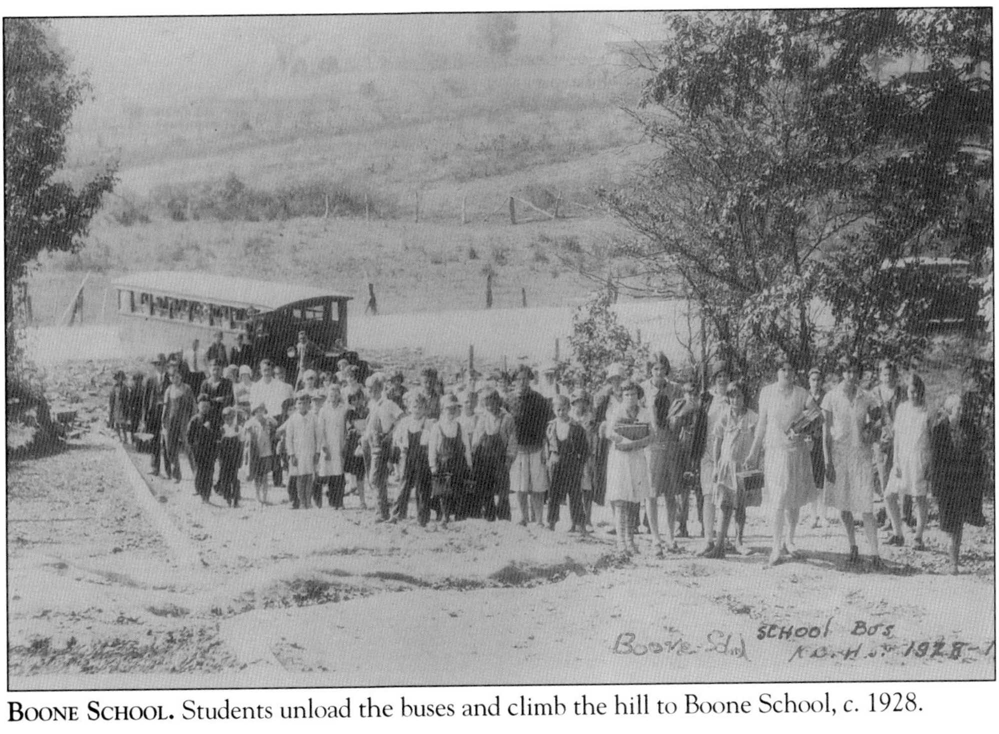

Boone School. Students unload the buses and climb the hill to Boone School, c. 1928.

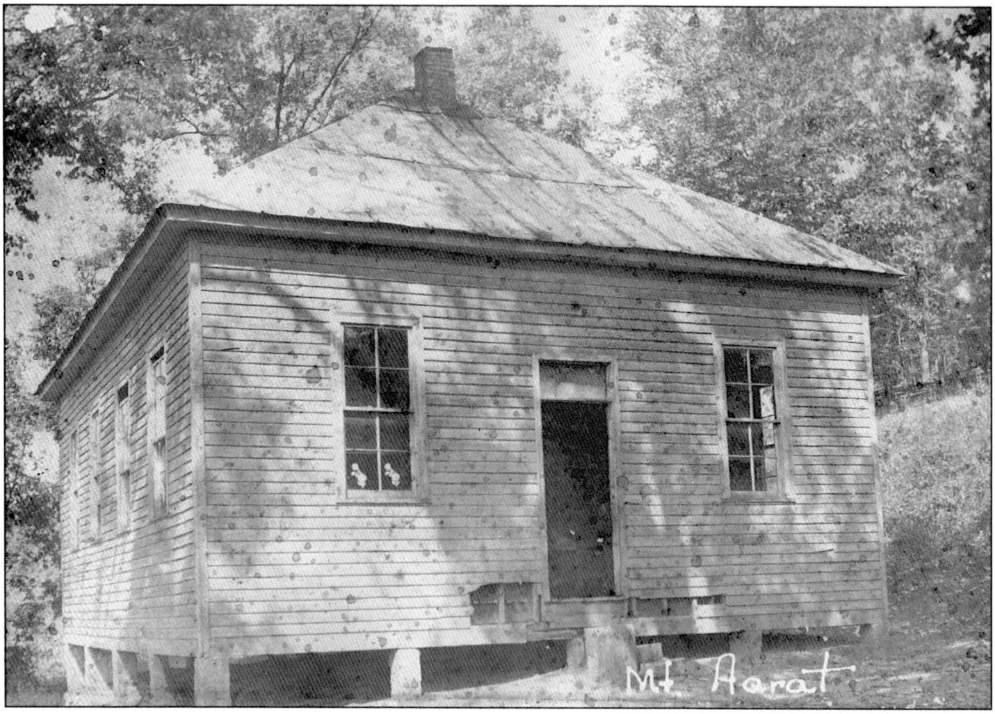

The Old Mt. Aarat School Building. This was typical of the many one-room schools that were found up and down the hollows of Knox County near the Laurel County line during the early 1900s.

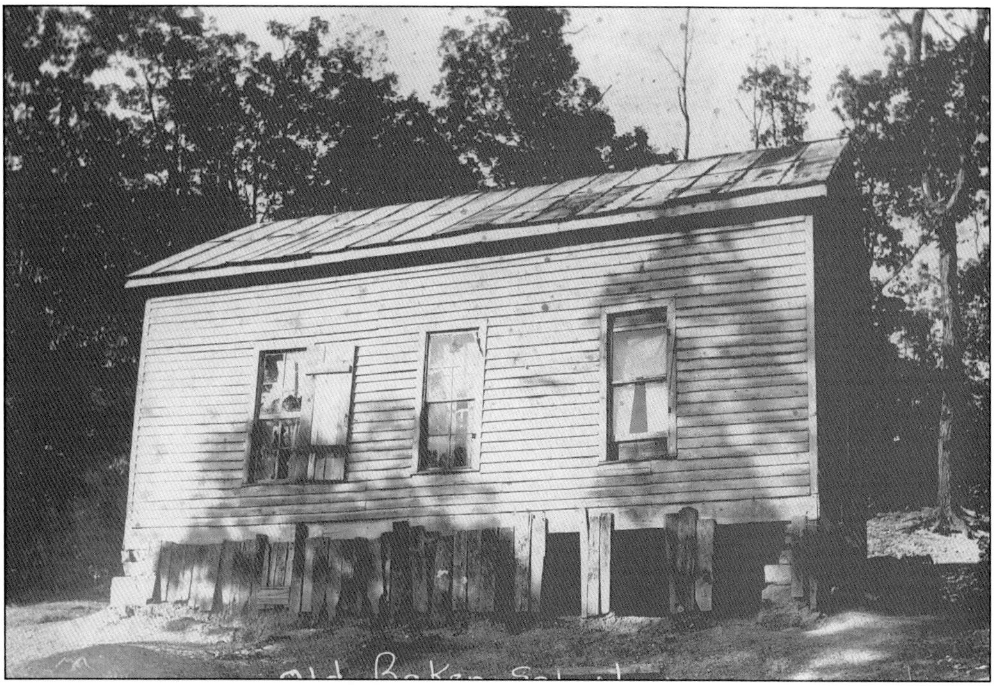

The Old Baker School. This school was also weather boarded and consisted of one room. It was located on Little Richland Creek.

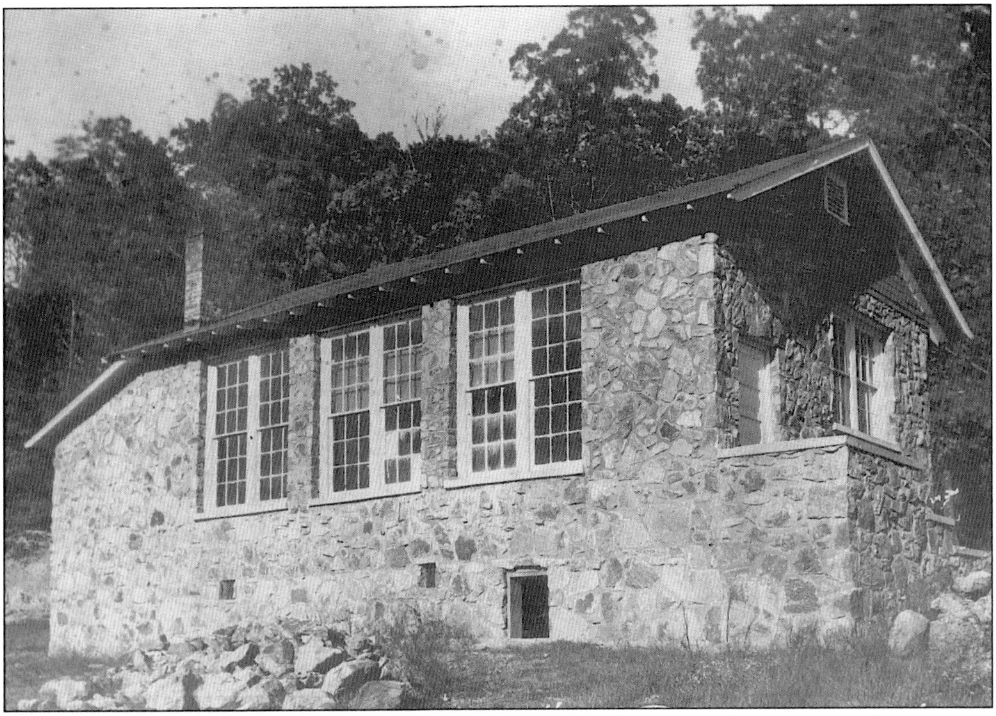

The "New" Baker School. By the 1930s, stone was used to cover the exterior of many one-room schoolhouses.

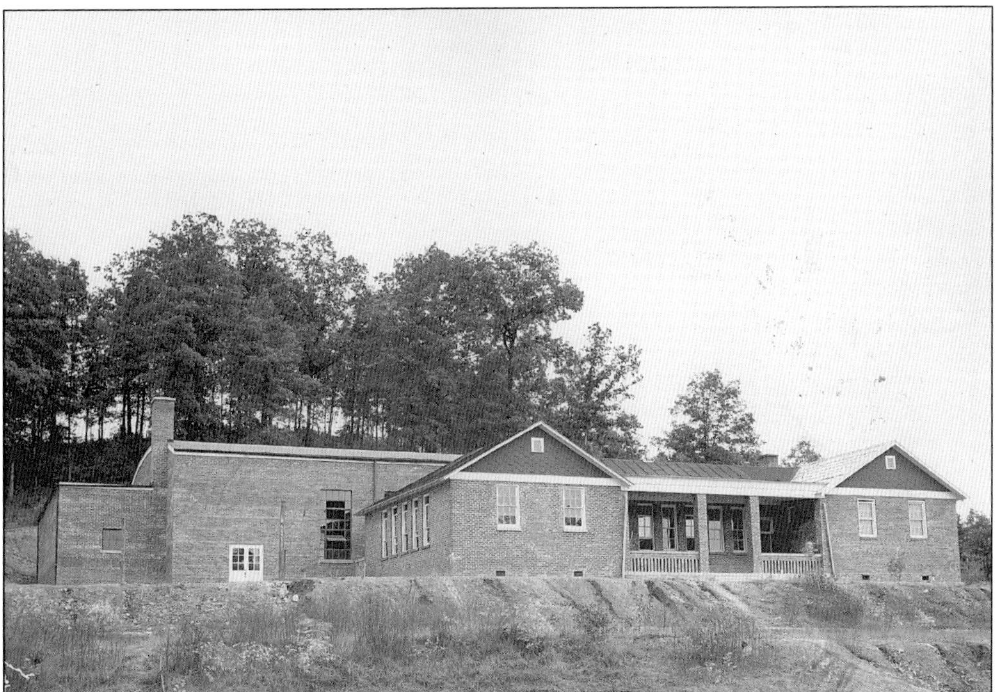

School at New Bethel. By the late 1950s, some school buildings were brick. This one had a gymnasium.

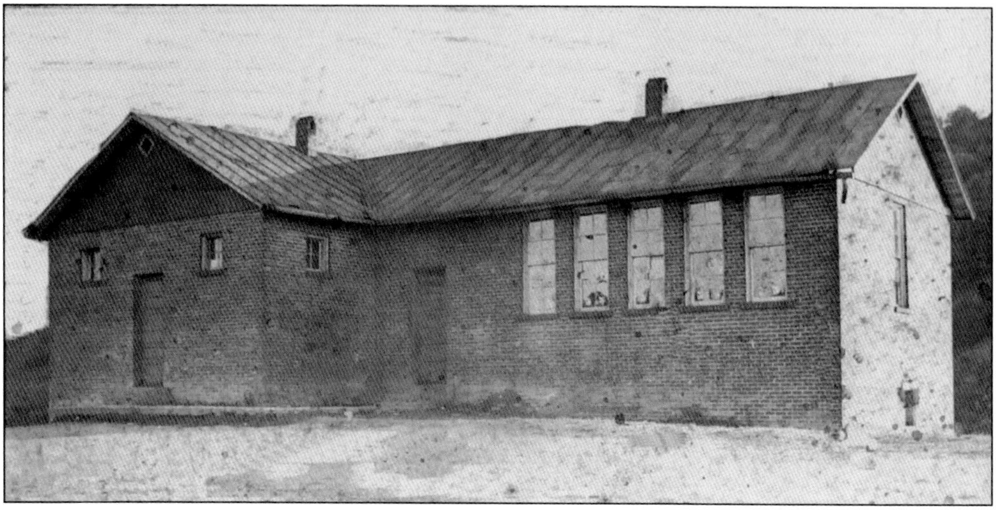

School at Bailey Switch. This school was not only brick but had more than one room.

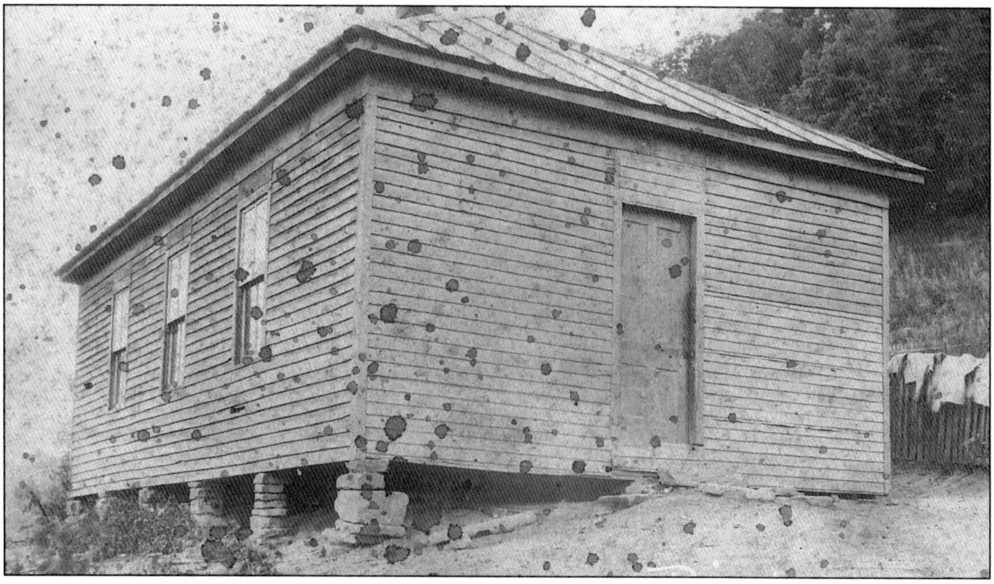

The Binghamtown School. This school was located near Dewitt, KY.

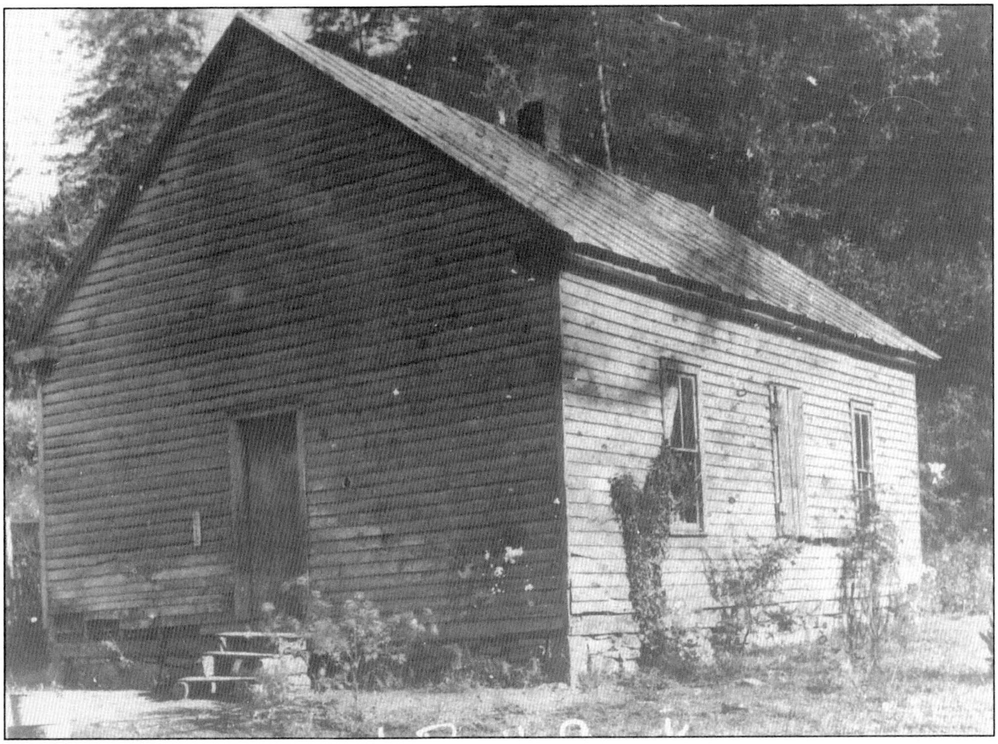

BULL CREEK SCHOOL.

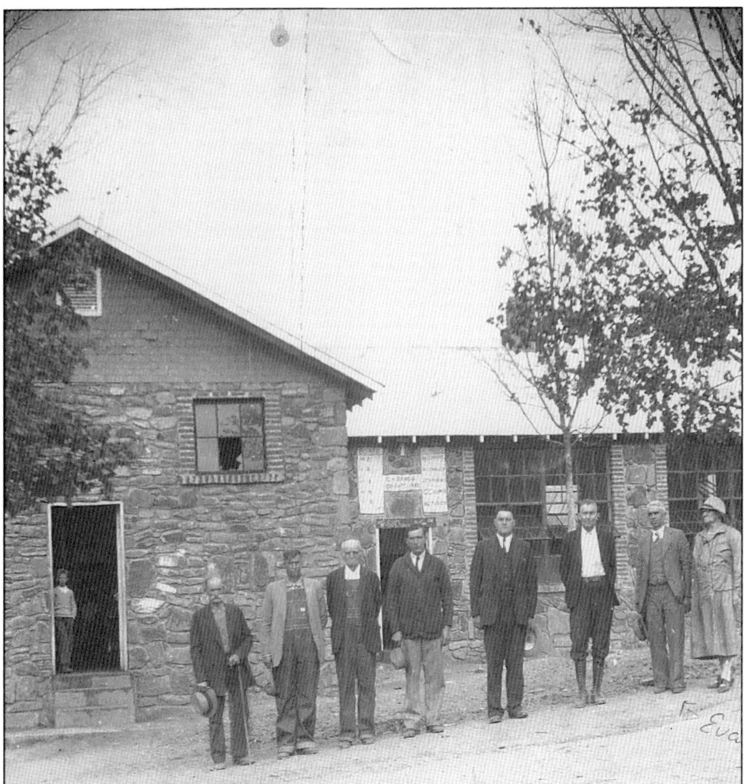

CALLIHAN SCHOOL. Superintendent Evans, second from the right, stands in front of the old school.

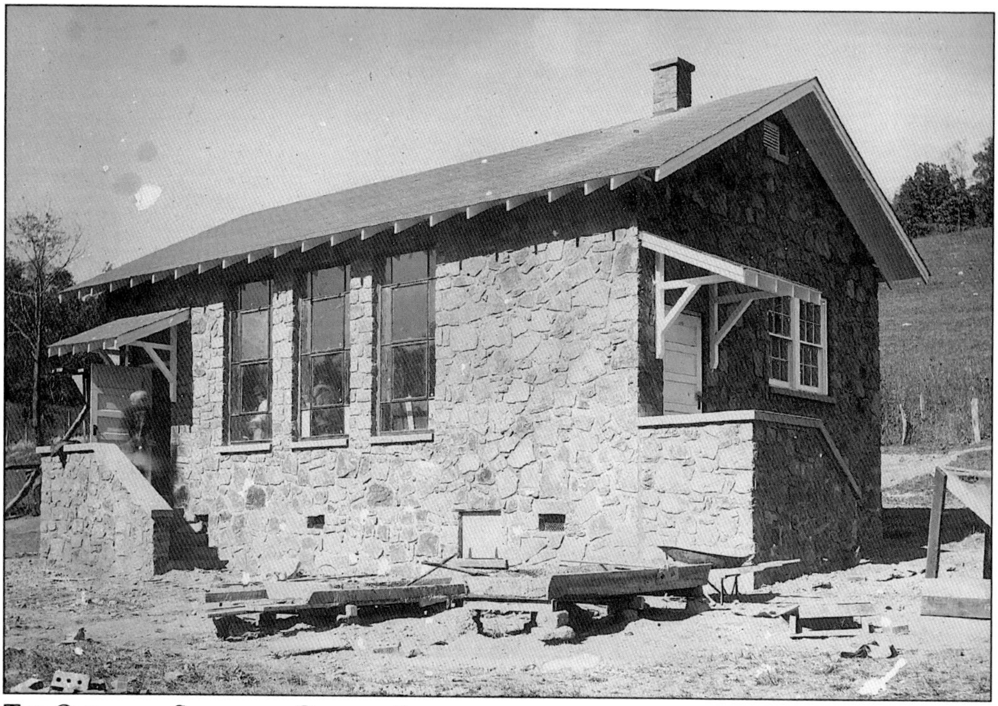

THE ONE-ROOM SCHOOL AT CALLEBS CREEK.

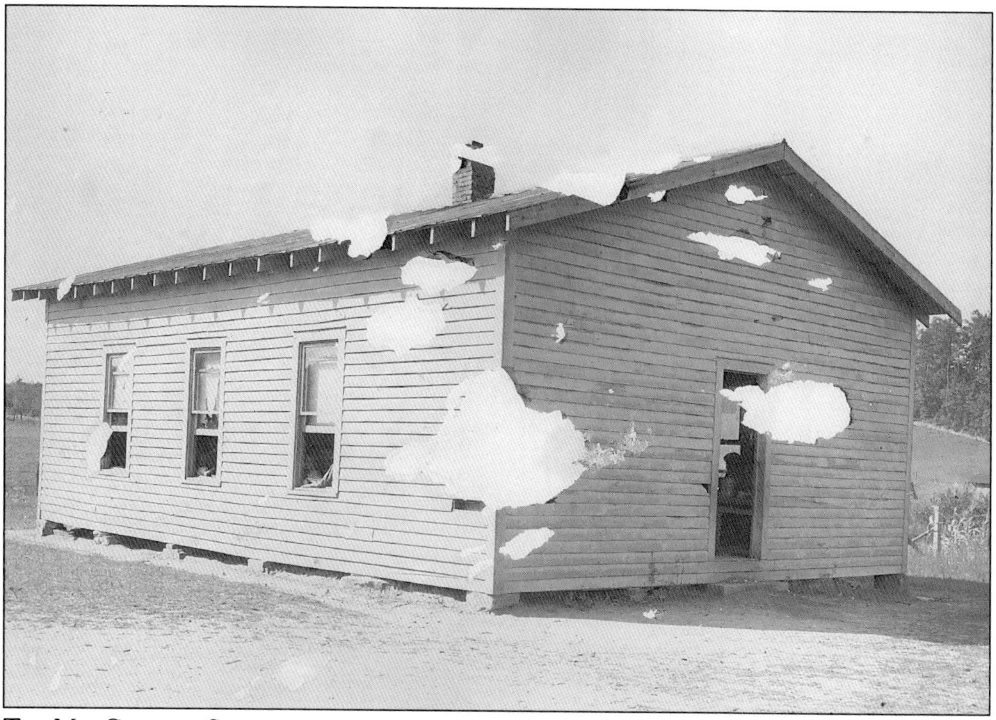

THE MT. CALVARY SCHOOL.

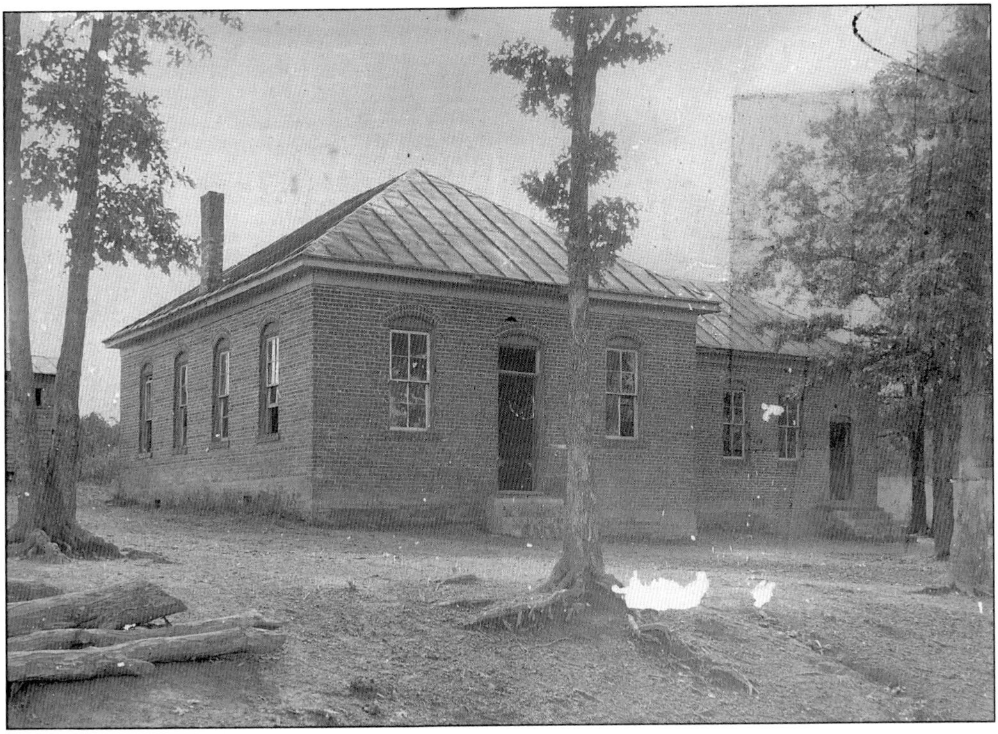

THE CALVARY SCHOOL.

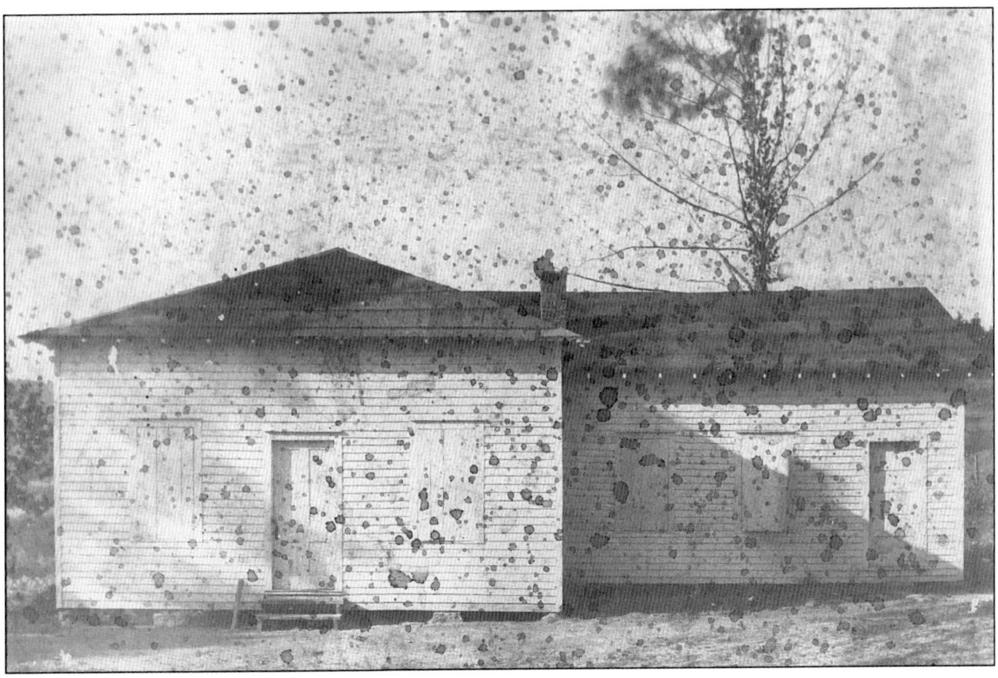

THE CAMPBELL SCHOOL.

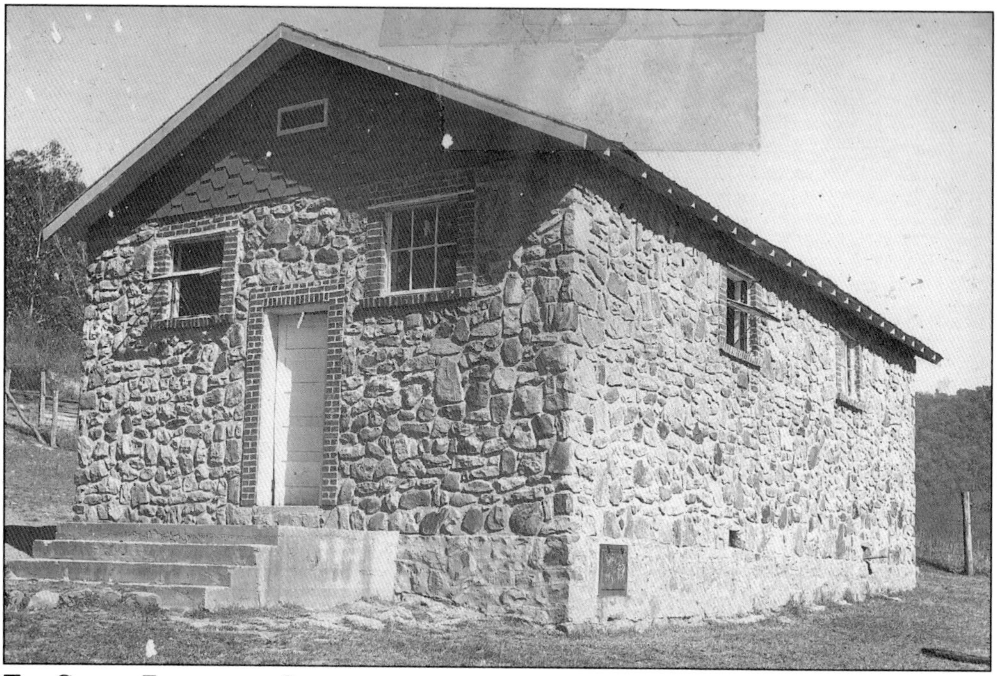

The Carnes Elementary School.

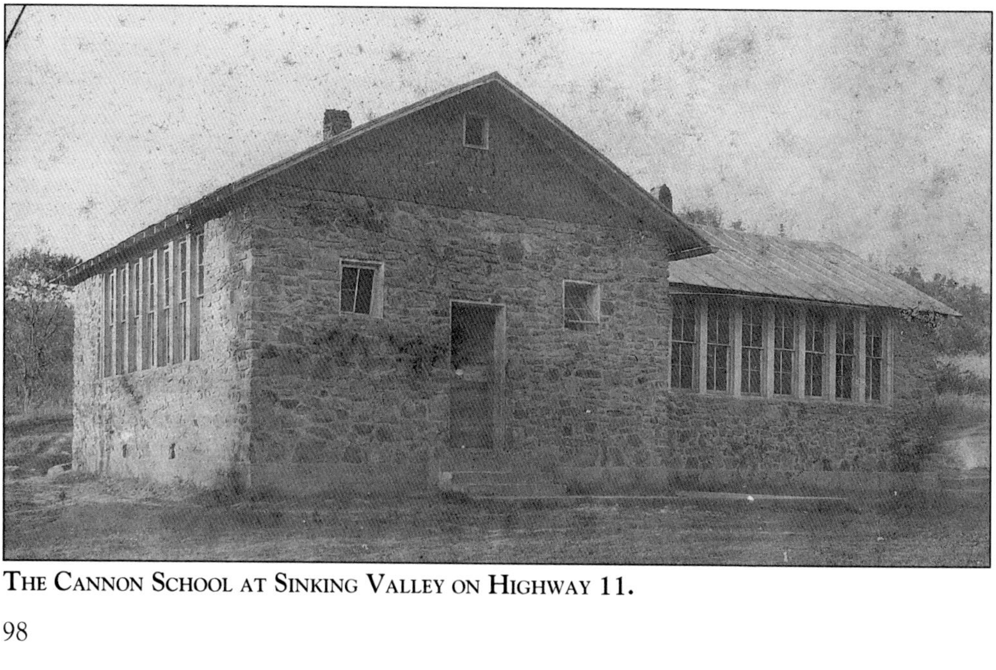

The Cannon School at Sinking Valley on Highway 11.

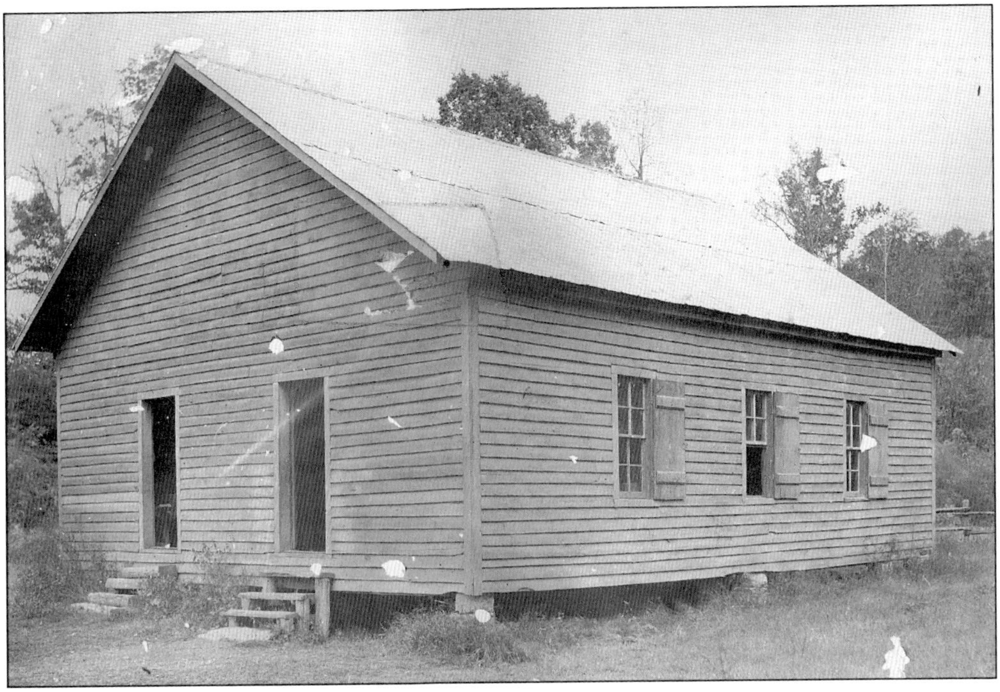

THE CRANES NEST SCHOOL.

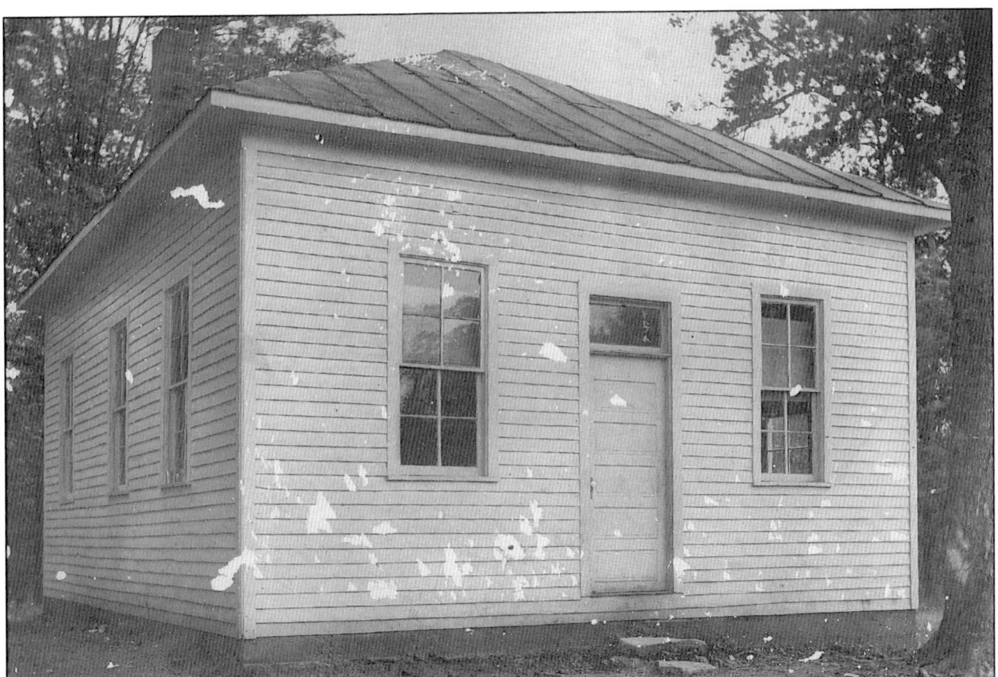

THE OLD CLATE SCHOOL BUILDING.

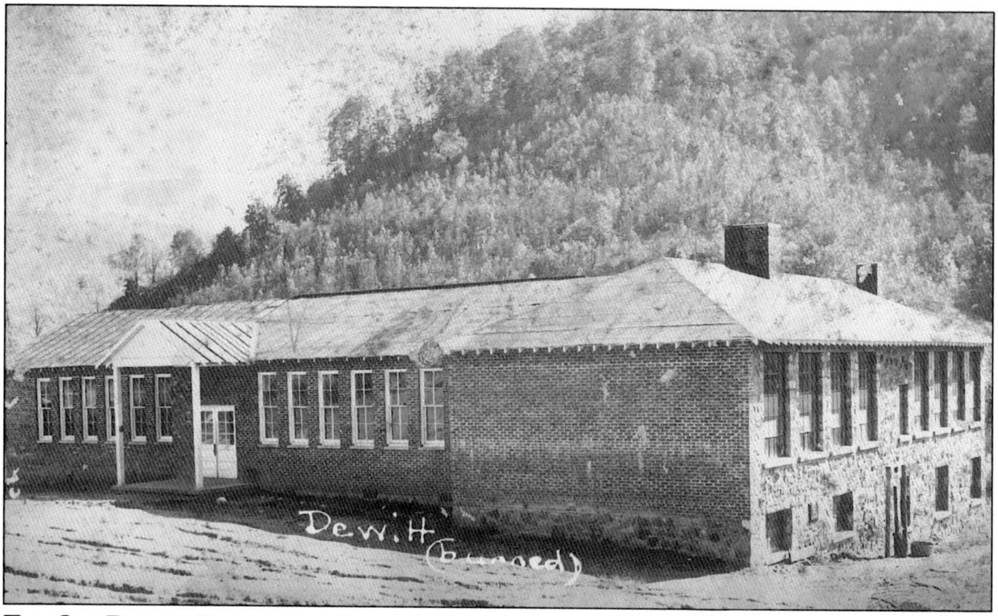

The Old Dewitt Elementary School. This school was destroyed by fire in 1954.

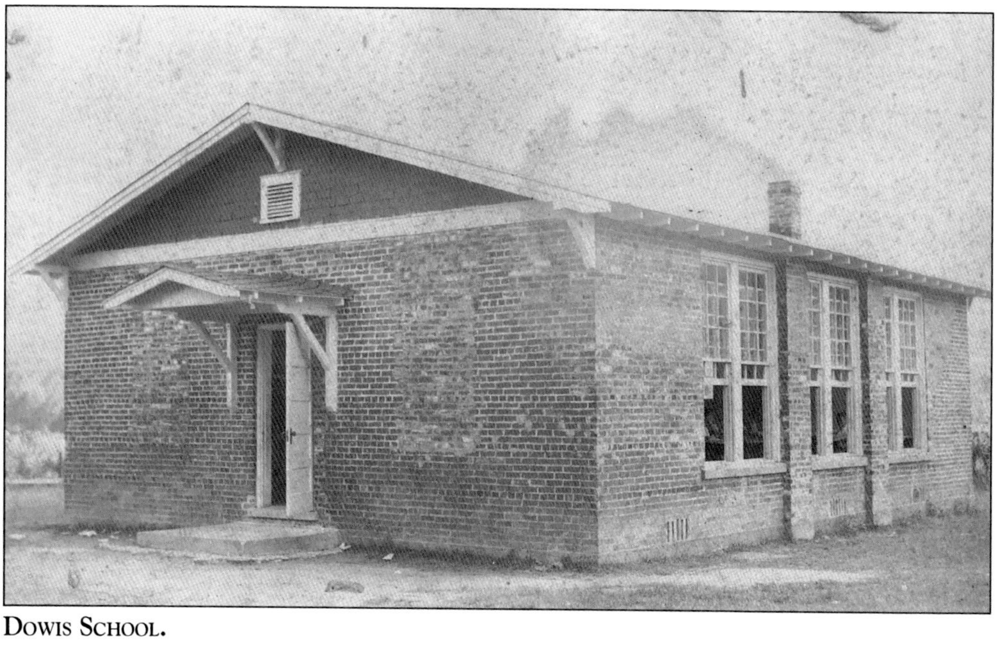

Dowis School.

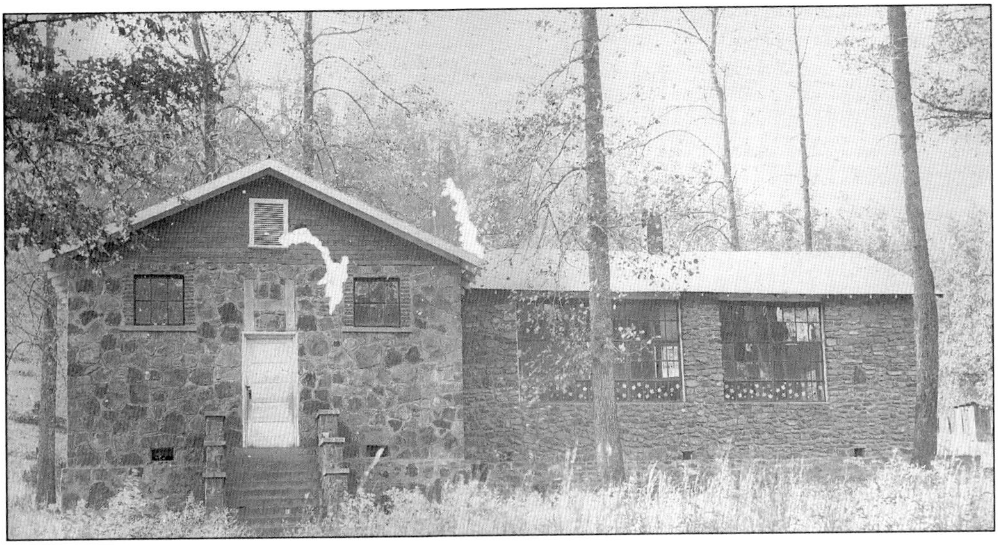

DOZIER SCHOOL.

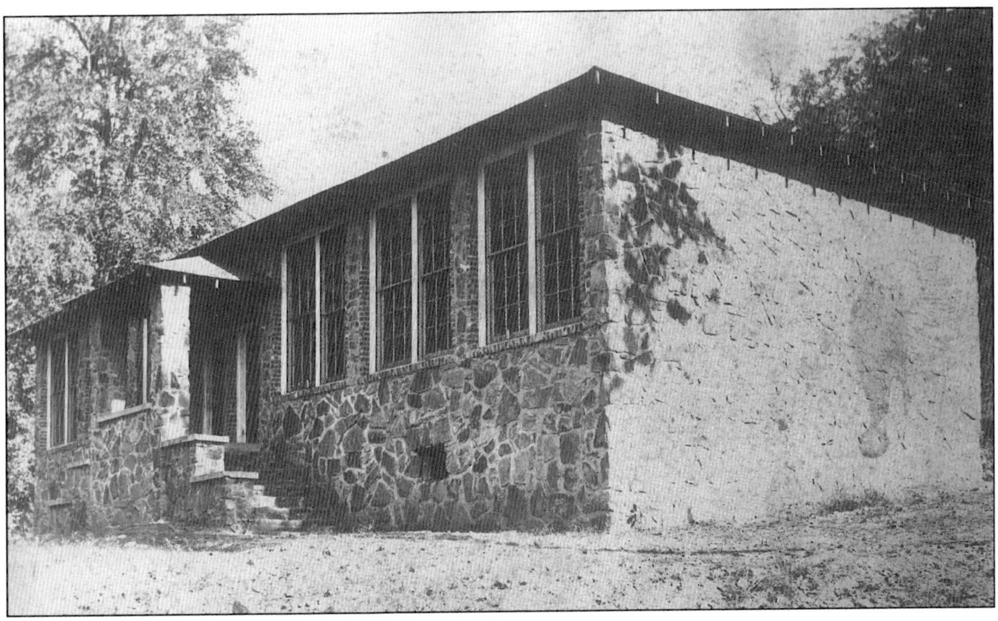

ELYS SCHOOL.

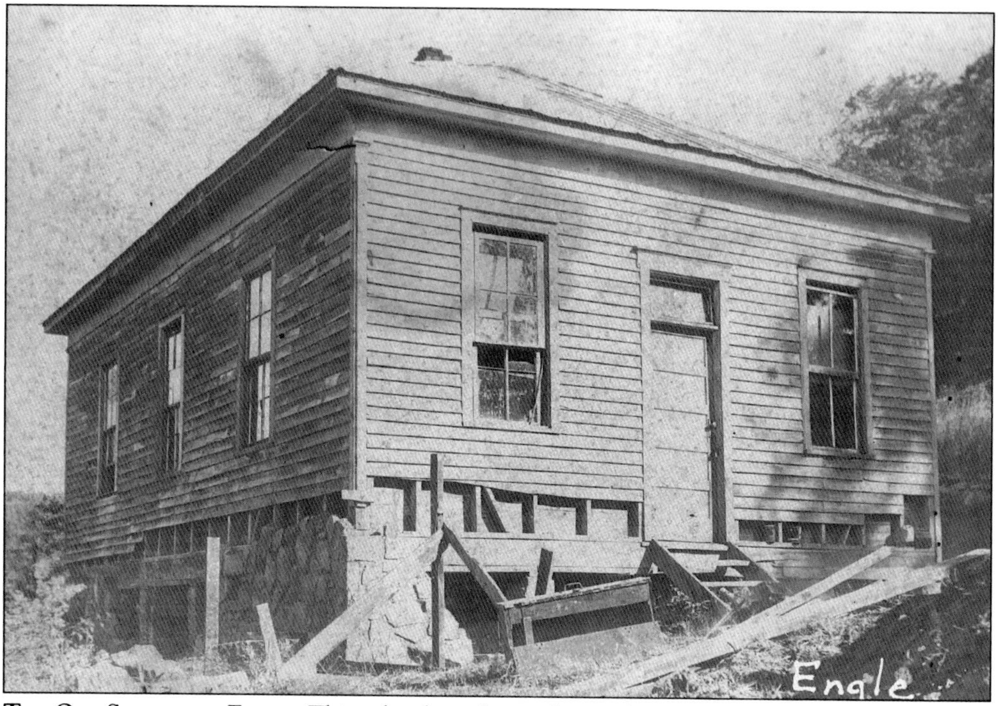

The Old School at Engle. This school was located on Indian Creek.

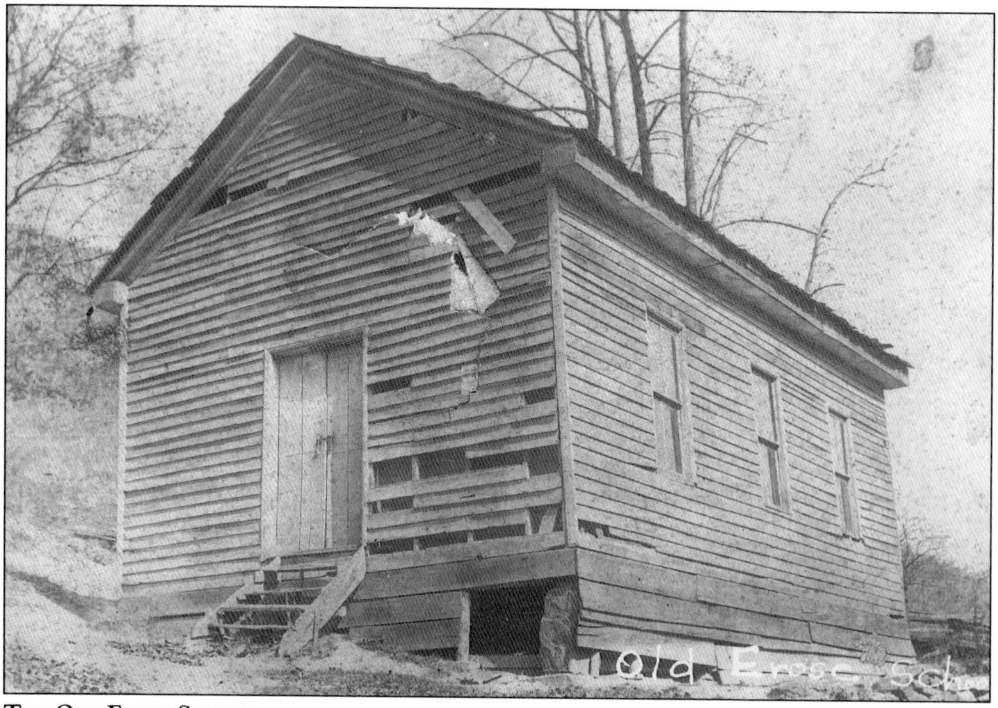

The Old Erose School.

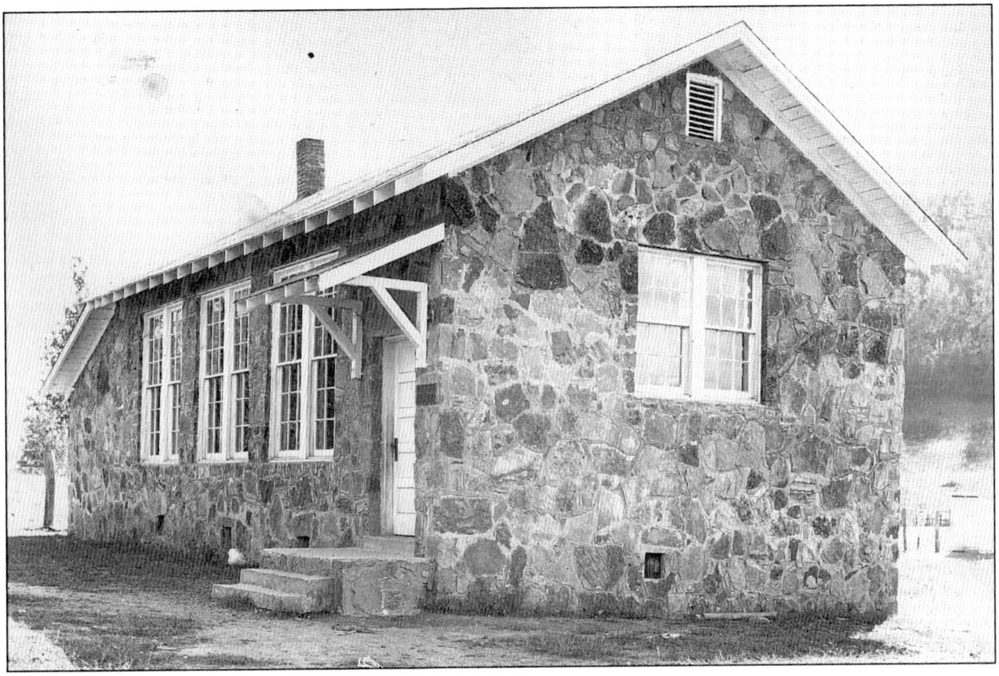

The Flat Creek School.

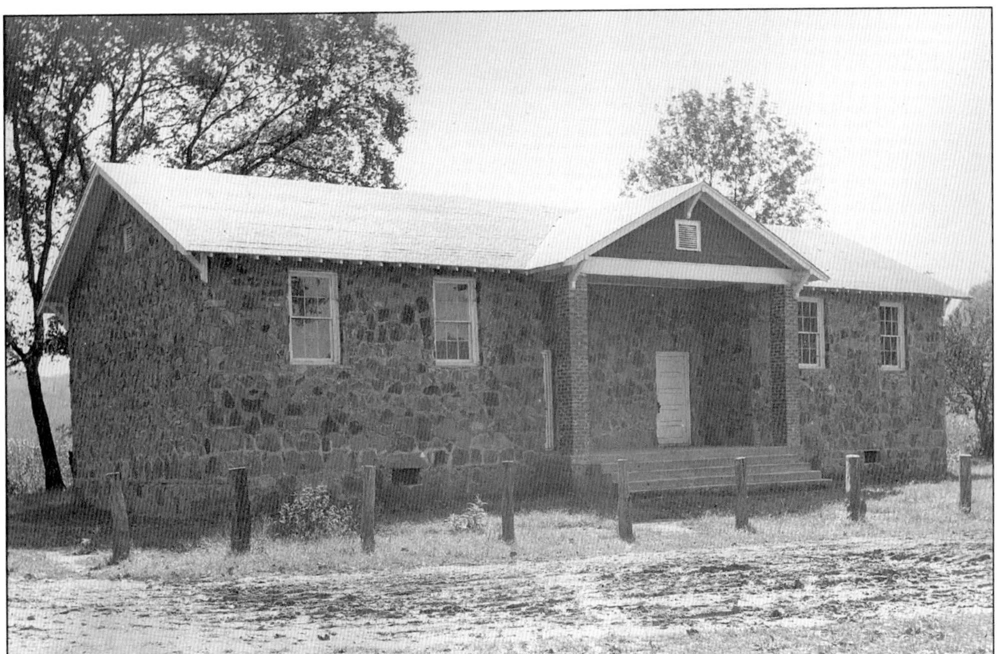

Fount Elementary School.

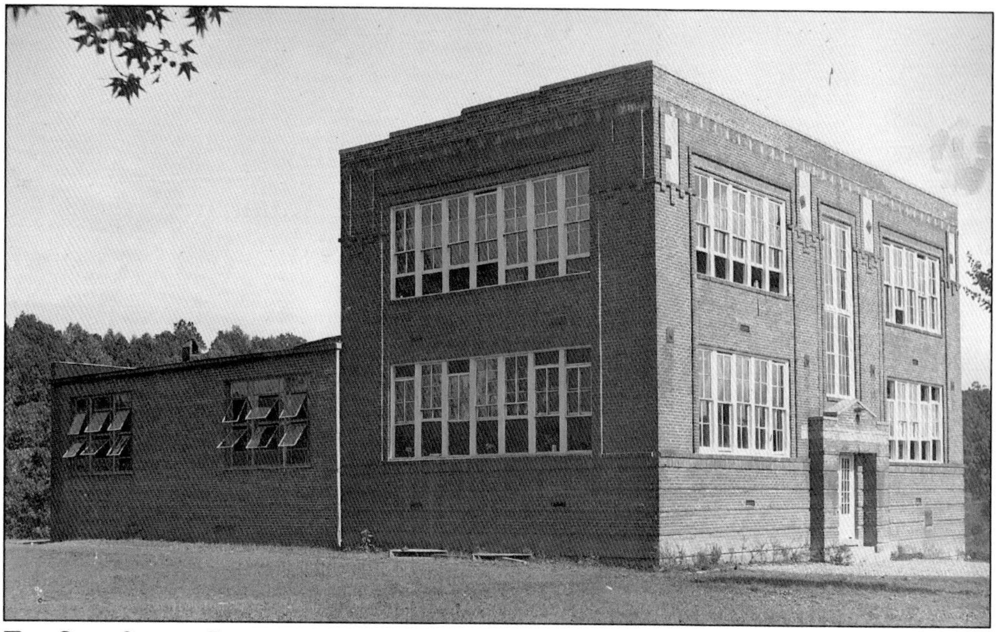

THE GRAY SCHOOL BUILDING, 1937.

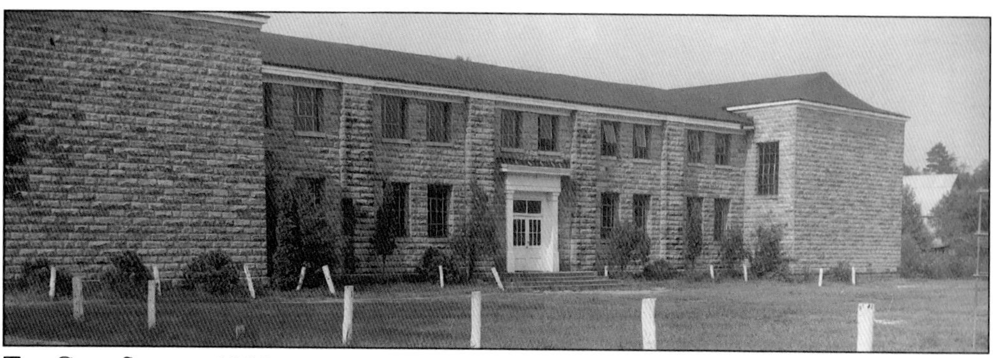

THE GRAY SCHOOL, 1960S.

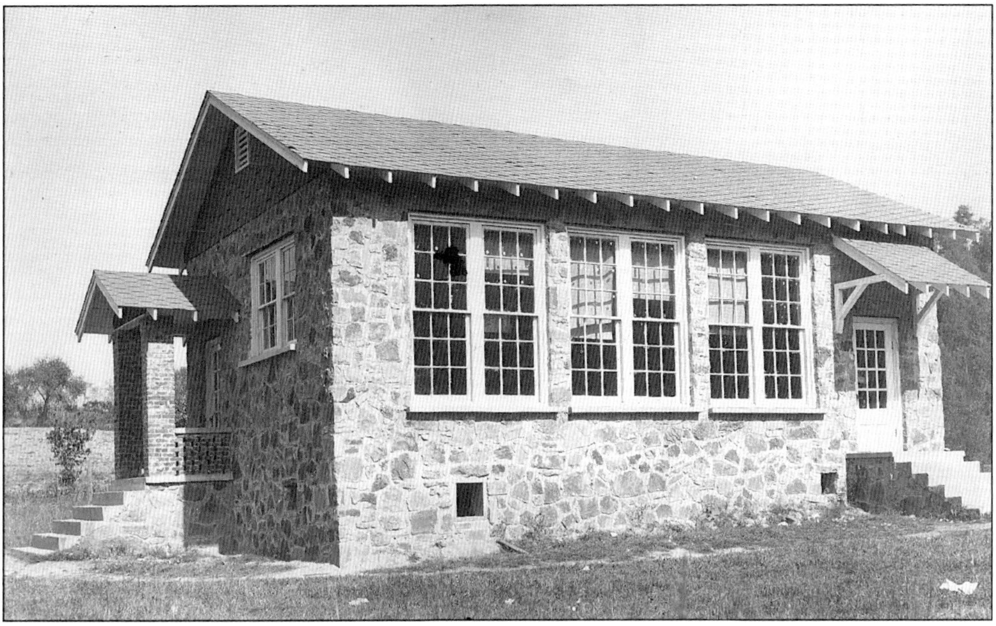

THE GREEN GROVE SCHOOL.

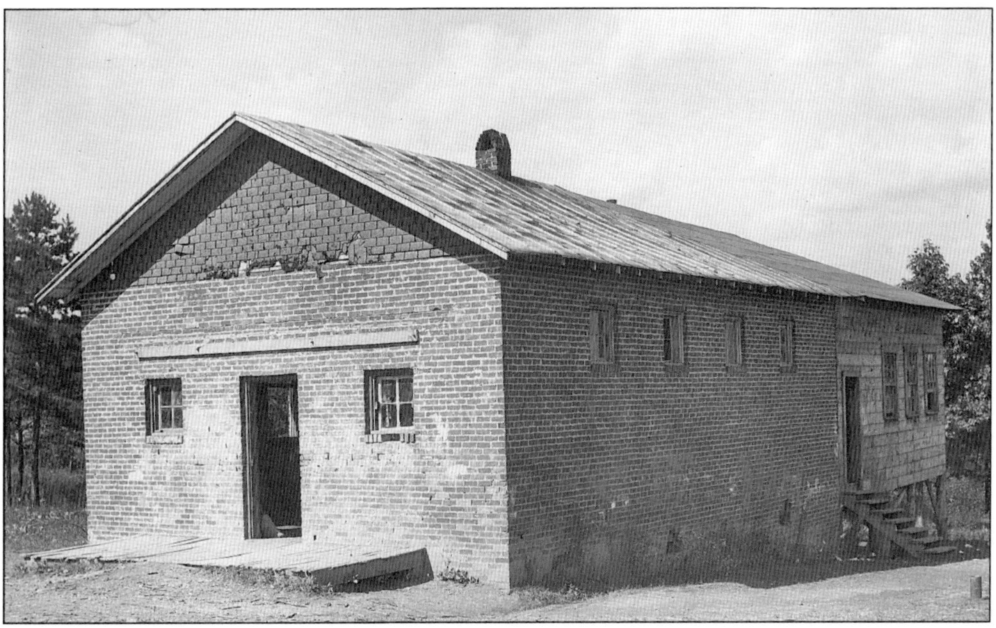

HART SCHOOL.

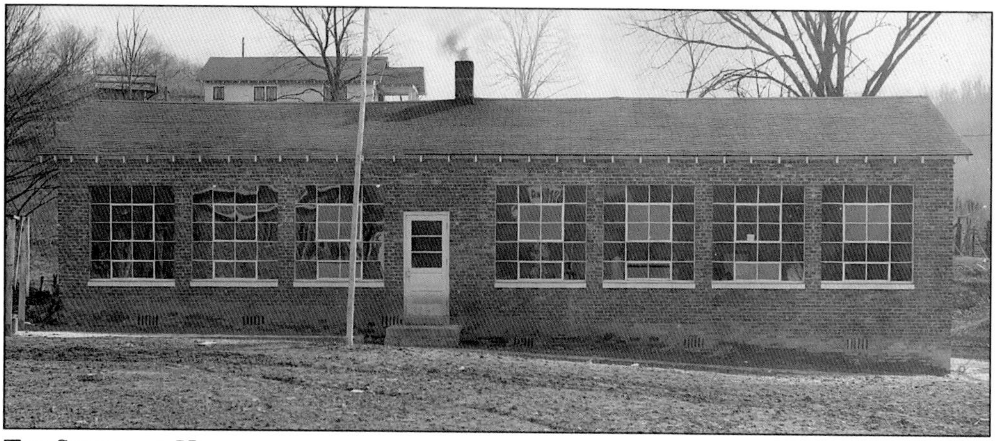

THE SCHOOL AT HEIDRICK.

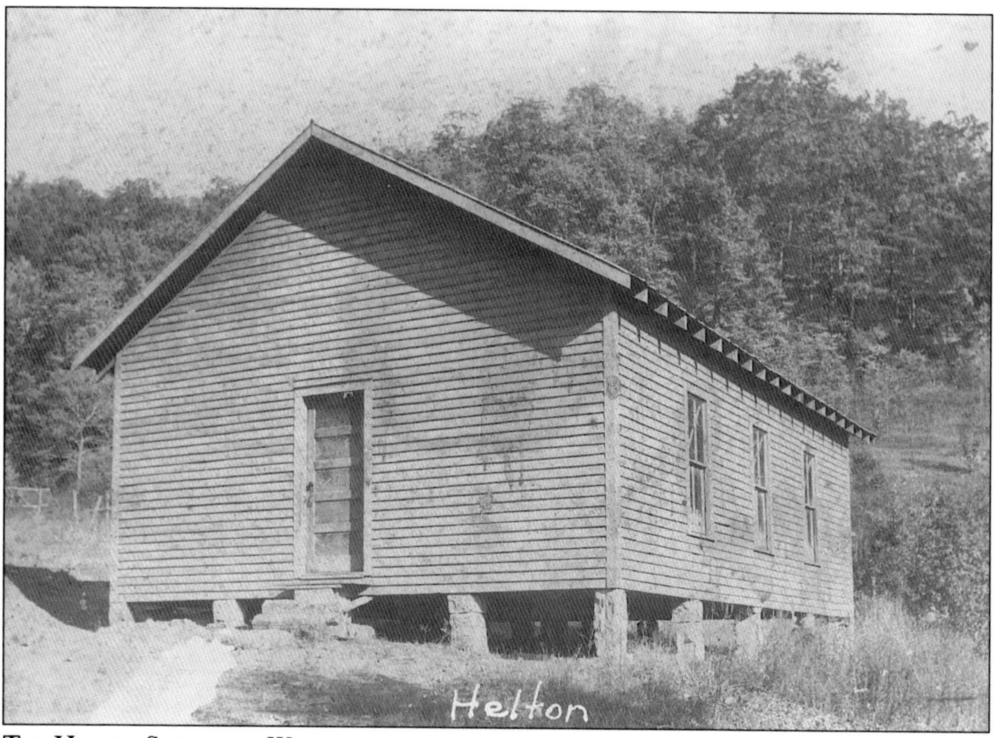

THE HELTON SCHOOL AT WILTON.

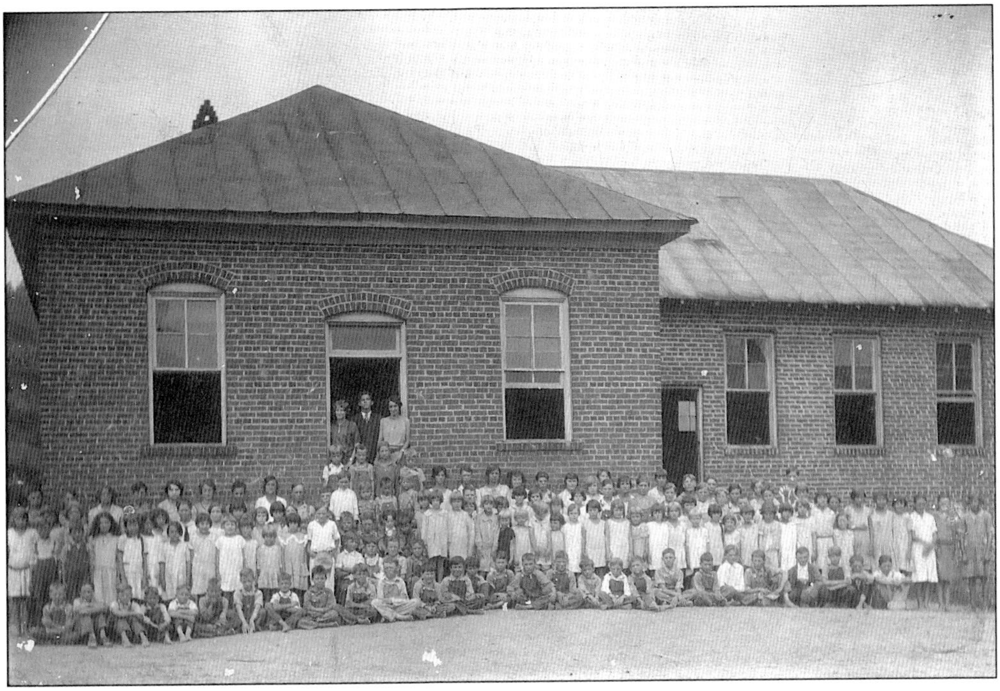

THE HIGHLAND PARK SCHOOL BUILDING.

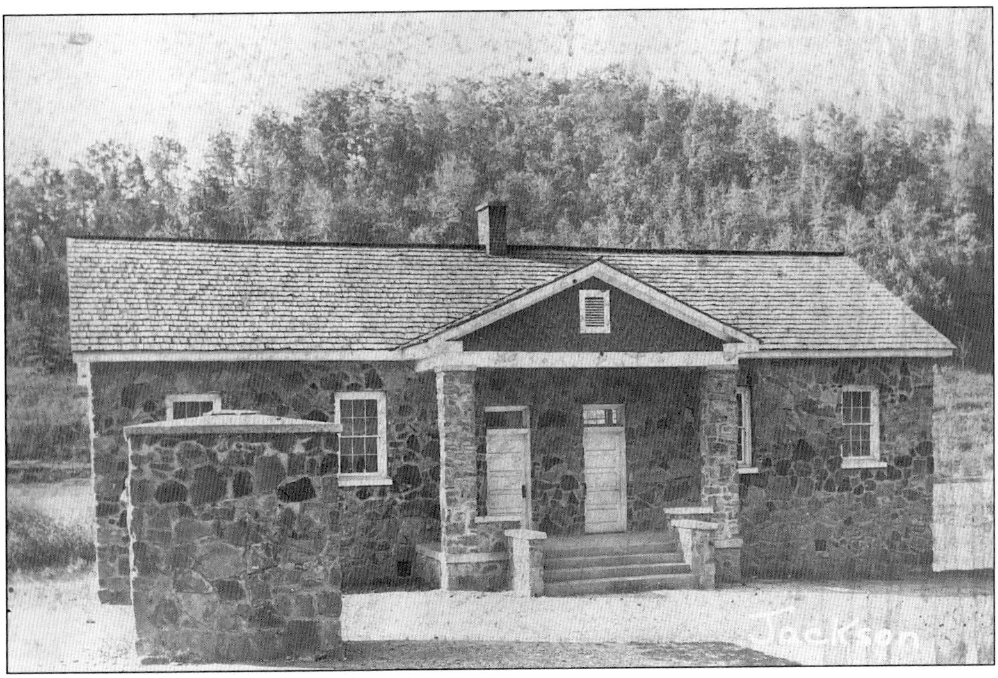

THE OLD JACKSON SCHOOL.

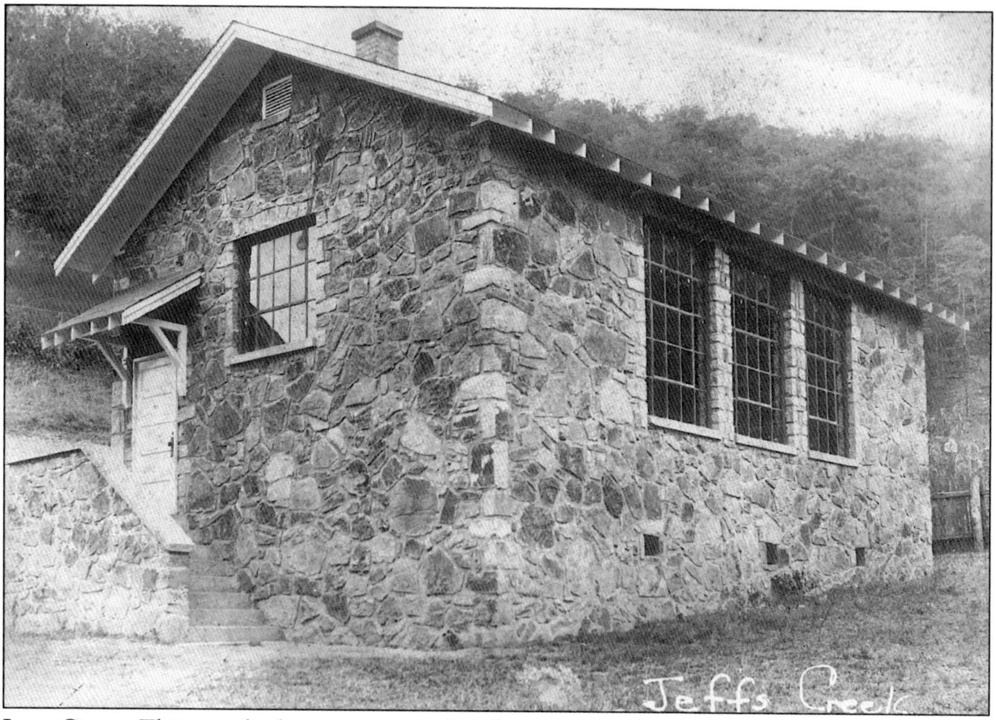

Jeffs Creek. This was the last one-room schoolhouse to be closed in Knox County.

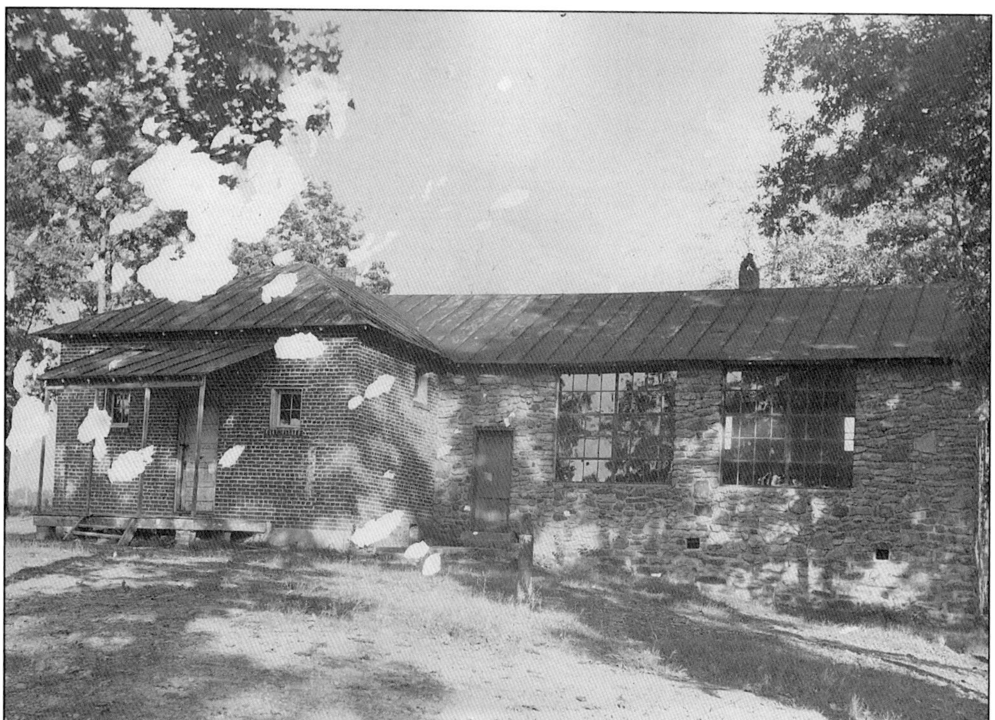

Keck School.

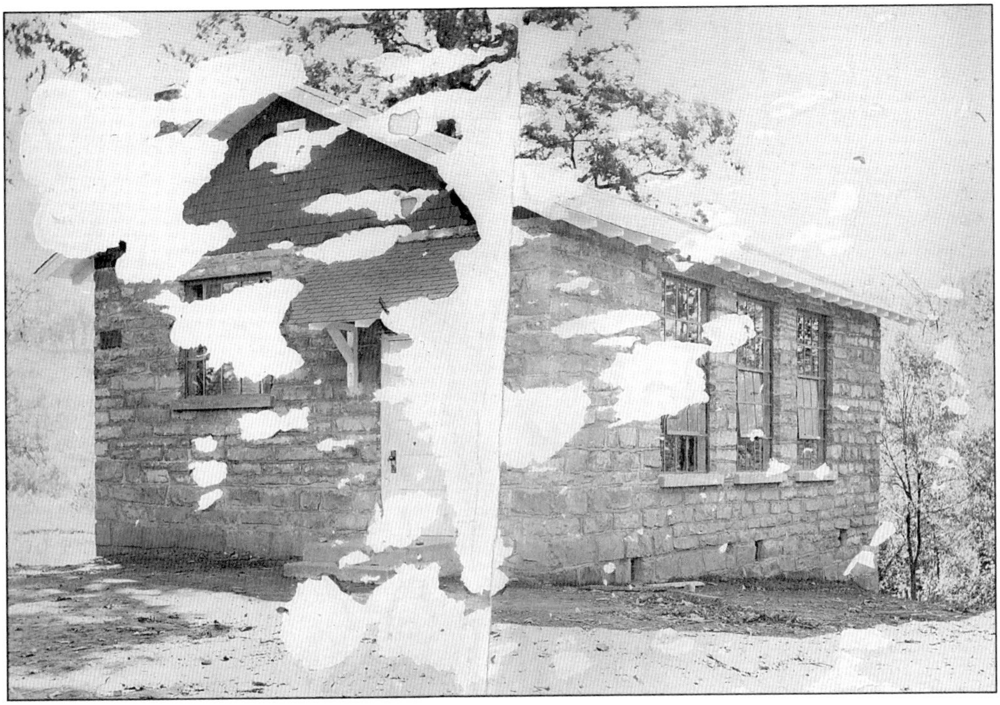

The Ketchen School.

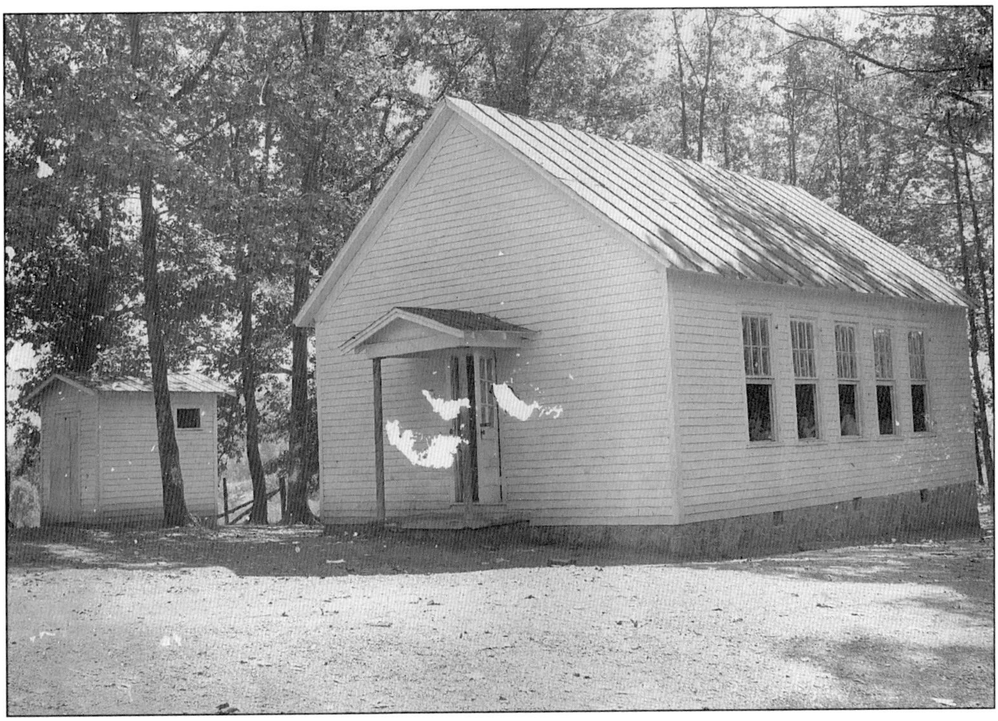

The Liberty School.

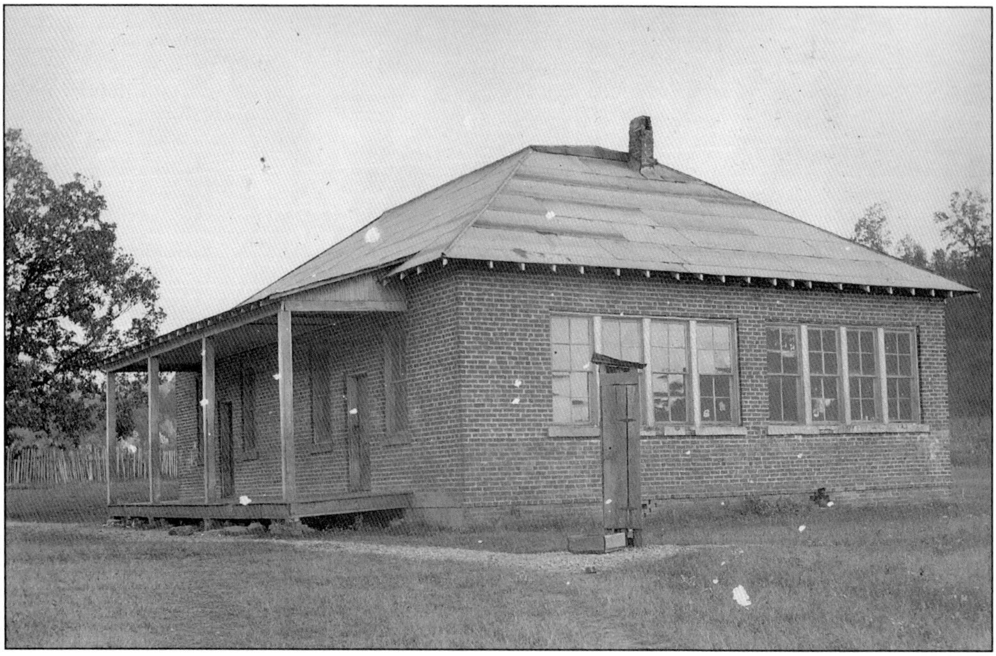

Locust Grove School.

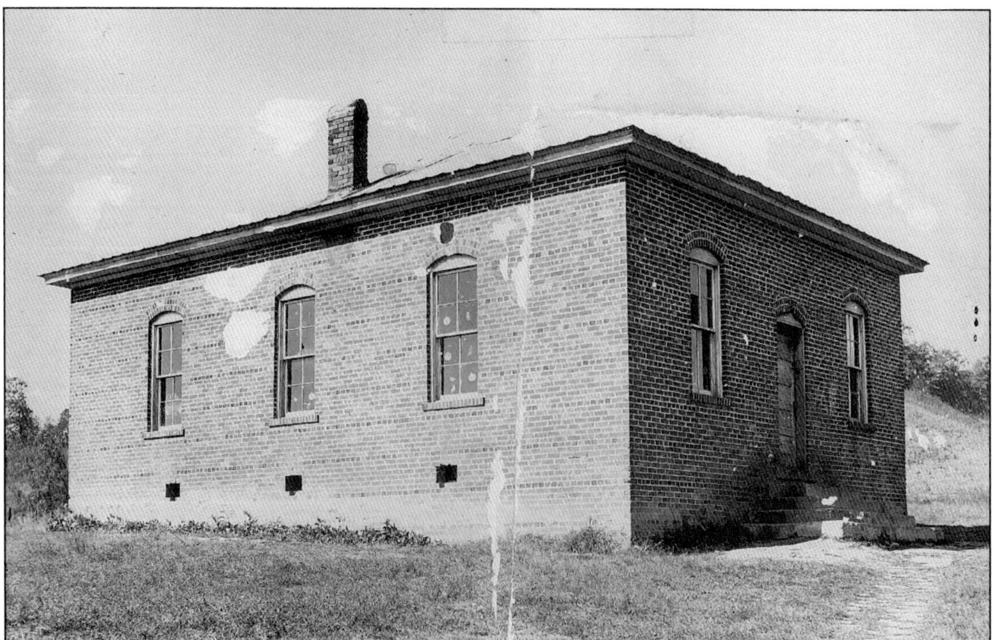

The Logan Gap School.

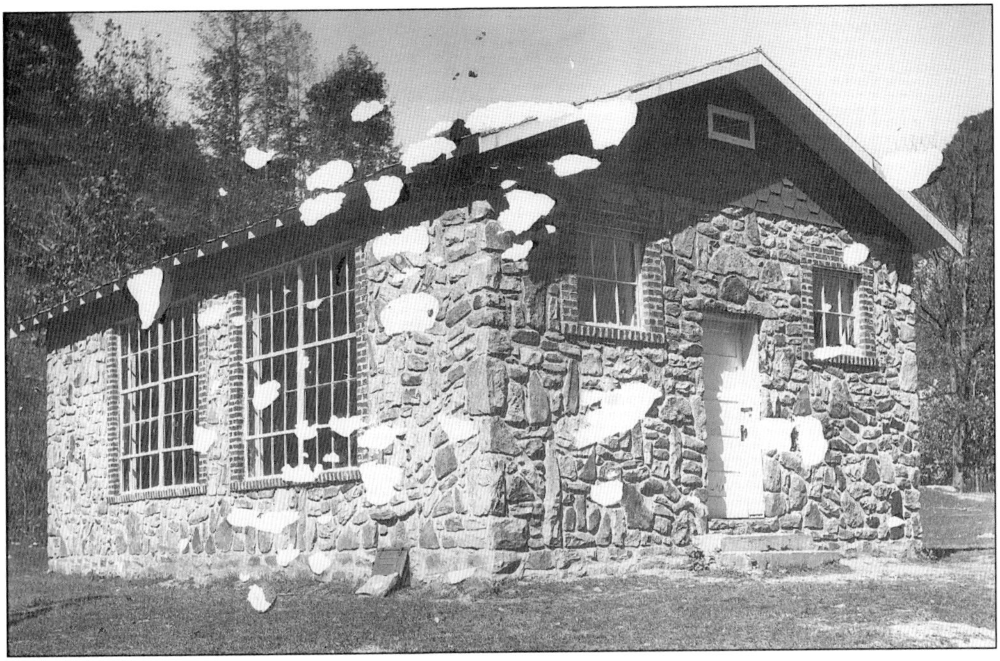

THE MESSER SCHOOL.

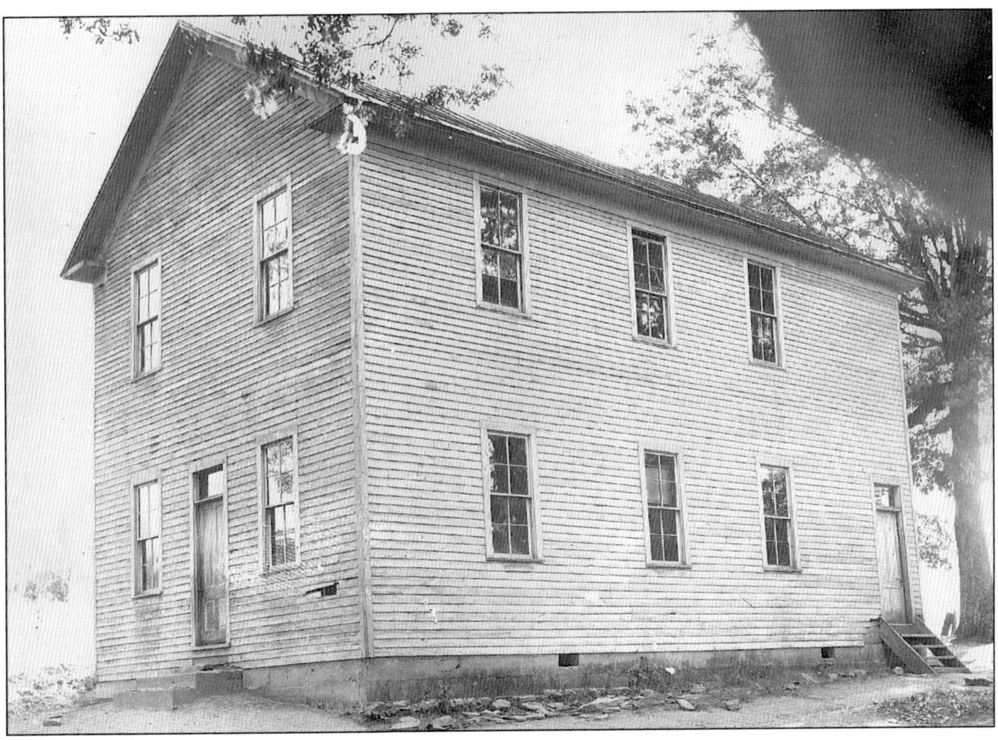

THE OLD SCHOOL AT MACKEY BEND.

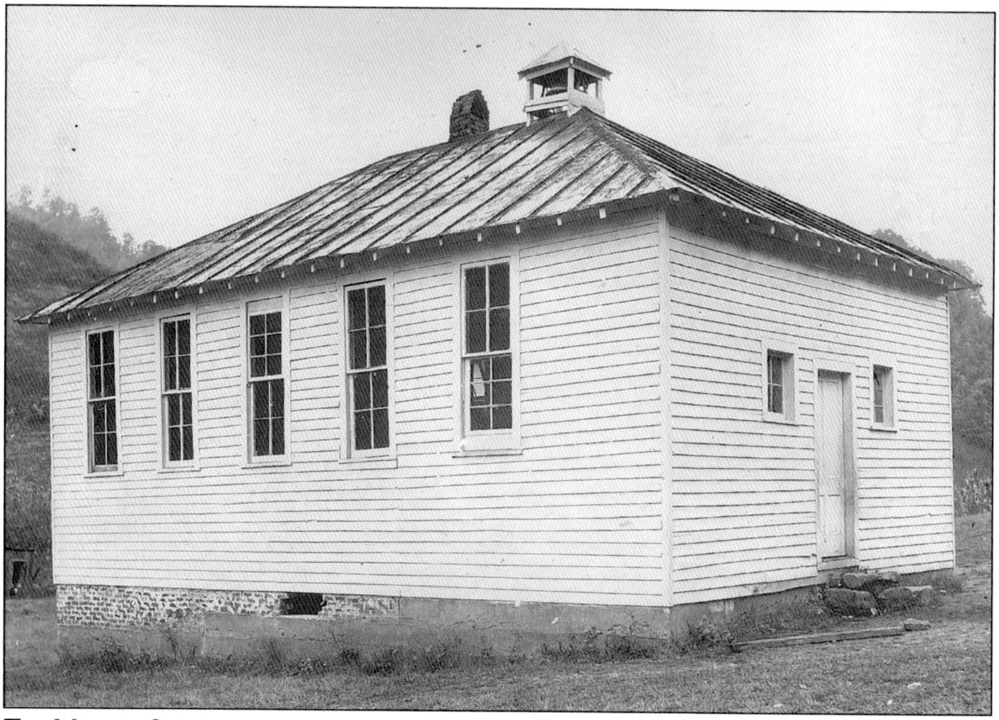

The Macroe School.

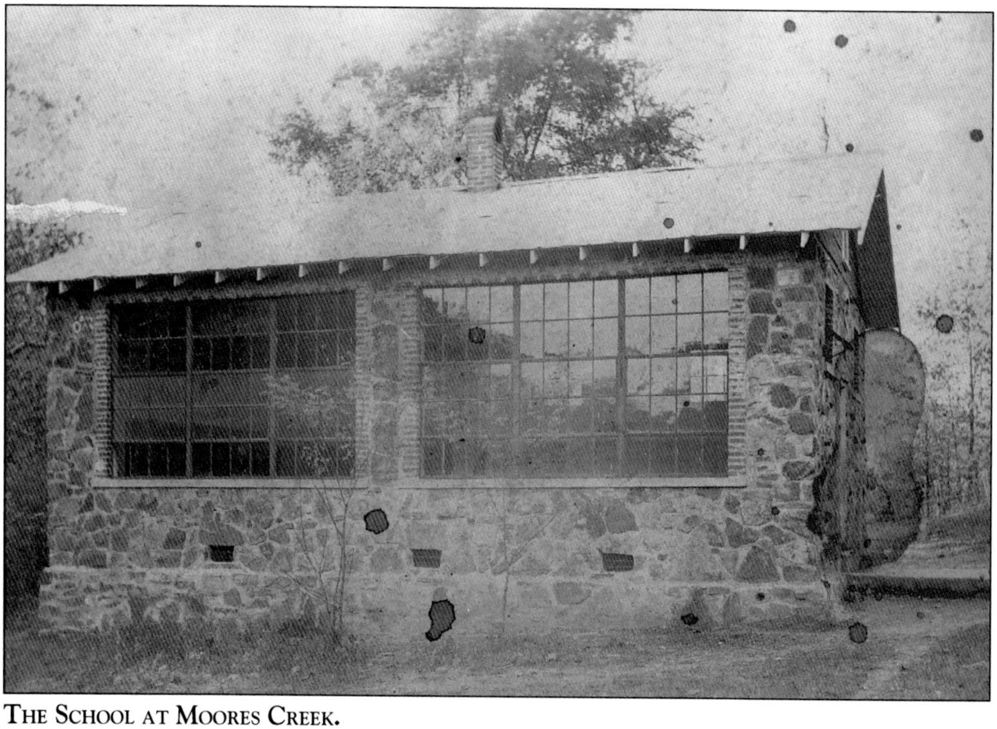

The School at Moores Creek.

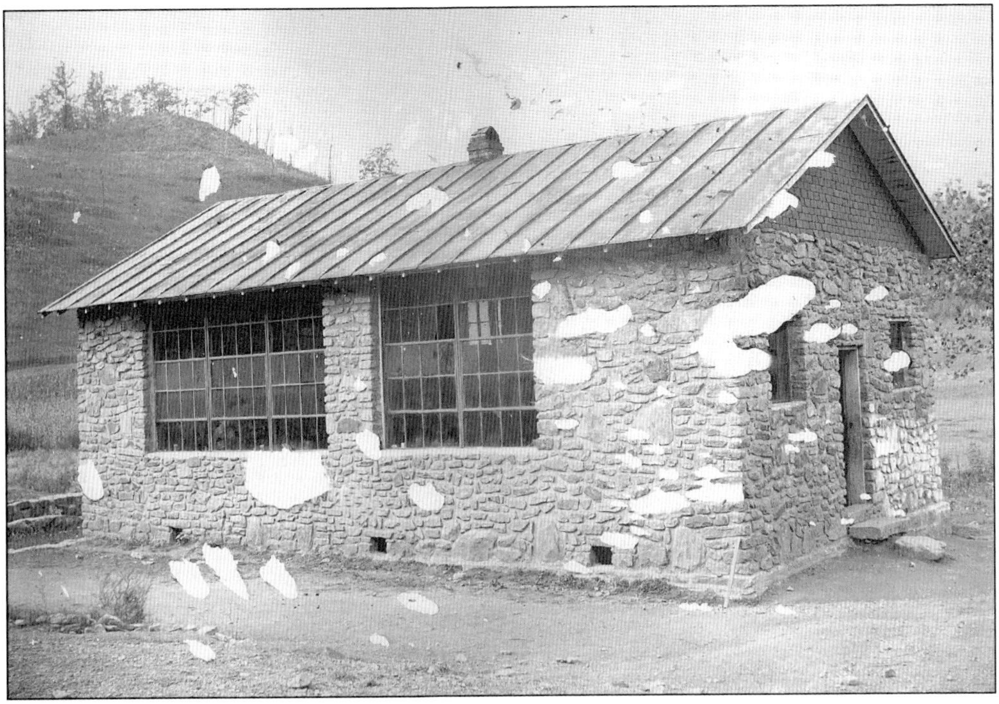
THE ROAD FORK SCHOOL.

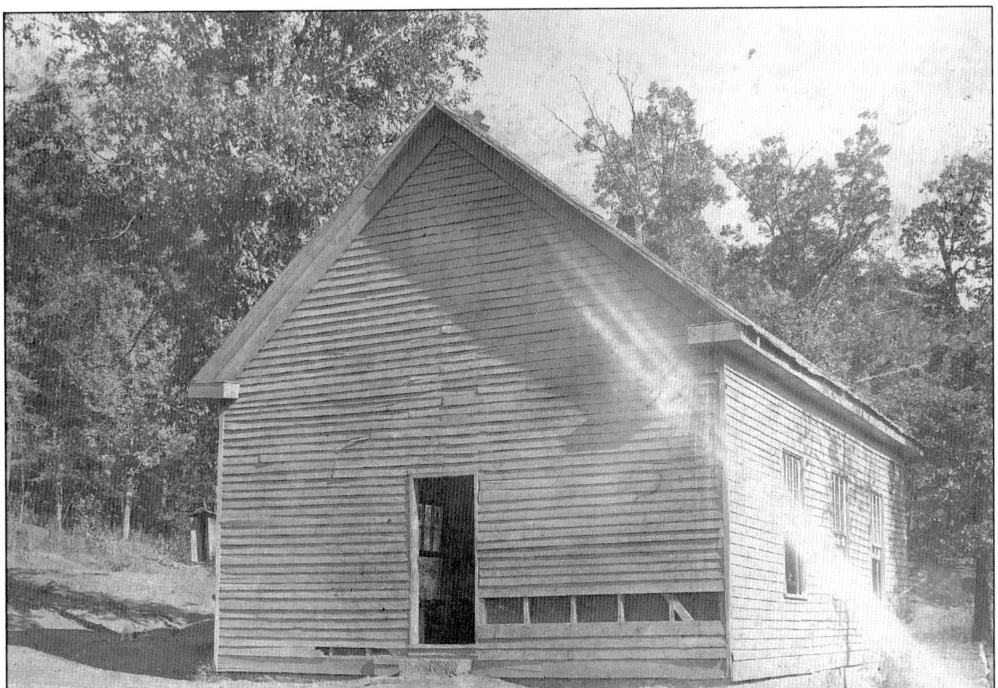
REECE ELEMENTARY SCHOOL.

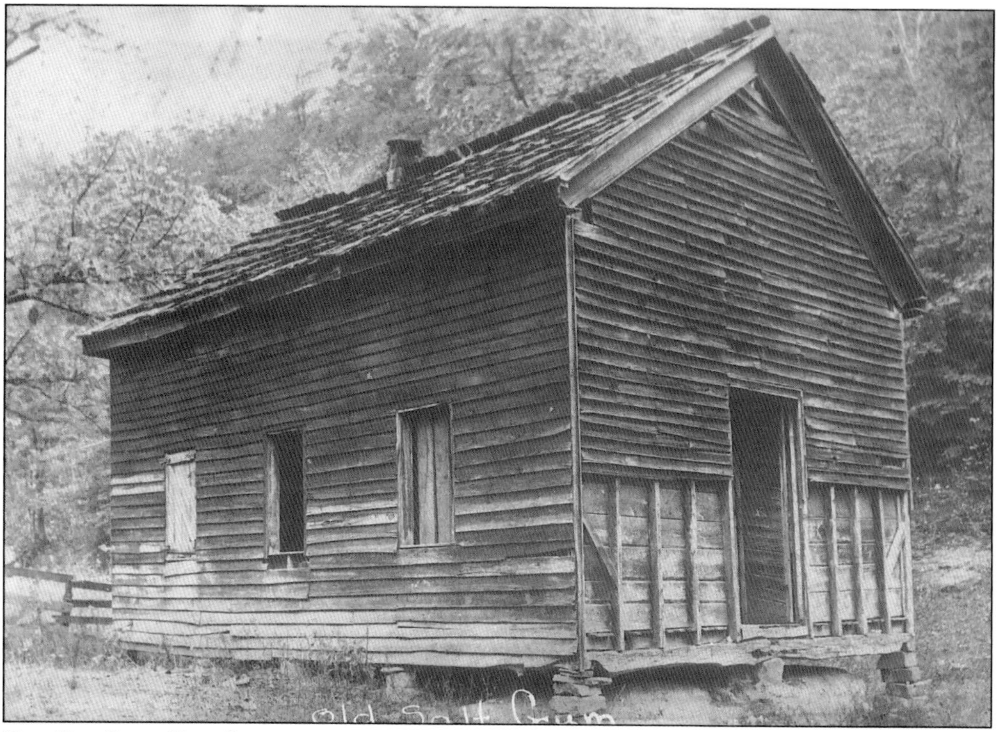

THE OLD SALT GUM SCHOOL.

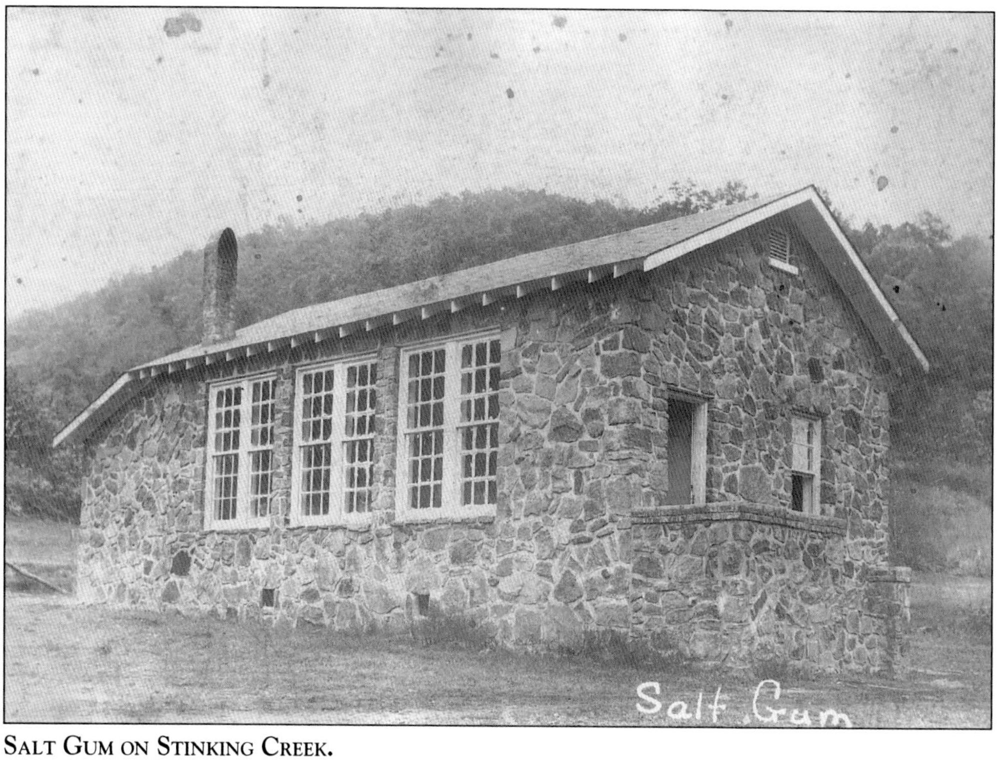

SALT GUM ON STINKING CREEK.

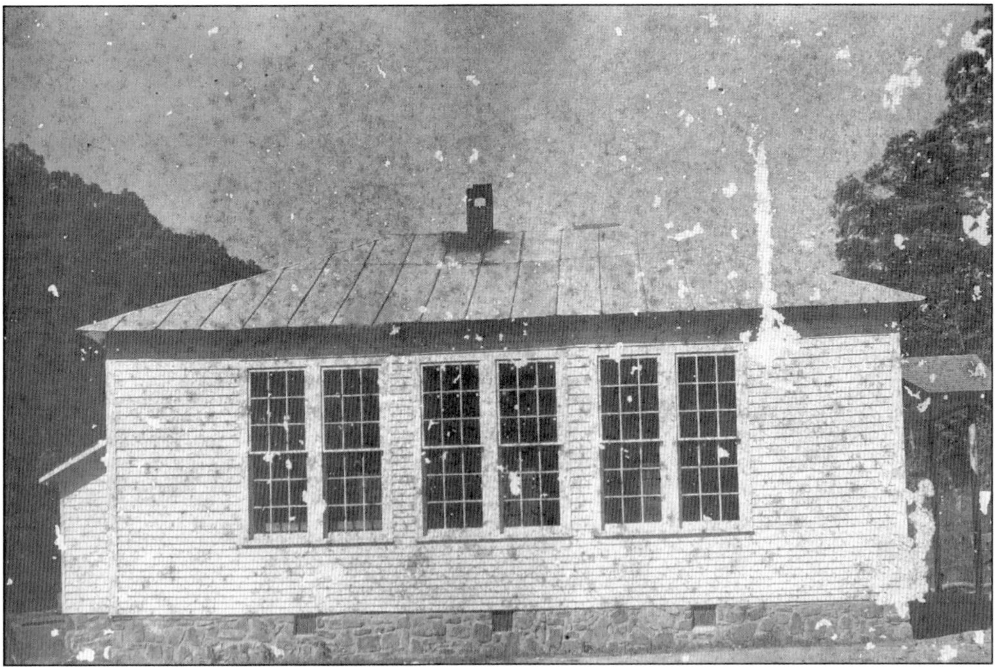

SHADY SCHOOL.

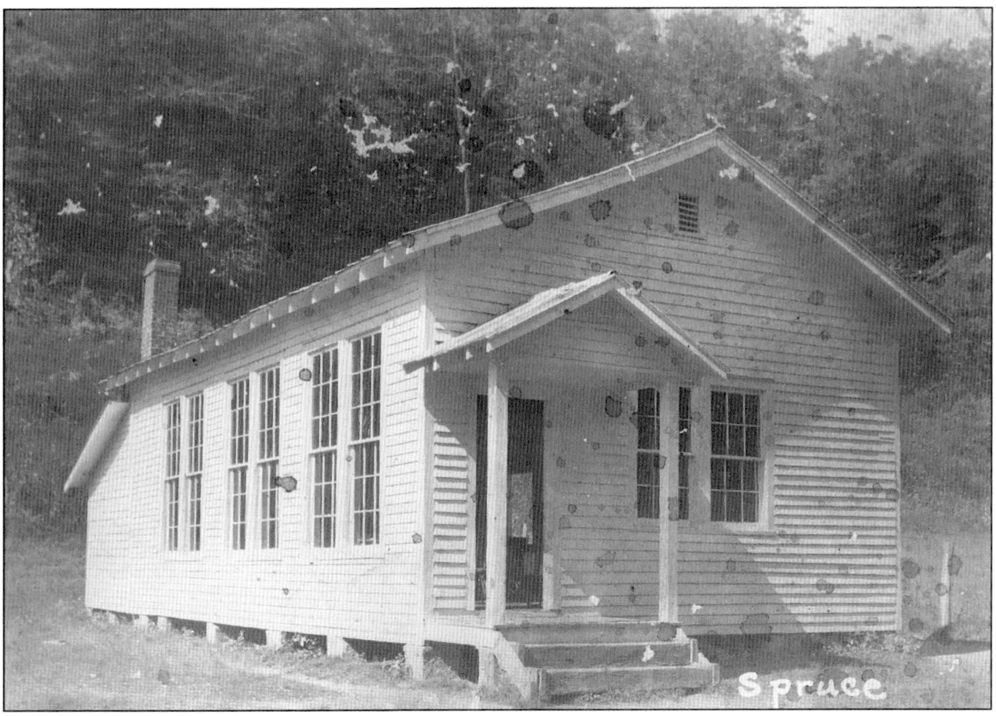

THE SPRUCE SCHOOL AT HAMMONS FORK.

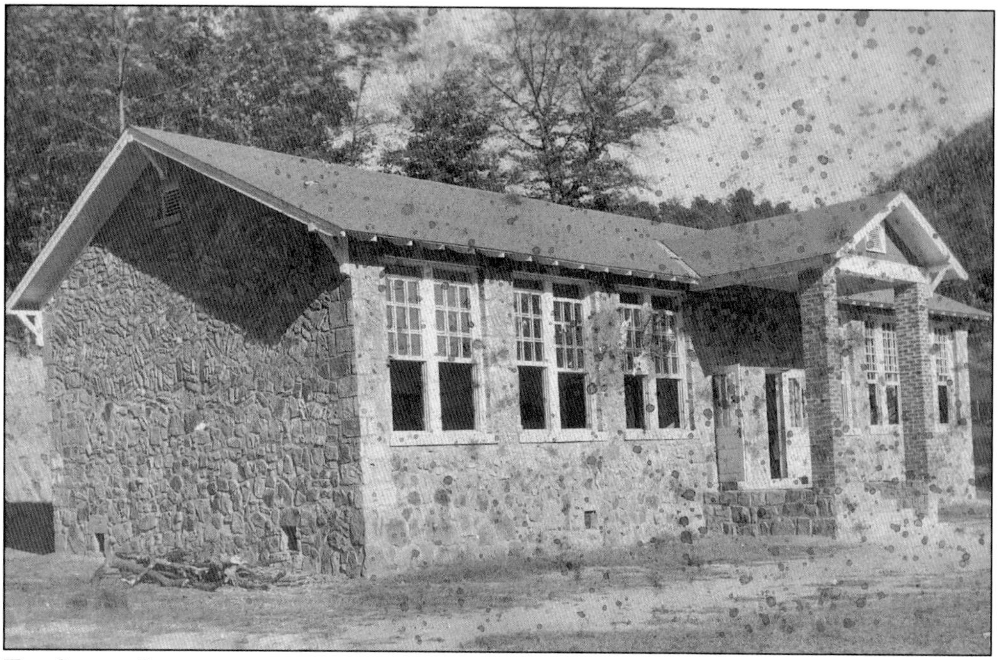

THE SPRULE SCHOOL.

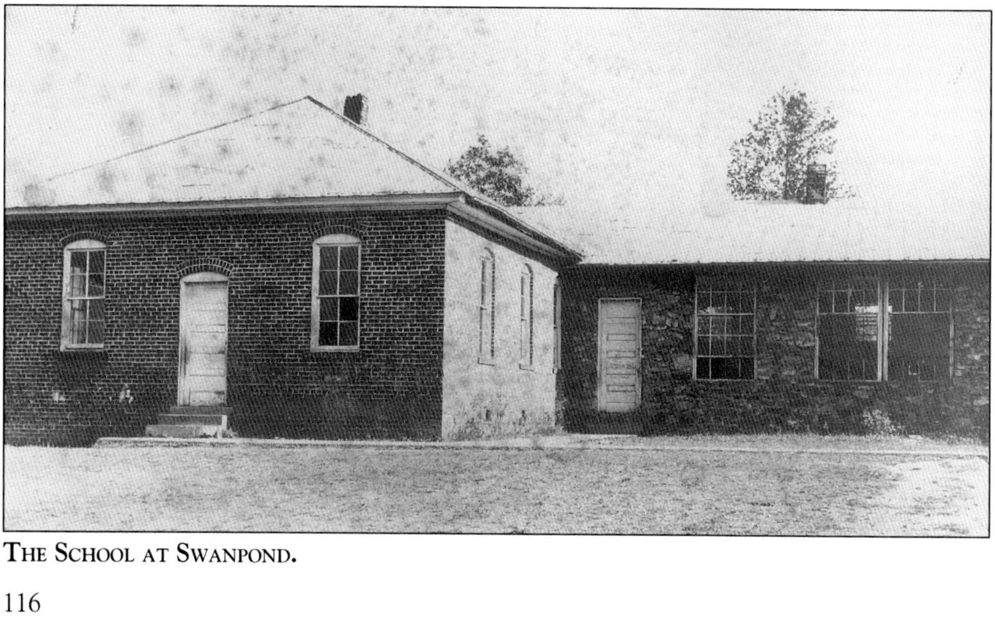

THE SCHOOL AT SWANPOND.

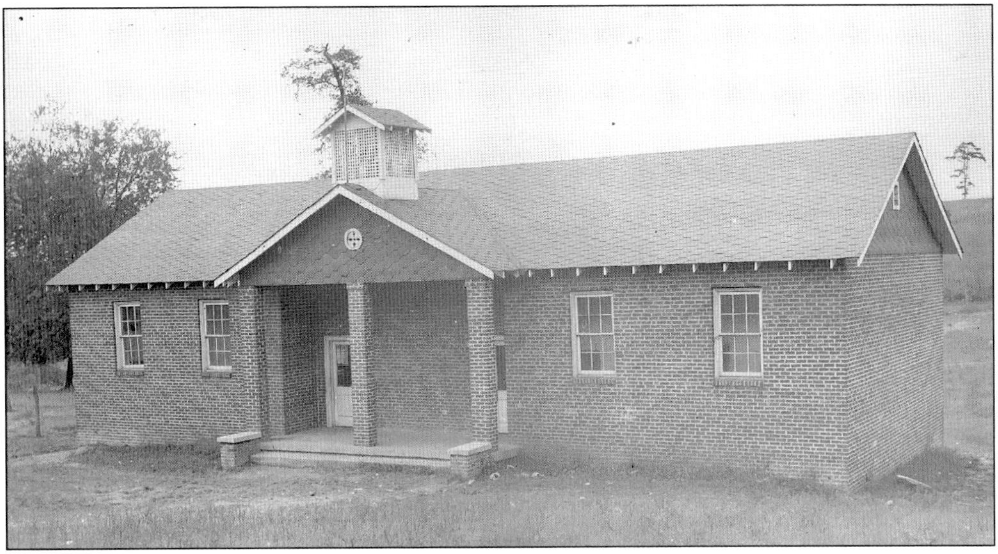

PARKHILL SCHOOL.

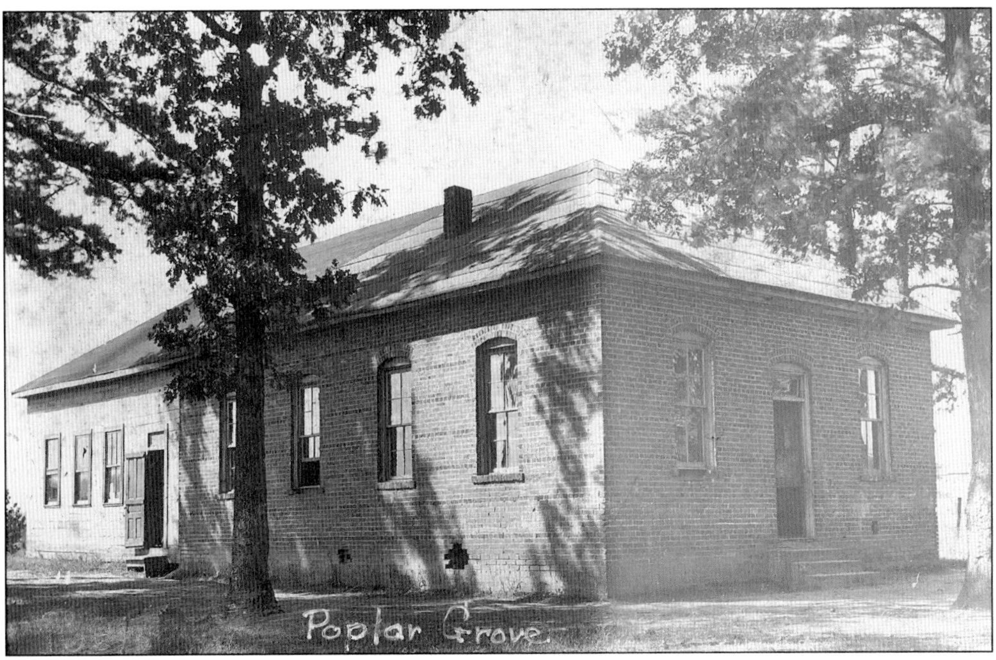

POPLAR GROVE SCHOOL. This school was located near the Lynn Camp community.

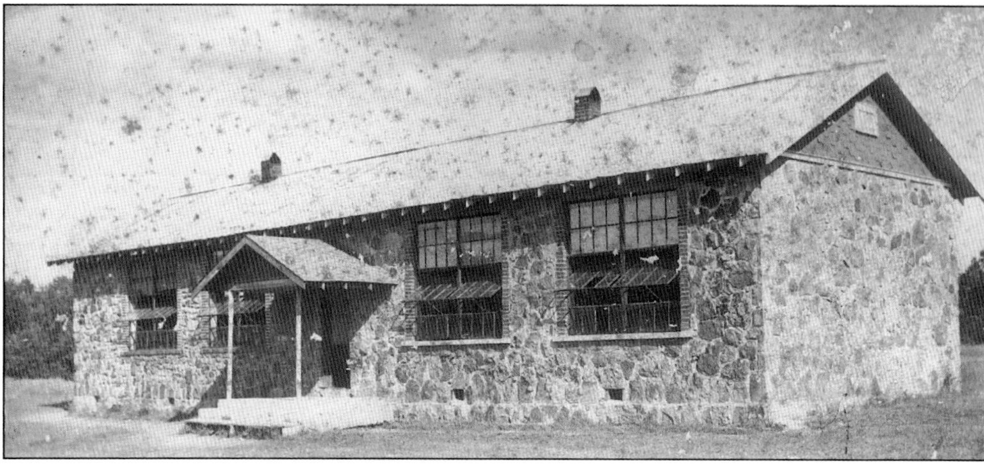

"NEW" POPLAR GROVE.

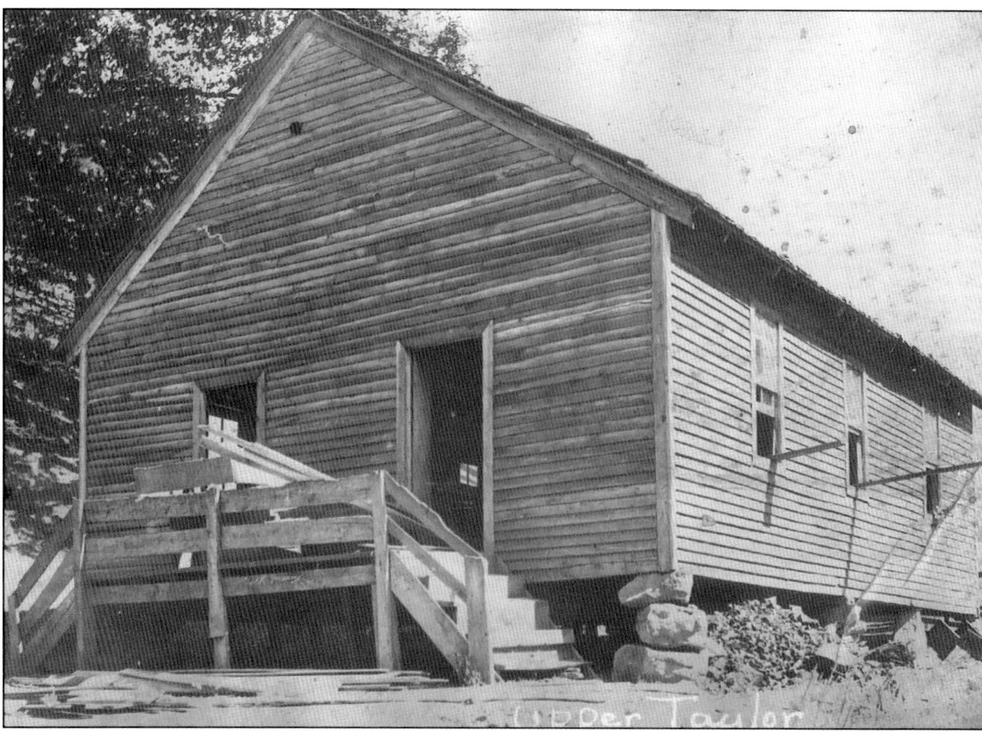

THE UPPER TAYLOR SCHOOL.

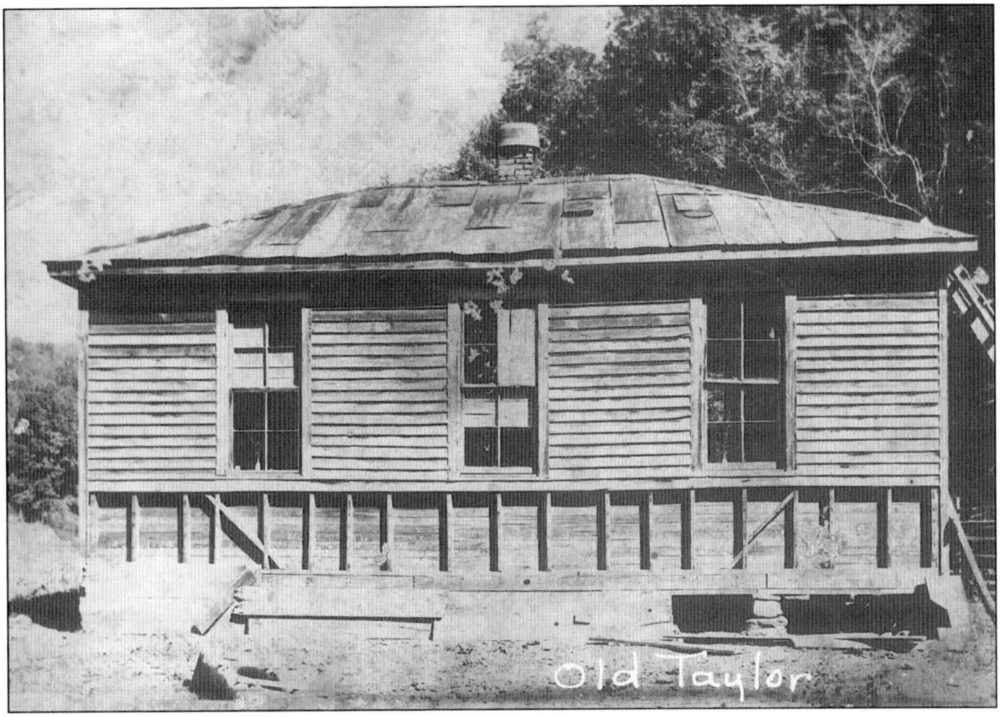

OLD TAYLOR, NEAR EROSE AND ALEX ON STINKING CREEK.

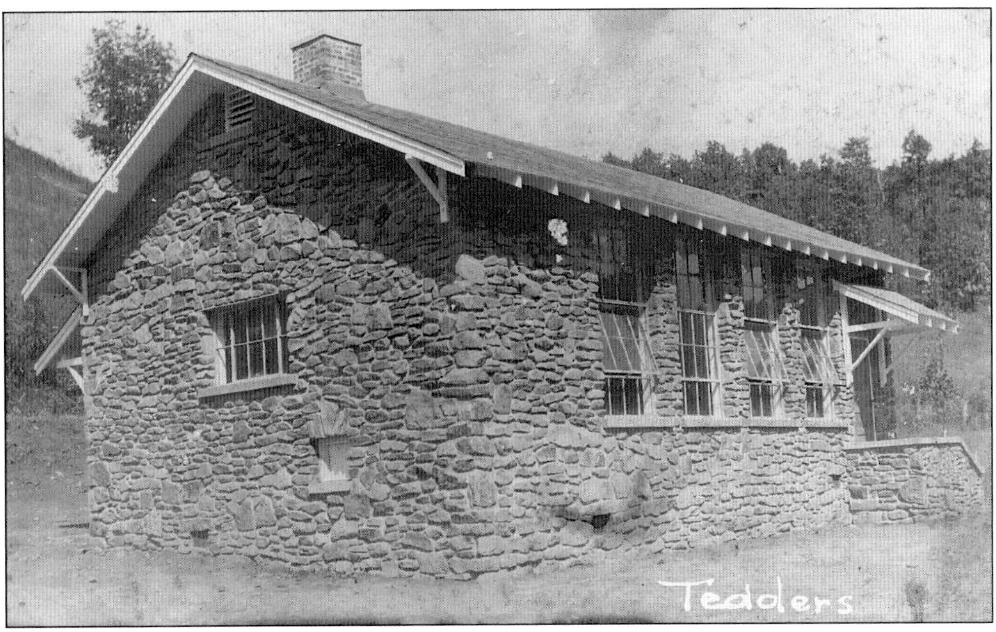

TEDDERS SCHOOL, LOCATED NEAR NEW BETHEL.

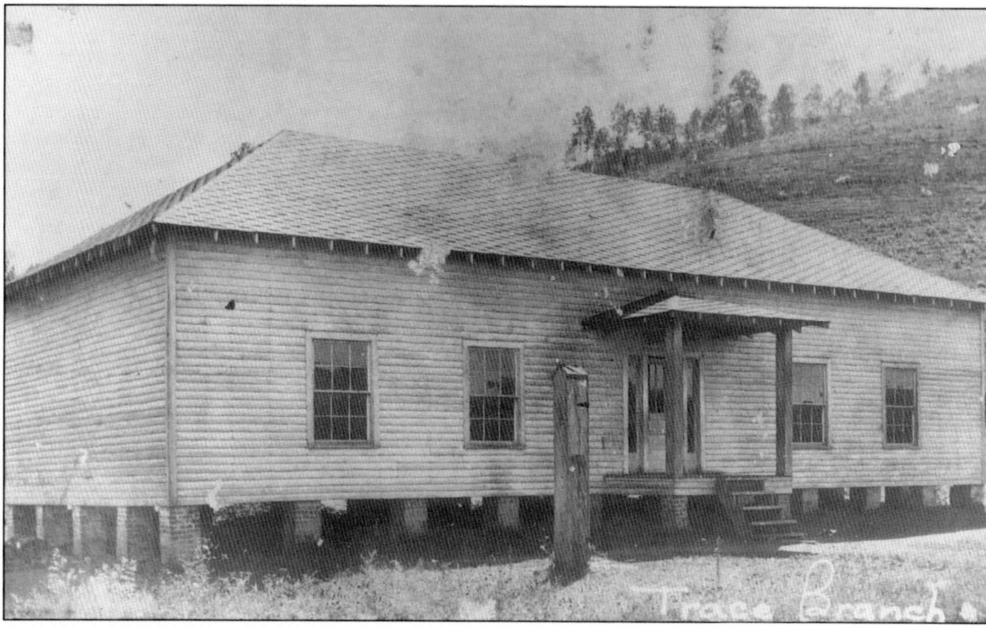

The School at Trace Branch.

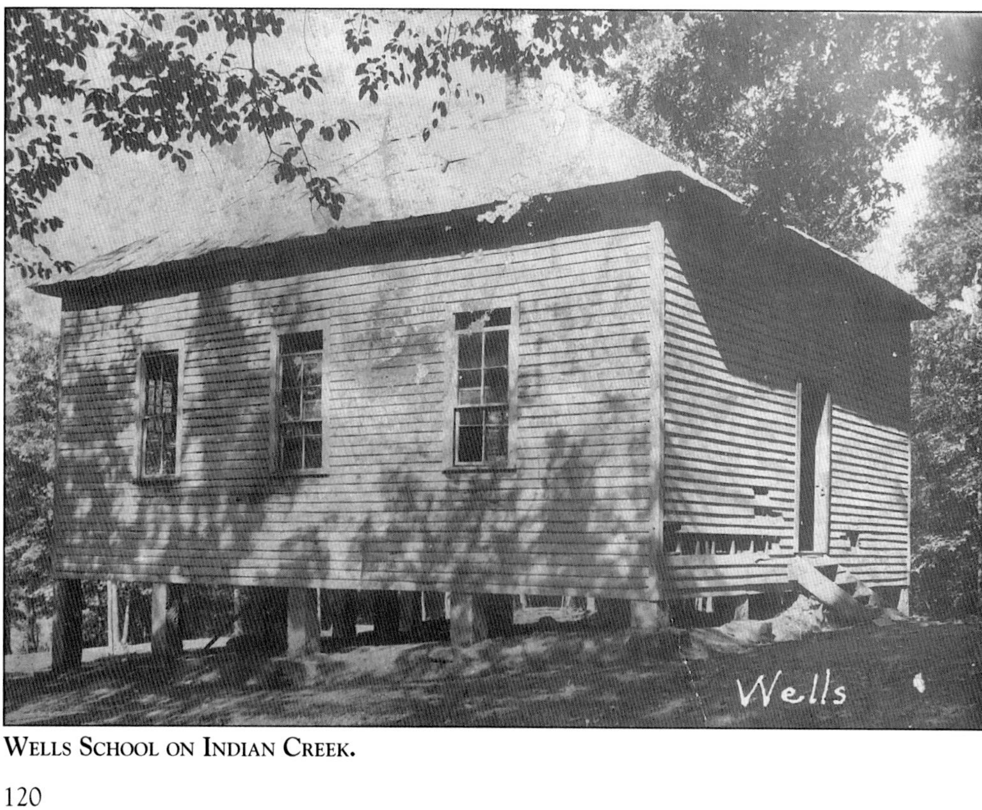

Wells School on Indian Creek.

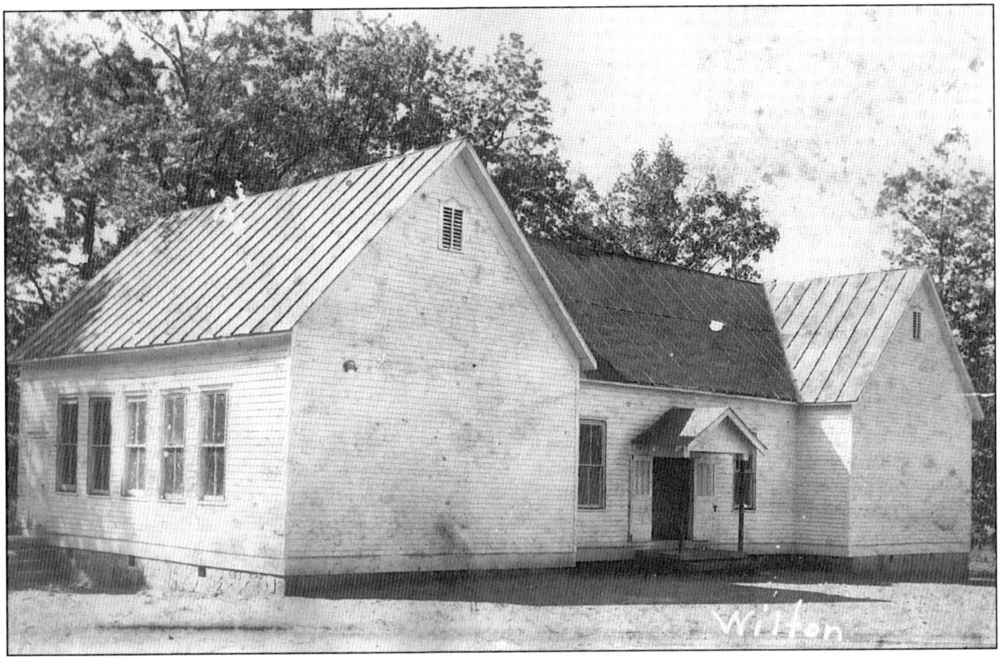

WILTON SCHOOL ON INDIAN CREEK.

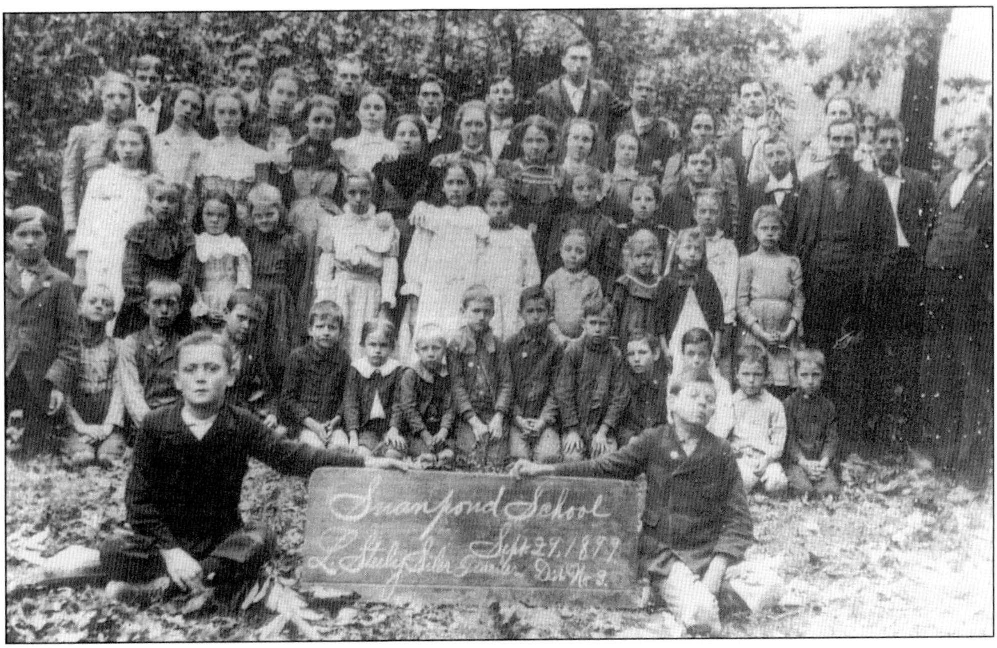

SWANPOND SCHOOL, SEPTEMBER 29, 1899.

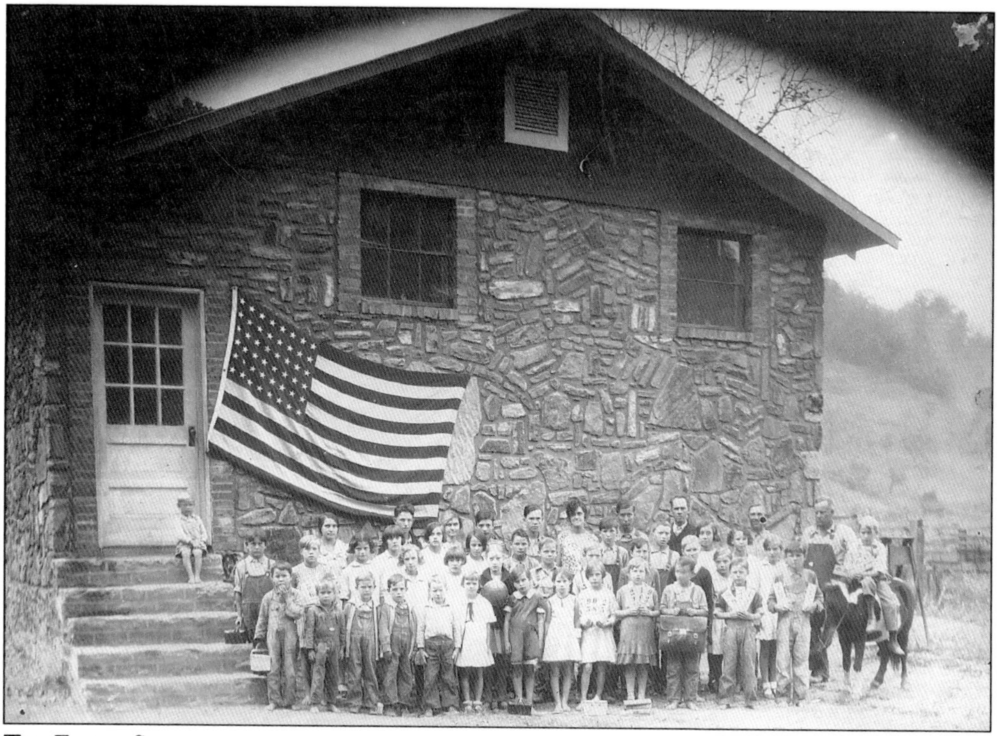

The Fount School.

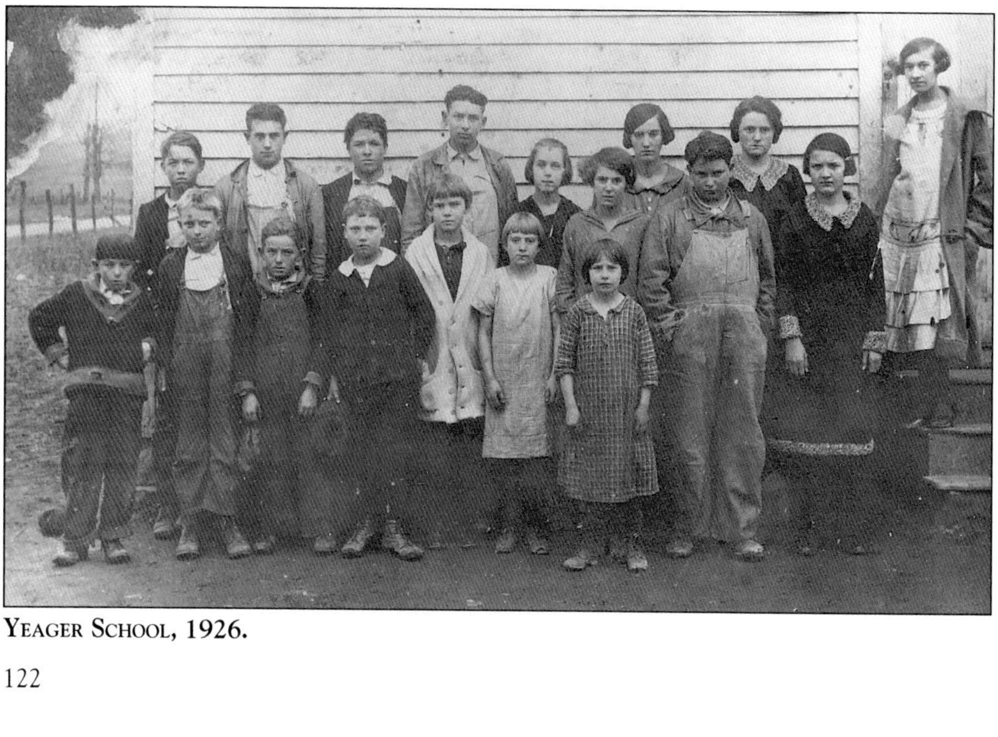

Yeager School, 1926.

Seven

CELEBRATIONS

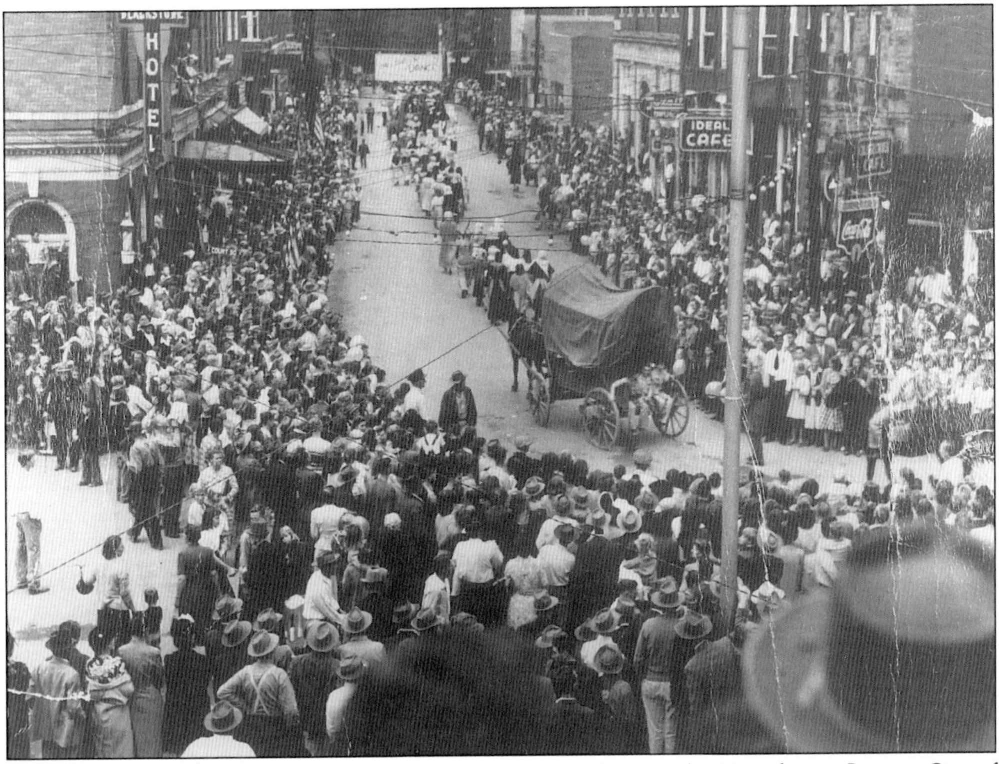

Barbourville and Knox County celebrations always take place on the Courthouse Square. One of the earliest celebrations was the May Festival in the late 1940s. Here, a queen was chosen, and a parade was the climax to the festival. In 1950, Governor Flem Sampson organized a celebration to honor Dr. Thomas Walker's exploration of this area in 1750. This was known as the Walker Bicentennial celebration, and it too was highlighted with a parade around Courthouse Square. The Daniel Boone Festival, held each October in Barbourville, was started in 1948. It also features a large downtown parade. The above photo was taken in 1950 at the Thomas Walker Bicentennial parade.

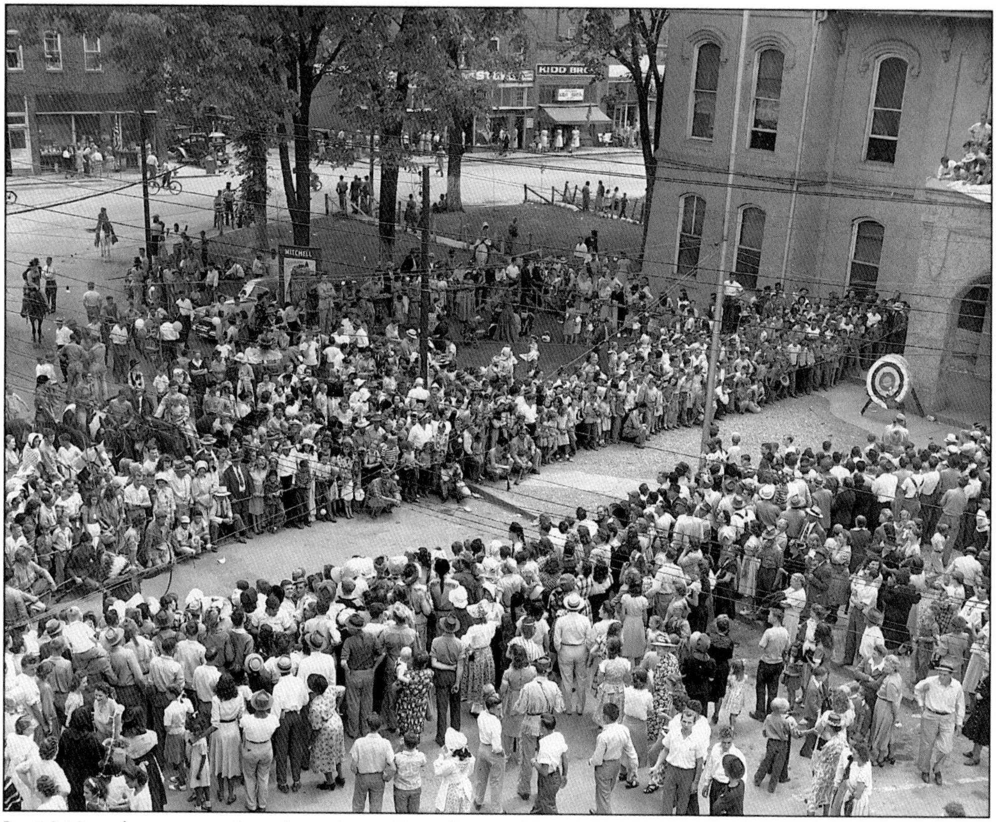

In 1948, a large crowd gathered on Courthouse Square to see Native Americans and watch them shoot arrows at targets.

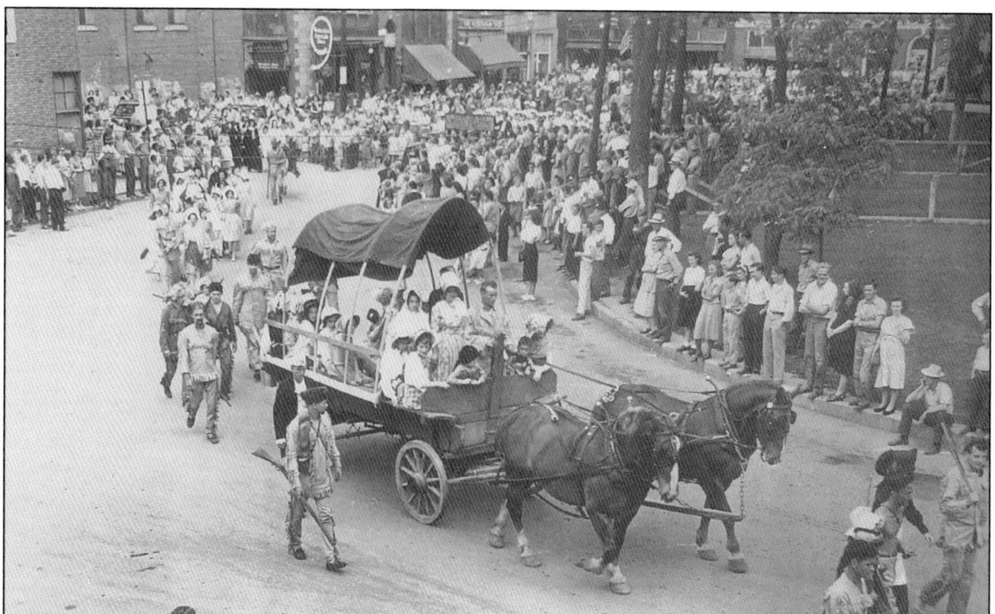

The Daniel Boone Festival parade in 1948 looked much like the Thomas Walker parade.

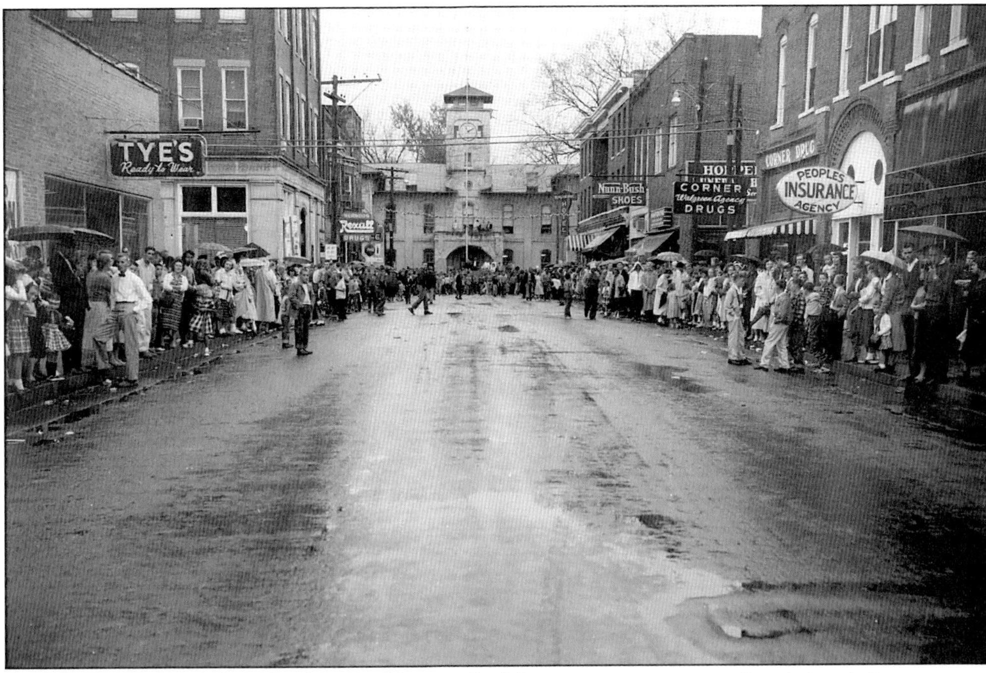

A crowd lines the sidewalks for a 1950s parade. No one seems to care that it is raining.

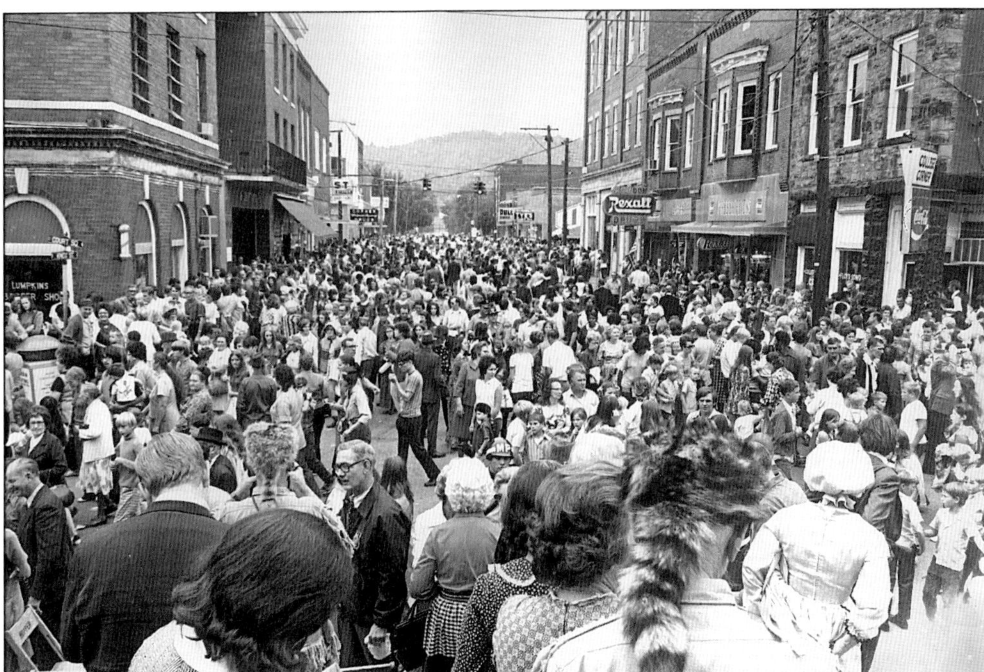

This crowd is typical of the large crowds that attend the Daniel Boone Festival each year.

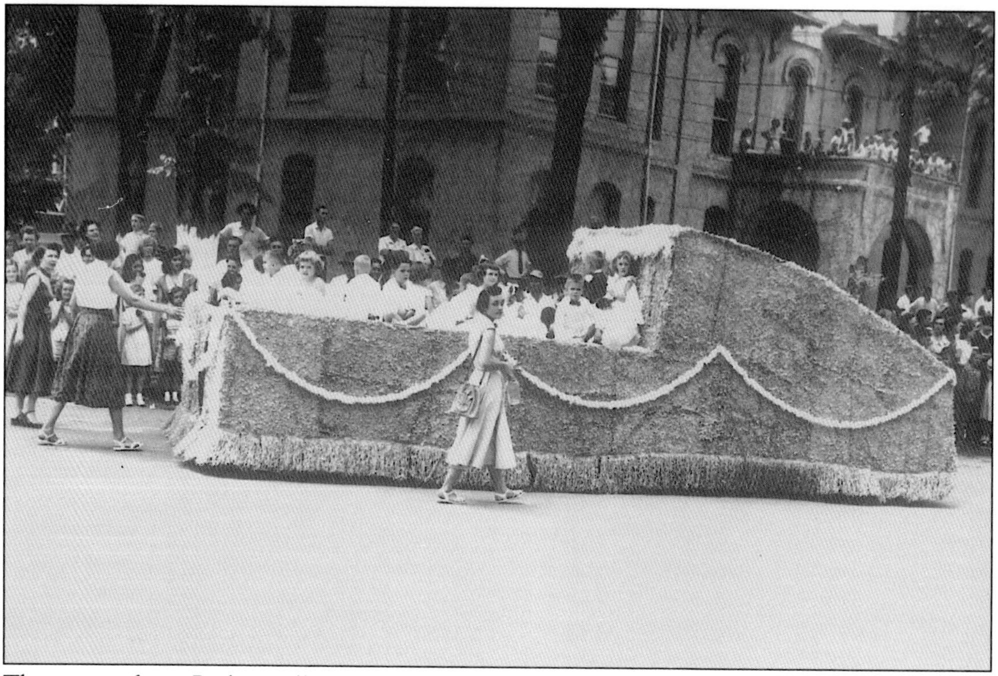

This scene from Barbourville's May Festival parade shows a float making its way around Courthouse Square.

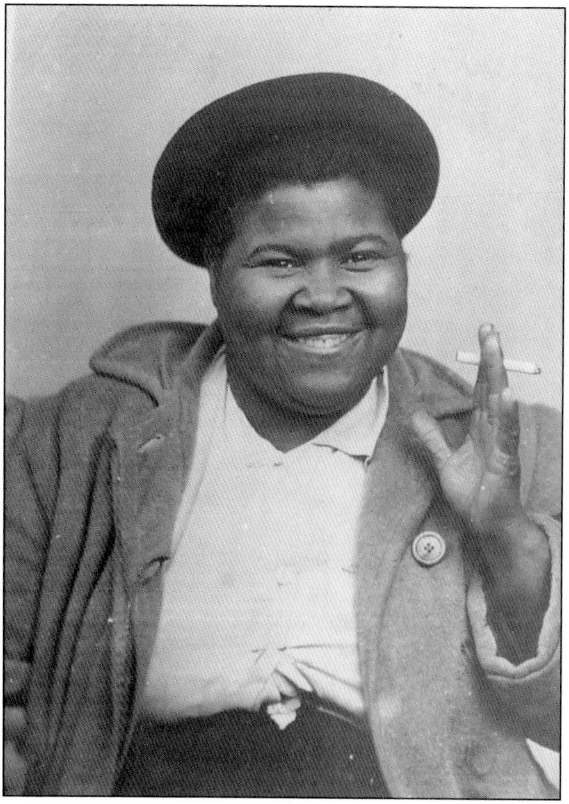

Pictured here is a "Barbourville personality" from the 1950s, known to all as Nancy Rabbit.

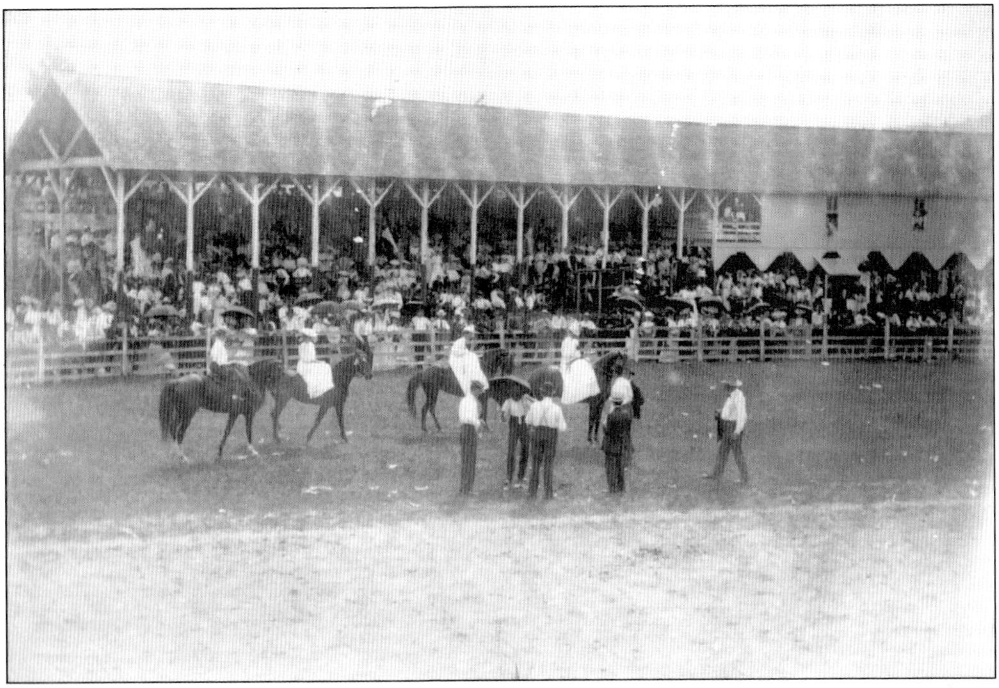

The old Knox County Fair Grounds was a favorite gathering place for city and county residents alike. Here, ladies ride side-saddled and enjoy a beautiful summer afternoon.

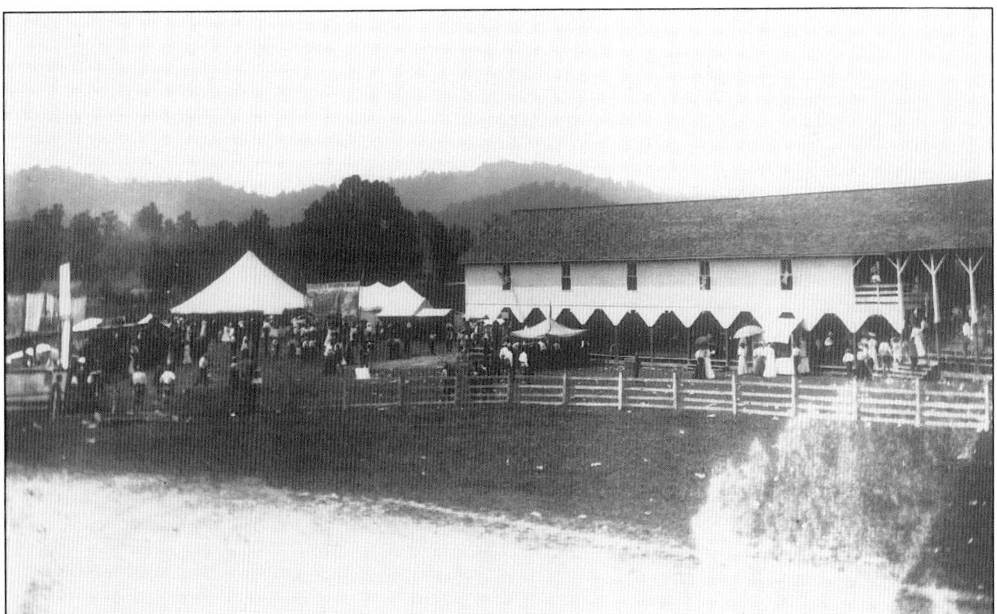

The fair grounds, pictured here, are now the site of Knox County's new hospital.

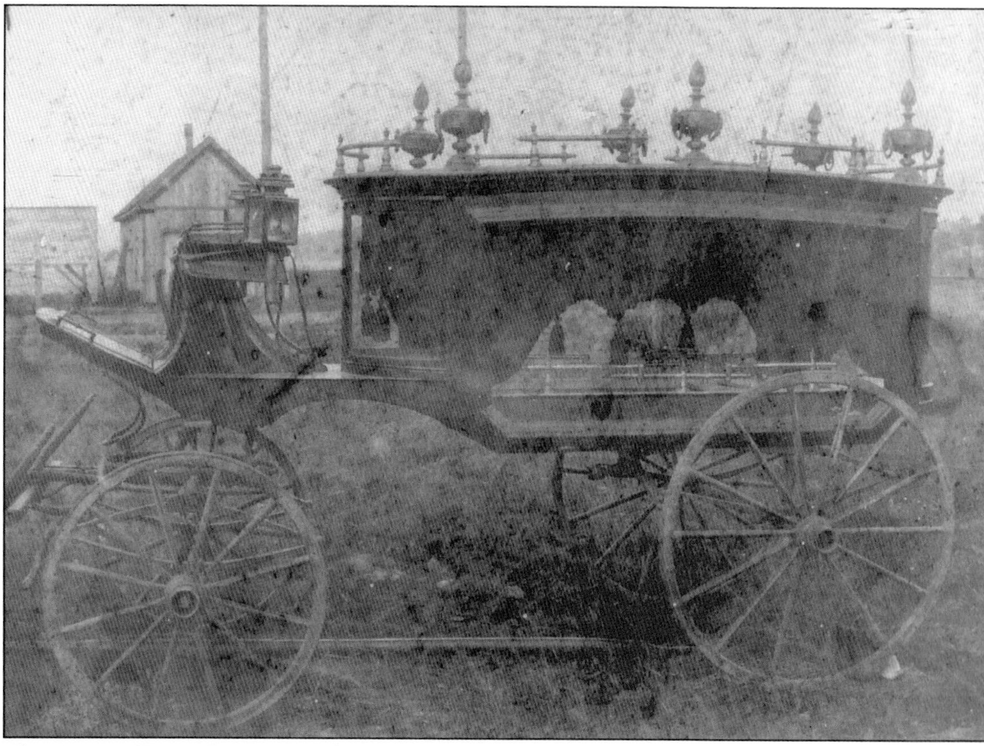

The Hopper Funeral Home, in days gone by, used an old horse-drawn funeral hearse.

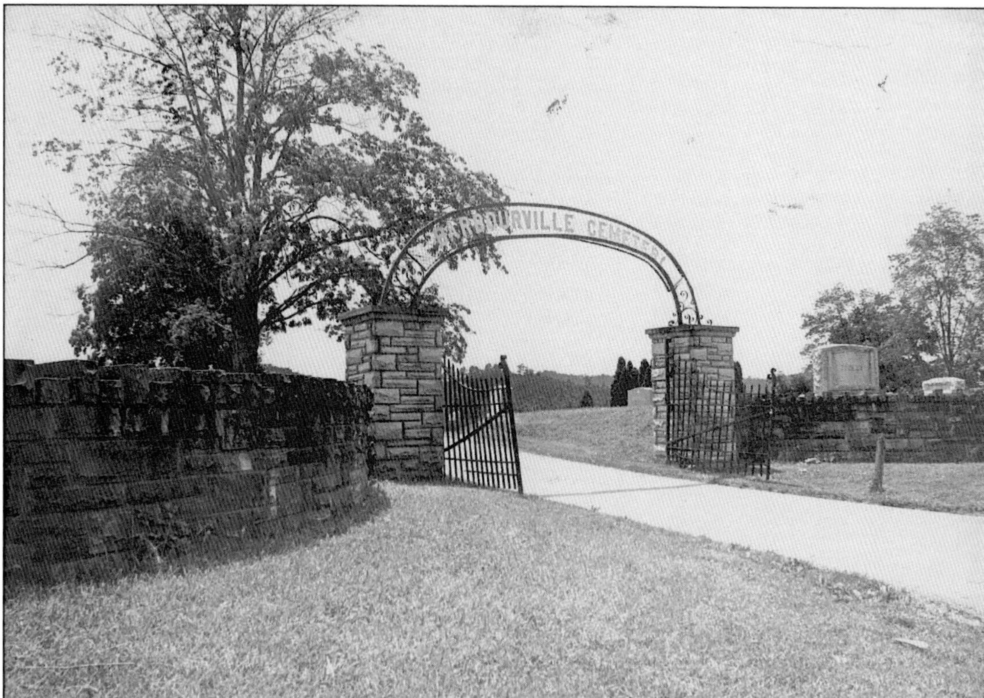

A trip in the old funeral hearse would most likely take you to the Barbourville Cemetery, and that would be "the end!"